BEAU BRUMMELL

Beau Brummell: engraved from the miniature by John Cook

Beau Brummell

HUBERT COLE

MASON / CHARTER   NEW YORK 1977

First published in the United States by
    Mason/Charter Publishers, Inc.

Printed in Great Britain

Library of Congress Cataloging in Publication Data

Cole, Hubert.
    Beau Brummell.

    Bibliography: p.
    Includes index.
    1. Brummell, George Bryan, 1778–1840. 2. Great
Britain–Court and courtiers–Biography. 3. London–
Social life and customs.
DA538.B6C54   1977   941.07′3′0924 [B]   77-2462
ISBN 0–88405–593–0

To Richard

Contents

Illustrations

ILLUSTRATIONS

A*

CHAPTER ONE

Coming Up in the World

It was a warm Wednesday night in June 1780 and London was in flames. On the previous Friday the Member of Parliament for Luggershall, Lord George Gordon, had summoned a great rally of the Protestant Association in St George's Fields to support his petition for the repeal of Lord North's Catholic Relief Act of 1778. The 50,000 demonstrators marched eight abreast to Westminster, going the long way round over London Bridge and the City and sweeping up the riff-raff of the rookeries and grog-shops as they went. In New Palace Yard they assaulted Members and prevented them from leaving Parliament until ten o'clock at night. The drunks and mischiefmakers then began smashing the Catholic chapels attached to foreign embassies. They did the same on three succeeding nights, destroying private houses in Moorfields, where there was a large Irish Catholic colony.

On Tuesday they set fire to Newgate and released three hundred prisoners. They moved farther afield to Clerkenwell, where they broke into the Bridewell and the New Prison, and to Bloomsbury, where they burned the houses of the Archbishop of York and the Lord Chief Justice. Any citizens in the neighbourhood who did not illuminate their houses in honour of these achievements had their windows shattered. On Wednesday morning regular soldiers and militiamen marched in from the Home Counties; on the advice of the Privy Council the King issued a Royal Proclamation authorising troops to fire without the presence of magistrates; artillery rumbled through the streets; by

evening all was calm. Until suddenly a mob attacked the Bank of
England, troops opened fire, rioting broke out in a score of
places, in the City, at Southwark, at the prisons across the river,
the toll-houses on Blackfriars Bridge, a distillery which the
drunken looters set on fire, thus burning themselves alive.

In Downing Street Lord North was entertaining friends to
dinner. Earlier the rioters had been cleared from outside the
house by a troop of dragoons, and those who returned were
informed that twenty Grenadiers were stationed on the top floor
with loaded muskets and orders to use them. The situation was
not new to Lord North, who the previous year had been forced
to take refuge upstairs when another mob attacked the house in
protest against the court-martialling of Admiral Keppel; the
London slums hid some of the most violent ruffians in Europe
and they never missed an opportunity to run amok. Before his
guests left for home, the Prime Minister took them up to where
the soldiers still stood on watch. 'We beheld London blazing in
seven places', recalled John Macpherson, the Member of Parliament for Cricklade, 'and could hear the Platoons regularly firing
in various directions.' They had their fill of the sound and spec-
tacle and then went downstairs, got into their carriages and were
driven peaceably home, the West End having been closely
patrolled throughout the disturbances.

A short time later they were followed by 'Mr Brummell, Lord
North's private secretary, who was in attendance but did not make
one of the Company.' For him it was an evening of more than
usual significance. The rioting had brought nearer the resignation
of the master whom he had closely and faithfully served for more
than ten years; it was also forcing him to spend the night at the
house he rented a few paces away, next to that of Lord Sheffield,
North's son-in-law. A devoted family man, William Brummell
would have much preferred to leave earlier and ride out to
Hampton Court, to join his wife and children in celebrating the
birthday of his younger son, who was one day to be famous
throughout Europe as 'Beau' Brummell.

The boy had been born here in Downing Street two years
before and christened George Bryan at St Margaret's, Westminster. Later in life, when the Beau's extraordinary domination

of fashionable society attracted the inevitable envy, the snobs put it about that he was the son of a footman, a pastrycook, jumped up from the gutter. There were similar rumours about his father, briskly efficient William, who was known to have such a strong influence with the Prime Minister when it came to allocating sinecures and places and distributing bribes. When Lord North came under fire in the Commons for partiality in farming out the Budget Loan to his friends and supporters, the *Public Advertiser* carried a small paragraph stating that 'the Exaltation of Mr Brummell, the Secretary of Lord North, is entirely the Creation of Mr Jenkinson; Mr B——— being the Son of the Person with whom Mr J———, when a Commis, and very early in life, used to lodge.' That same day, Saturday 21 March 1781, the editor, Mr Woodfall, received a note signed 'Veritas' and sent from St James's: 'Your account of Mr Brummell, Lord North's secretary, is by no means correct. I have sent you his origin: his father was footman to Mr Pelham and his mother an industrious washerwoman–the late Charles Townshend gave him the run of the kitchen and after that he became an under commis in the Treasury thro that gent's interest.'

Mr Woodfall's original item was accurate; but the vindictive Veritas, except that he got all the names wrong, was not far off the trail either. Little George Bryan had been born into the comfortably padded lap of upper middle class luxury, but the two previous generations of Brummells had made a very rapid rise in the world.

The William Brummell who was George Bryan's grandfather and father to Lord North's secretary had a close connection with the Monson family: Charles Monson, MP for Lincoln, his elder brother the first Lord Monson, and his younger brother Henry Monson, Regius Professor of Civil Law at Cambridge. A letter published in *Notes and Queries* in 1850 shows this William Brummell to have been on intimate terms with Charles and Henry in 1757; a letter in the British Museum addressed either to him or to his son refers to advice given about the sale of Lord Monson's house in 1763. Lady Monson claimed that he had been a servant in the family and it seems likely that, at whatever level he may have begun, he ended as a sort of major-domo to Charles Monson. Somewhere along the way he acquired a house on the east corner of Bury Street and Jermyn Street, which he first rented and then bought leasehold from the Crown. He married a Miss Jane Garret who bore him a son and daughter, William and Mary, and some years later the appropriately named Benjamin. In 1761 he decided to take as a lodger at his Bury Street house the newly elected MP for Cockermouth, Charles Jenkinson. It was one of the most important decisions of his life.

Jenkinson had made his way to Parliament without money or influence. For his services in increasing the King's control over the Cabinet he was to be created the first Earl of Liverpool. He was a scholarly, humourless man of great application; and he recognised many of his own qualities in his landlord's elder son, William. When he was made Joint Secretary to the Treasury in 1763 he took young Brummell with him as a sort of unestablished office-boy.

In February 1765 William Brummell senior, describing himself as a 'Gentleman, being sick of body but of sound mind, memory and understanding', made a will leaving his house, furniture and an annuity of £60 a year to his wife, with the reversion of this and the rest of the property to be divided equally between his three children. As executors he appointed 'my said wife and my honoured friend Charles Jenkinson Esq' (of whom he desired 'his acceptance of Twenty Guineas for his trouble') and gave them 'liberty to apply any reasonable part of the share of my said son Benjamin during his minority to bring him out apprentice or Clerk to some Trade or Profession'. Sick though he was, William Brummell did not die for another five years, during which Jenkinson proved himself to be a friend indeed. In July he got young William Brummell officially appointed to the Treasury establishment as a Supernumerary Clerk, and when he lost his office a year later he ensured that Brummell should be raised to the grade of Under Clerk at a salary of £100 a year.

'I cannot conclude this letter', he wrote to Charles Townshend, Chancellor of the Exchequer in the new government, 'without returning you thanks for having taken under your protection Mr Brummell. He acted under me as a clark for many years with great diligence, skill and fidelity, and I am persuaded that you will have the same reasons to be satisfied with him.' Townshend died and was succeeded in October 1767 by the Tory Lord North; by the time North became Prime Minister he had been so impressed with Brummell's diligence and discretion that he appointed him his private secretary. On the last day of March that year, 1770, old William Brummell died and was buried in the churchyard of St James's, Piccadilly. His wife lived for another eighteen years, during which Charles Jenkinson continued to discharge his duties as executor.

North, like Jenkinson, was a leading member of the 'King's Friends'. He was an amiable man of considerable ugliness, exceeded only by that of his family. A popular story of the time described how a man at a party asked North, 'Who is that frightful woman?' 'That,' North replied, 'is my wife.' 'Good heavens, no,' said the man, trying to cover up his *faux pas*, 'I didn't mean her–I meant the monster next to her.' 'Oh,' said North, 'that monster is my daughter.' (A later Prime Minister, Frederick Robinson, told the story one evening to his dinner partner, Lady Charlotte Lindsay. 'I know,' she replied, 'I am Lord North's daughter.') North's policy as Prime Minister was simple: he regarded himself as the King's servant with the duty of carrying out the King's wishes by the extensive use of bribery. Because of this he was much criticised but also well rewarded. In June 1771 the King gave him the Rangership of Bushey Park (an appointment he held in his wife's name to avoid having to resign from the Commons).

With the Rangership went the attractive Ranger's House in Bushey Park. It was convenient for Lord North to have his private secretary living near at hand, and in March 1772 William Brummell was allotted grace and favour apartments in the royal palace of Hampton Court. The King disliked the place and never lived there (it was said he had unhappy memories of his grandfather, George II, boxing his ears in the State Apartments). The rooms were neglected, and some of them considerably defaced by tenants converting them into sculleries and kitchens. But they still provided good accommodation as well as an excellent address. (Dr Johnson unsuccessfully applied for 'such rooms as shall seem proper' to the Lord Chamberlain four years later.)

William Brummell moved into Suite Thirty, second floor on
the east side of Clock Court, bringing his mistress with him. The
King, however, was a man of high moral standards with a sharp
eye for goings-on of this sort, even in those of his palaces which
he did not frequent. It was made clear to Mr Brummell that he
must either regularise the situation or move out again. Thus he
came to marry the youngest daughter of the Keeper of the Lottery Office and they lived happily and devotedly ever after and
were rewarded with the additional accommodation of Suite
Twenty-five in which to bring up their family of William, Maria
and the yet-to-be-famous George Bryan. The bride claimed
descent from Sir Thomas Richardson who had been a Chief
Justice in the reign of James I; she had at least two brothers and
three sisters, one of whom married an actor, Joseph Vernon, and
another an innkeeper named Samuel Brawne, who later moved
from his hostelry in the Strand to a farm at Kilburn. One of the
earliest anecdotes about George Bryan Brummell is that on a visit
to Aunt Brawne he ate so much of her delicious damson tart that
he could eat no more—yet had enjoyed it so much that he could
not bear to leave off, and consequently broke into howls of tearful frustration. Aunt Brawne's granddaughter Frances was later
to inspire unrequited passion of a more refined nature in the heart
of John Keats.

Lord North's administration endured for twelve years. He had
taken over the King's quarrel with the American colonists—
they resenting the foolish policy of taxation without representa-
tion introduced five years before, George III outraged at their
ingratitude after he had spent so much in men and money saving
them from conquest by the French. This North fomented by
allowing the full blast of the King's high-principled vindictive
indignation to play upon it. In India he substituted systematic
control for the East India Company's chaos by his Regulation
Act, but the fighting and confusion was still fierce and general
when he decided to resign. His noble and overdue measures for
lifting some of the more extreme penalties from Roman Catho-
lics resulted in the Gordon Riots. He was in many ways a luckless
man.

Not so his private secretary, whose position gave him influence among politicians of all colours and friendship with many of them—with the brilliant spendthrift Charles James Fox for instance, who quarrelled with North and surrendered his post as a Lord of the Treasury in 1774; with Richard Brinsley Sheridan, the playwright, who became Secretary to the Treasury. He was on calling terms with two of the best-known painters of the day; the President of the Royal Academy and the American-born Historical Painter to the King. 'Breakfast with me tomorrow, after which I shall be happy to accompany you to Sir Joshua Reynolds and Mr [Benjamin] West's,' he said in a letter to Caleb Whitefoord at the end of December 1781. A short time afterwards he commissioned Sir Joshua to paint the portrait of the two Brummell boys that now hangs in Kenwood.

He busied himself with favours for his friends and his friends' friends. 'Dear Brummell, if you can be of any use to the poor man who is the bearer of this, I shall be much obliged to you,' wrote his old benefactor, Charles Jenkinson, now Secretary of State at War. 'I have always pitied his case, yet have no means of making any provision for him.' Brummell could always find the means. For Sheridan's brother-in-law, the poet Richard Tickell, he procured a commissionership of stamps and also handed over to him an extra set of apartments that he had acquired at Hampton Court (Suite Seventeen in the Gold Staff Gallery on the South Front). He told another suitor 'I have just received the enclosed from Sheridan [then Secretary to the Treasury]. If I have not soon some other and more explicit answer from the same quarter, I shall renew my attacks and I doubt not that they will meet with success.' With ministers he used polite persistence; with ordinary members of both houses he adopted a more direct approach. He was the principal channel of governmental corruption.

It was accepted practice. For fifty years the second edition of the Geneva Bible had been known as the Whig Bible because of its misprint, 'Blessed are the placemakers.' Politicians were of two kinds: the leaders who jockeyed for power and the Garter, the draff who could be bought with places and hard cash. There was very little hypocrisy about it. A man elected with votes bought or bullied from the pot-wallopers and forty-shilling freeholders who

made up less than four per cent of the population was unlikely to
waste his breath denying that he was the corrupt product of a
corrupt system, though he would vehemently claim it was in the
public interest that the system be preserved. Consequently the
political scene, though just as dirty as it is today, was a great deal
less disgusting.

Dining at Lord Bessborough's house in 1790, and well filled
with champagne, Ross Mackay admitted that when he was
Treasurer and Paymaster of the Ordnance in 1763 the House of
Commons had been persuaded to accept the unsatisfactory terms
of the Treaty of Paris only by 'a pecuniary distribution. I was
myself the channel through which the money passed. With my
own hand I secured above one hundred and twenty Votes.
Eighty thousand pounds were set apart for the purpose. Forty
members of the House of Commons received from me a thousand
Pounds each. To eighty others I paid five hundred Pounds apiece.'
Sir William Wraxall, who recorded the conversation, added:
'The same system certainly continued during the period of the
American War when John Robinson [Junior Secretary of the
Treasury], and under him Brummell, were its Agents.' A recent
historian has denied the truth of this story on the odd ground that
no corroborative evidence can be found in government records,
but there can be little doubt that, as Mackay insisted, money in one
guise or another–lottery tickets, bonds, jobs, contracts–'formed
the only certain and effectual method' of controlling the House of
Commons.

With so many sweetmeats passing through Brummell's hands
it was natural that some should stick to his fingers. He had in
addition many opportunities to collect commissions and per-
centages. In one year, for instance, the Treasury bill for stationery
totalled £5000, an enormous sum–and the contracts had all been
placed by William Brummell. He feathered his nest with such
efficiency that, when Lord North finally left politics in 1783,
Brummell was rich enough to quit at the same time.

With him into retirement Brummell took a fine collection of
sinecures: Joint-Receiver of the Duties on Inhabited Houses in
London and Middlesex, Comptroller of the Hawkers' and Ped-
lars' Office, Agent and Paymaster to the Out-Pensioners of

Chelsea Hospital, Agent to the Navy. They brought him £2500 a year–an income probably not surpassed by more than six hundred people in the United Kingdom, and well ahead of the many country squires and substantial merchants who rightly regarded themselves as rich, and may indeed have had greater capital assets. In addition Brummell had the dividends from the savings that he had built up over the years and invested in government stock and West Indian ventures, and a number of smaller sources of income, such as the agency for the Horse Grenadiers, which the King gave him when appointing his son, the Duke of York, to the colonelcy in March 1782.

He gave up the Downing Street house and moved to the more fashionable area of Charles Street, Mayfair. He was still paying the rates on 10 Bury Street (they had gone up from tenpence to half-a-crown in the pound during the North administration) though his sister Mary, now Mrs Tombs, was the occupant. He exchanged Suite Thirty at Hampton Court for Number Twenty-nine in the Silver Staff Gallery, on the top floor north side of Fountain Court. And as his principal home he bought and enlarged a house called The Grove at Donnington in Berkshire. He acquired the neighbouring manor of Church Spleen in 1784 and the manor of Chieveley in 1787, and in 1788 he was appointed High Sheriff for the county. To set the final seal on a successful life, he sent both his boys to Eton.

George Bryan was eight, William nearly two years older, when they entered the First Form in 1786, and were introduced to the system of fagging, flogging and construing or composing Latin and Greek which formed the backbone of eighteenth-century education. They lodged with the parsimonious Dame Yonge, and on ordinary schooldays (there were partial holidays on Tuesday, Thursday and Saturday, plus many red-letter days, Founder's Day and Royal Birthdays) they attended school from eight to nine, from eleven to twelve, from three to four, and from five to six. In the summer the Lower School had also to get up early for a lesson from a quarter to seven until half past. The First Form learned nothing but Latin grammar on regular days, with an hour or so of writing or arithmetic on holidays.

The Headmaster, Jonathan Davies, was noted for his wit, his loud voice, his habit of monopolising the conversation and his delight in spending much time in London when he should have been at Eton. He got on so badly with his dozen or so assistant masters that three years before the Brummell boys arrived the masters had walked out of the school. This left Dr Davies facing a mob of boys who soon realised they had nothing to fear from him, chased him out of Upper School and, while he took refuge in Provost's Lodge, split the birching-block into pieces with red-hot pokers.

The Lower Master, William Langford, was also Canon of Windsor and Chaplain to the King. It was his practice not to punish boys individually at the time of their offences, but to wait until there was a sufficiently large batch to be marched up the hill to the Castle and flogged in his residence. This must have delighted the King, who took a great interest in the school and had a thoroughly Teutonic belief in the efficacy of corporal punishment. He enjoyed living at Windsor (in the Queen's Lodge, which he had specially built to accommodate his family while the Castle, neglected by both his predecessors, was refurbished) and whenever he crossed the river to Eton he would rein in his horse and jovially shout: 'Well, well, well, my boy! When were you flogged last, eh eh?' or 'Put him in the bill, Praeposter; he must be flogged.' George III practised on his own sons what he preached for others. His daughter, Princess Sophia, retained throughout her life the memory of seeing her two brothers, the Prince of Wales and the Duke of York, 'when they were boys of thirteen and fourteen, held by their arms to be flogged like dogs, with a long whip'. Another brother, Augustus Frederick, was 'afflicted with asthmatic breathing, which his tutor "required him to stop" '. He failed to do so; this defiance of authority, 'after various rebukes and threats, ended in a sound flogging'.

If the young Etonian managed to avoid the birch for indiscipline or inattention in school, he still ran the risk of a beating for failing in his duties as a fag when he returned to the boarding-house kept by his Domine or Dame. There were forty boarders at Dame Yonge's. George had the good fortune to have as his fag-master the House Captain, a good-natured boy who remembered him long after as an excellent toaster of bread and cheese. 'As head of the house I had two suppers of cold meat and pastry, and a double portion of bread and cheese. George Brummell nightly toasted mine most delicately for three years.' The task could be much more hazardous than it sounds: a future Duke of Bedford suffered permanent damage to his fingers because his fag-master beat him every time he found him effeminately using a toasting fork. On the other hand it could bring benefits–the House Captain used to share the toasted cheese with George, a boy of naturally large appetite who claimed that the seniors at his table took all the meat and left the juniors with nothing but bread and gravy.

'He was a general favourite. I do not remember that he ever fought or quarrelled with anyone; indeed, it was impossible for anybody to be more good-natured than he was.' He did as little work as possible, but was smart enough to keep level with his older brother all through the school. 'He was a very *clever* and a very *idle* boy, and very *frank*; and then, whatever he became afterwards, not in the least conceited, though nature seemed to have supplied him with a quadruple portion of amusing repartee.' This earned him special attention from one of the assistant masters, Joseph Goodall, later to become Headmaster and then Provost. Goodall combined 'a dignified demeanour, a tall and well-shaped figure, a sincerity of manner and a pleasing, and occasionally humorous, mode of expression'. It was a pattern that George copied and refined.

Out of school hours there was a wide choice of activities. The Ram Hunt, in which an unfortunate animal provided by the college butcher was chased through the street (latterly carted, hamstrung, to Weston's Yard) and battered to death with clubs, had been discontinued; but there was cricket and football, boating and real tennis, fives played between the chapel buttresses, marbles and hide-and-seek, hare-and-hounds, swimming, shooting and billiards, badger-baiting on Eton Common and cock-fighting in Bedford's Yard. Among the spectator sports for those willing to risk a birching for being caught out of bounds, there was horse-racing at Datchet or Ascot, bull-baiting at Windsor. In his school-work, George moved on to the Latin Testament in

the Second Form, then through Lower Greek and Upper Greek
to the Greek Testament in the Fourth Form. By 1793 he had progressed through the Remove to the Fifth Form, under the direct
tuition of the Headmaster, the formidable Dr George Heath
who had recently succeeded Davies. Heath, preparing the way for
the record flogging achievements of John Keate, gave fifty boys
a round dozen strokes each on one occasion and on another
administered ten cuts to each of seventy boys, after which 'he
was laid up with aches and pains for more than a week'.

George Brummell was now entitled to a fag of his own, who
later recalled 'his gaiety and good nature to lower boys, his fair
florid complexion, and a quantity of light curly hair, which it
was the fashion in those days to wear long enough to hang upon
the shoulders. He was a strong muscular boy, with short limbs;
and I can even now distinctly recollect seeing him, with thick
shoes and striped worsted stockings drawn over his knees (quite
clean and tight), going to play at football–in summer he used to
be on the river, not at cricket in the playing fields.' So much for
those vivid memories of the best days of our lives–George not
only played cricket but was in the Eton eleven in the summer
of 1973.

The first time his fag saw him was when, with two other senior
boys who played a hurdy-gurdy and a triangle, George seren-
aded the Headmaster's daughter, Susan, from the street beneath
her window. All three were wearing carnival costumes and George
was playing the French horn. He delighted in practical jokes and
showing-off, but not usually to extremes. The personality that he
was constructing for himself was pert but fastidious. His contemporaries remarked on 'the anxiety with which he eschewed the
dirty streets on a rainy day, his white stock with a bright gold
buckle behind, and the measured dignity of his step. His language, dress and deportment were always in perfect keeping.'
The pose was that of a young man cultured beyond his years,
innately superior to the mob–a languid assumption of authority.

There was constant friction between the boys who used the
Thames for sport and the bargees who had more serious business
on it. One afternoon George came upon a band of his school-
fellows who had seized an unwary waterman and were about to

throw him over the bridge–with a fair chance of being drowned. Brummell had a sympathy with the underdog that was often to get him into trouble later in life. On this occasion he eased his way into the shouting, struggling, sweaty scrum, tapping on shoulders and waving a disdainful hand, until he stood beside the proposed victim. He turned to address the boys.

'My good fellows,' he said, 'don't send him into the river; the man is evidently in a high state of perspiration, and it almost amounts to a certainty that he will catch cold.' There was a shout of laughter and the bargee was released. But there were, of course, some who found nothing to admire in such schoolboy nonchalance. 'I knew him well, sir,' said another contemporary. 'He was never flogged; and a man, sir, is not worth a damn who was never flogged through the school.'

George's mother died in March 1793; his father came up to London shortly afterwards and made a new will. He left the house in Bury Street with the furniture and £50 a year to his sister Mary Tombs. Annuities of £50 each to his wife's sister Margaret Vernon and niece Jane Mary Ann Underwood (alias Vernon), and one hundred guineas each. To another of her sisters, Grace, a spinster of Charing Cross, a gift of £200, which he doubled in a codicil the following year. To three clerks in the Chelsea Agents' Office and the Navy Agents' Office £100 each. 'for the trouble they will respectively have in settling my office accounts after my decease'. To William Francis Johnston, an Extra Clerk in the Secretary of State's office, the very large amount of £1000 for unspecified services. To his daughter Maria 'all my Jewells Watch and Diamonds and Trinkets now in a Box in the Possession of Messrs Drummond [the Charing Cross bankers] which I hope she will keep and wear in Memory of her ever to be lamented and never to be forgotten Mother'.

He gave one year's wages to each of his servants and £50 to Miss Sarah White, who was probably the sister of his friend Joseph White, a spinster on whom Sheridan had played a typical trick at Donnington. Persuaded by Sheridan that another guest, Thomas Harris the proprietor of Covent Garden Theatre, was falling in love with her and needed only to see her in a romantic situation to declare himself, she 'dressed herself in the costume of one of those pastoral beauties immortalized in Chelsea china and, attired in a stiff dress of primrose brocade and gipsy hat, with pale blue ribbons, sat by the side of a pond in the grounds, with a fishing-rod in her hand, the best part of a broiling summer's day'—until she at last realised that she was the victim of another of Sheridan's callous jokes.

To Harris himself Brummell left a mourning ring, as he did to the Earl of Guilford, eldest son of Lord North who had died in 1792, Charles Dundas MP for Berkshire, Sheridan, Tickell, John Palmer, whose system of Royal Mail coaches revolutionised road passenger transport when Pitt adopted it in 1794, and several other friends. His brother Benjamin got only £20 to buy mourning clothes because 'I some years since resigned unto him some appointments or offices which afford him an ample provision.' One of these was the Under-clerkship at the Treasury which William had nominally held until the end of the North administration. Benjamin took this over in March 1782 and, thanks to brother William's continuing influence, shot up to the top grade of Senior Clerk by December 1783. There was fifty guineas each for his four executors, headed by Sir John Macpherson; and after a few other minor gifts the residue was to be equally divided between his three children when they reached the age of twenty-one or, in the case of Maria, if she married earlier.

After the Michaelmas term neither of the boys returned to Eton. Their father brought them up to Charles Street, to be introduced to such elements of society as remained in London during the winter, and to the others who returned in the spring. After that they were to go on to Oriel College, Oxford.

The world had been manufacturing history at a great rate in the seven years since William Brummell sent the boys off to make useful friends at Eton. France, bankrupted by her support of the American revolutionaries, galloped from autocracy to ochlocracy with scarcely a pause at democracy on the way. The Americans confirmed their independence at the Peace of Versailles and wise men everywhere realised that Britain, slothful and exhausted, would never again be a world power. Clarkson and Wilberforce began their campaign for the abolition of the slave trade; the industrial revolution marched on, bringing wealth to the nation and misery to individuals; Warren Hastings was impeached for administering too well the sub-continent that was to be the core of Britain's next empire. Frederick of Prussia had died and Catherine the Great was about to do the same. The King of France had been beheaded by his subjects; the King of England had lost his wits almost unaided.

This last event was the one that most directly touched the young Etonians. The King was a popular and frequent visitor; they made great celebrations on his birthday and continued to do so after his death (though the cynics said this was because his successor's birthday fell during the holidays). He extended a standing invitation to the boys of the Upper School to visit him on Sundays, when he paraded up and down the terrace in his blue Windsor uniform, chattering on and on and on without remission, accompanied by his irritable wife, forever dipping finger and thumb into her gold snuff-box and mournfully scattering the filthy powder over her small monkey face and ill-used bosom, and escorted–on those occasions when they were on speaking terms–by the rake-helly Prince of Wales.

They were an unhappy family. The King, when a young man, had sacrificed his deep love for Lady Sarah Lennox to his political and dynastic responsibilities and accepted marriage with the unprepossessing Princess Charlotte Sophia of Mecklenburg-Strelitz. Since his sexual appetite was as strong as his sense of duty, he rewarded Queen Charlotte with fifteen children, most of whom she detested, and none more so than her eldest son, George Augustus Frederick, Prince of Wales. The Prince, whipped from boyhood into habits of disloyalty and deceit, opposed his parents as a matter of principle and Hanoverian tradition. When Lord Thurlow, the gruff, bullying Lord Chancellor, once said to him 'You, Sir, will never be popular; your father is, because he is faithful to that ugly woman your mother,' the remark delighted the Prince, who saw no virtue in faithfulness and hated his mother. His companions were loose-living aristocratic louts such as the Duke of Norfolk, his equerry Colonel George Hanger, and three other Irish bullies–'Hellgate' Lord Barrymore, his lame brother 'Cripplegate' and a third brother nicknamed 'Newgate' because that was the only prison he had not been inside. (Their sister, Lady Melfort, was 'Billingsgate' because of her foul mouth.) At sixteen he bought a twenty-year-old actress, Mary Robinson, as his mistress with a bond for £20,000 which he dishonoured. He created drunken scandals with his reprobate uncle, the Duke of Cumberland, whose marriage to the notorious Lady Anne Luttrell incensed the King into driving the Royal Marriage Act through Parliament in 1772.

When he came of age in 1783 and set up his own establishment, he engaged the fashionable Whig architect, Henry Holland, to remodel Carlton House, which he intended to make a rival, subversive court to the one in Buckingham House at the other end of the Mall. His spendthrift habits and the enormous debts they produced became a public scandal. He was a bewildering mishmash of charm and coarseness, taste and vulgarity, a good classical scholar, a lover of books and paintings, a drunken sot. He was a braggart and a coward: 'I thank God that there is but one of my children who wants courage,' said his father, 'and I will not name him because he is to succeed me!' He was charitable to strangers, disloyal to his friends and family: 'That bandy-legged bitch, my sister' was how he described the Princess Royal in a letter to one of his mistresses.

In 1784 he took measures which were to have a considerable effect on his own life and George Brummell's. To hide the swollen glands that had appeared in his throat (and were perhaps symptoms of the rare complaint, porphyria, that caused his father to go mad from time to time) he began to wear very high neckcloths. And to relieve the condition he decided to take a course of sea-bathing and sea-drinking at Brighton, where the water was said to be especially efficacious in cases of 'asthma, cancer, consumption, deafness, ruptures, rheumatism and madness', in addition to impotence.

He had visited the town the year before, loyally greeted with a royal salute from the ancient battery which killed one of the gunners. It was still a small place, known by its original name of Brighthelmstone, living more from fishing than from summer visitors. 'The streets are not paved; the houses chiefly built of the round sea-pebbles pitched in mortar. There is a pretty theatre, but neither of the two public rooms is equal to those at Southampton.' The Marquess of Queensberry, notorious 'Old Q', and Sir Harry Fetherstonhaugh, Emma Hamilton's first protector, had recently organised horse-racing on the downs; the Prince's uncle Cumberland had a house down by the Steine, the strip of green on which an orchestra played. The Prince found it all a welcome change and, after spending ten weeks there from July to September, decided to look around for permanent lodging. He was still aping the horsey set who dressed, drank, spat and swore like the coachmen from whom they delighted in taking over the ribbons, and he won much applause this year by setting up a record–London to Brighton and back in a day, driving a three-horse phaeton.

This was also the year that he met the fascinating Mrs Fitzherbert who, at twenty-eight, was six years his senior. It was his habit to fall in love with women older than himself and previously married. Mrs Fitzherbert had had two husbands, both now dead, and was not perhaps quite as ingenuous as her admirers have made her out to be. She was a Catholic. It was therefore impossible for the Prince to marry her and a grave offence for any person to abet the marriage or any priest to carry it out.

Nevertheless, the Prince's passion being irresistible and the lady's moral scruples immovable, a secret wedding did take place on 15 December 1785 at Mrs Fitzherbert's house in Park Street. This was an outright defiance of the Act of Settlement because of the bride's religion, and of the Royal Marriage Act because the bridegroom was under twenty-five. Mrs Fitzherbert moved to St James's Square and was accepted as the Prince's mistress– until in some unexplained fashion word got round that she was in fact his wife. They spent the summer and autumn of 1786–George Brummell's first term at Eton–like any other placid newly-married couple at Brighton, with the exception that he ostensibly lived in the former farmhouse that he had rented on the Steine and she in a small villa nearby. One of those who knew that there must be a strong possibility of truth in the marriage rumours was the discreet William Brummell, for Sheridan, a frequent guest at Donnington Grove, was also one of the few of the Prince's friends invited down to Brighton to visit him during these blissful six months.

It was a peaceful interlude too good to last. In the spring of 1787 the attention of the House of Commons was drawn to the extent of the Prince's debts. Indeed it could scarcely have ignored the subject, since he owed, and expected the national purse to pay, the impressive sum of more than a quarter of a million pounds. The debate produced hints and innuendoes about his marriage. Panicking at the realisation that if the truth came out he could never ascend the throne, he sent for Charles James Fox.

Fox, a Whig aristocrat of sharp wit and unprepossessing appearance, was one of the most compulsive gamblers in an age and society notorious for high play. Horace Walpole drew a sketch of his style of life.

He had sat up playing Hazard at Almack's from Tuesday evening, 4th February, till five in the afternoon of Wednesday 5th. An hour before he had recovered £12,000 that he had lost, and by dinner, which was at five o'clock, he had ended losing £11,000. On Thursday he spoke [in a debate in the House], went to dinner at past eleven at night; from thence to White's, where he drank till seven the next morning; thence to Almack's, where he won £6,000; and between three and four in the afternoon he set out for Newmarket. His brother Stephen lost £11,000 two nights after, and Charles £10,000 more on the 13th; so that in three nights the two brothers, the eldest not twenty-five, lost £32,000.

At Almack's, the gaming-club in Pall Mall, it was customary to play only for rouleaus of coins worth £50, and there was often £10,000 on the table. The gamblers 'began by pulling off their embroidered clothes, and put on frieze great-coats, or turned their coats inside outwards for luck. They put on pieces of leather (such as worn by footmen when they clean the knives) to save their lace ruffles; and to guard their eyes from the light, and to prevent tumbling their hair, wore high-crowned straw hats with broad brims, and adorned with flowers and ribbons; masks to conceal their emotions when they played at Quinze.'

Fox incurred the implacable hatred of the King. It was this that prompted the Prince of Wales to court his friendship 'in the most indecent and undisguised manner'. The Prince supported the Whigs for the simple reason that his father supported the Tories. If Fox was the King's enemy, then he was automatically the Prince's friend. There was also an aura of distinction about him, and the Prince constantly cultivated persons of distinction in the secret hope that some of that quality would rub off on himself.

It was not physical distinction. Fox, rising late and blear-eyed in his lodgings in St James's Street and preparing to struggle along to Brooks's (for he now spent more time in the Whig club than in the Tory White's), was a gruesome sight: 'his bristly person and shagged breast quite open and rarely purified by any ablutions, wrapped in a foul linen night-gown, and his bushy hair dishevelled'. Yet as soon as he opened his mouth he was an angel of wit, capable of charming the birds out of the trees and duchesses out of dower houses. His greatest admirer was indeed the most attractive duchess of her day, Georgiana Duchess of Devonshire, who, in canvassing for him in the Westminster election of 1784, went round visiting 'the most blackguard houses in Long Acre' offering 'kisses for votes of men some of them worse than tars', and so inflaming one coal-heaver that he vowed, 'I could light a pipe at your eyes.'

Since the Prince's succession to the throne would mean the Whigs' return to power, Fox was delighted to receive his royal friend's formal denial that any marriage existed between himself and Mrs Fitzherbert. On 30 April 1787, Fox rose in the House and, on the Prince's authority, declared that 'there never had been the slightest ground for this slander, either legally or illegally'. It was, George Selwyn remarked, as if the Prince had given him the same instructions as Othello gave to Iago: 'Villain, be sure thou prove my love a whore!' The Prince was very conscious of this and, calling on Mrs Fitzherbert next morning, he took both her hands in his and said: 'Only conceive, Maria, what Fox did yesterday! He went down to the House and denied that you and I were man and wife! Did you ever hear of such a thing?' Fox, suddenly discovering how he had been deceived and disowned, and fearful of the effect on Whig fortunes, tried to placate Mrs Fitzherbert by promising to create her a duchess as soon as his party came to power. She refused to receive

him, and for the rest of her life never again admitted him to her
house.

The marriage crisis was far from over. During the remarkably
dry summer of the following year–'everything in russet, not in
green'–the King took the Queen for a drive through Windsor
Great Park. He had been behaving rather peculiarly of late, talking unceasingly, switching with bewildering inconsequence from
one subject to another, punctuating the flow of words with 'Eh?
eh?, what? what?', but never waiting for a reply. On this particular afternoon, he suddenly stopped chattering and ordered the
coachman to halt the carriage. He then got out, advanced to an
old oak tree, removed his hat and bowed profoundly. Tucking his
hat under his left arm, he took a couple of paces forward and
shook hands with one of the branches of the tree. Having, as he
thought, paid his respects to the King of Prussia, he returned
contentedly to Queen's Lodge, but his madness grew steadily
worse and by October it was clear that he was unfit to govern.

On Guy Fawkes night, 1788, the Prince of Wales came up from
Brighton to Windsor and the King enlivened the dinner by grab-
bing him by the collar and throwing him against the wall. On the
whole, however, reported Lord Sheffield, William Brummell's
former neighbour in Downing Street, 'the King's illness is not
melancholy or mischievous; at times it is rather gay. Yesterday
se'night he talked incessantly for sixteen hours. He fancies
London is drowned and orders his yacht to go there. In one of his
soliloquies he said, "I hate nobody, why should anybody hate
me?"; recollecting a little, he added, "I beg pardon, I do hate the
Marquis of Buckingham." '

A Regency could not be long delayed. The two political parties were already arrayed: Pitt's Tory government, supported
by the Queen, claimed that the Regent must be appointed by
Parliament and consequently be subject to parliamentary control;
the Whigs claimed that the Prince should assume the Regency by
right, just as he would accede to the throne. If the Whigs gained
the day, there was no doubt that the Prince's first action would
be to throw out the Tories, despite their large majority.

The argument grew bitter. The Tories raised the bogey of an

unfettered Regent making the Catholic Mrs Fitzherbert queen. The Prince joyfully proclaimed at a supper party that his brother the Duke of York had said to their mother, 'Madam, I believe you are as much deranged as the King.' The Prince's secretary, Jack Payne (who shared with Harry Fetherstonhaugh the distinction of being the presumed father of Emma Hamilton's first illegitimate child) brought up the Whig libel that the Queen was having an affair with Pitt and added, 'Mr Pitt's chastity will protect the Queen's'–a reference to Pitt's lack of interest in women and alleged impotence. Whereupon the Duchess of Gordon, the only Pittite present, with true feminine loyalty, said, 'You little, insignificant, good-for-nothing, upstart, pert, chattering puppy, how dare you name your royal master's royal mother in that style?'

The joke went round that the Tories were trying to put the straitjacket on the Prince instead of the King. And Fox nearly went out of his own mind when he learnt that Sheridan, escaping with his wife from the bailliffs, had taken refuge in Mrs Fitzherbert's house, where he was making himself so popular that he was already regarded as 'Prime Minister of Carlton House'. Fox tried to lure the Prince with the actress Anna Maria Crouch, but she failed to attract (for one thing, she was younger than he was).

The quarrelling, jockeying and backbiting continued into the winter; but then, as mysteriously as it had come, the royal malady began to fade away. 'I am informed that the King is perfectly well,' wrote the Archbishop of Canterbury on 20 February 1789, 'calm, collected, accurate in his recollections. On this ground the Regency Bill was yesterday put off.' White's gave a celebratory ball at the Pantheon at which no Whig ladies appeared; Brooks's, dejected but unwilling to appear less overjoyed, gave theirs at the Opera House in the Haymarket and no Tories attended; the nation offered thanks to God at St Paul's on St George's Day.

Across the Channel the lords, clergy and commons were journeying towards Versailles for the first meeting of the States-General to be held in 165 years. The subsequent ominous rumbles and crashes brought the King and his eldest son closer together during the next year or two and provided the dominant subject of conversation, except for a panic period in the spring of 1790 when a man nicknamed the Monster made a series of attacks on women, stabbing fourteen and reportedly entirely clearing the London streets of prostitutes.

It is unlikely that George Brummell had any opportunity to see the Prince of Wales before 4 July 1791, when the school was given its usual holiday to celebrate the King's birthday–his fifty-third– and the Prince came to Windsor for the singing and dancing. He wore 'a bottle-green and claret-coloured striped silk coat and breeches and silver tissue waistcoat, very richly embroidered in silver and stones, and coloured silks in curious devices and bouquets of flowers. The coat and waistcoat embroidered down the seams and spangled all over the body. The coat cuffs the same as the waistcoat. The breeches were likewise covered with spangles. Diamond buttons to the coat, waistcoat and breeches, which, with his brilliant diamond epaulette and sword, made the whole dress form a most magnificent appearance.' Prince Charming still wears it to go to the ball in the costlier pantomimes. Its rich vulgarity must have set George Brummell's teeth on edge, but he still had a few years to wait before he could begin educating the Prince in the virtues of moderation.

Surprisingly dutiful, the Prince accepted his parents' invitation to return to Windsor on 12 August to celebrate his own birthday; he was twenty-nine. He behaved with such decorum and affability that *The Times* was inspired to one of the most unlikely comparisons even in journalistic history: 'Perhaps no heir to the Crown since the days of Edward the Black Prince...has been more generously admired for his amiable manners than the Prince of Wales.'

The generous admiration cooled a little in October when the Prince's horse, Escape, turned in two such contrasting performances on successive days at Newmarket that there was open speculation on how much money had been made out of the fraud, and by whom: the trainer, the jockey, or the Prince himself. The Prince took offence and never went to Newmarket again.

The fervour of the French revolutionaries and the fear and horror aroused in Britain by the Paris prison massacres and the

illiam Brummell, the Beau's father

Above   The Brummell children: William (*top*) and George, by Sir Joshua Reynolds

Opposite above   George III, with the Prince of Wales (sword raised) in his uniform Colonel of the 10th Light Dragoon Guards. On the King's left is the Duke of York Commander-in-Chief. Painting by Sir William Beechey

Opposite below   The entrance to Hyde Park on a Sunday

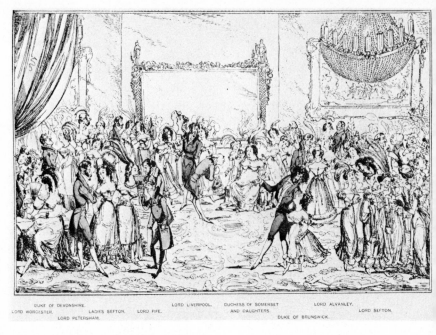

DUKE OF DEVONSHIRE.   LORD LIVERPOOL.   DUCHESS OF SOMERSET   LORD ALVANLEY.
LORD WORCESTER.   LADIES SEFTON.   LORD FIFE.   AND DAUGHTERS.   LORD SEFTON.
          LORD PETERSHAM.   DUKE OF BRUNSWICK.

Above   An aristocratic soirée at Almack's

Below   The first quadrille danced in London at the beginning of the nineteenth centur

guillotining of the King brought the two countries to open war in February 1793. In January the King had appointed the Prince of Wales Colonel Commandant of the 10th Light Dragoons: a move which, without precisely striking terror to the heart of the French nation, at least momentarily satisfied the Prince's desire to appear to be doing something in the imminent hostilities. The envy and enmity that he had hitherto focused on his father were now being diverted to his brother Frederick Duke of York. Frederick, his father's favourite, had been trained as a soldier in Germany, had married at the age of twenty-eight Frederica Princess Royal of Prussia, and was Commander-in-Chief of the Army in Great Britain. The war would bring him much public attention. To compound this offence, his wife—'pretty little Princess Fred'—refused to accept Mrs Fitzherbert as her sister-in-law.

Even the dragoons that the Prince of Wales had been given—formed in 1715 and previously known as Viscount Cobham's Regiment—could not vie in seniority or martial traditions with the Coldstream Guards of whom the Duke was colonel-in-chief. But the Prince could at least ensure that it became one of the most fashionable regiments. As vacancies occurred he filled them with his close friends. On 17 May 1794 he gave a cornetcy to George Bryan Brummell.

CHAPTER TWO

Princely Patronage

The story of how young Brummell, still three weeks short of his sixteenth birthday, managed to get himself gazetted to this very modish regiment has as many variations as that of his ancestry. Captain Gronow of the Coldstream Guards, who knew and disliked Brummell, maintained that George had an aunt, Mrs Searle, who was gatekeeper in the Green Park, and that when the Prince was strolling in the park one day she presented her nephew to him. Instantly impressed with George's style and wit, the Prince offered him a commission on the spot. There is no record of George having had an aunt named Searle and the story sounds highly improbable. Indeed, little Captain Gronow (he was so small that his friends called him 'Nogrow' behind his back) was so unfettered by consistency that he produced an entirely different version in another of his several books of reminiscences.

This was that, at Eton, Brummell

had made many friends among the scions of good families, by whom he was considered a sort of Crichton; and his reputation reached a circle over which reigned the celebrated Duchess of Devonshire. At a grand ball given by her grace, George Brummell, then quite a youth, appeared for the first time in such elevated society. He immediately became a great favourite with the ladies, and was asked by all the dowagers to as many balls and soirées as he could attend. At last the Prince of Wales sent for Brummell, and was so much pleased with his manner and appearance that he gave him a commission in his own regiment.

This is rather more plausible. George had easy entrée to Devonshire House through his father's friendship with Fox and

Sheridan and other frequent visitors there. And it would have been elsewhere that he met the Prince, who was still on very cool terms with Fox, and with the Duchess, who on moral grounds refused to go to the opera with Mrs Fitzherbert: 'I never did and never will and she knows it.' (The Duchess, who had at least one illegitimate child, was happily living in a *ménage à trois* with her husband, the fifth Duke, and his mistress who later succeeded her as Duchess.) But all these encounters and successes at balls and soirées must have taken place during the London season, which ran from May to July or August. Brummell could not have created his dazzling impression in less than three weeks in 1794, and as for the previous season, even as precocious a boy as he certainly was could scarcely have conquered the *beau monde* while still hovering around his fifteenth birthday.

His own account was that 'he had been presented to the heir apparent on the Terrace at Windsor when a boy at Eton, and his subsequent intimacy with His Royal Highness grew out of the slight notice with which he was then favoured'. A glance at his father's will shows that there were friends in a position not merely to introduce him but also to keep him in the Prince's mind: Sheridan, for example, and in particular John Macpherson, the tall Scotsman who had dined with North in Downing Street at the peak of the Gordon Riots. William Brummell had played a large part in North's reorganisation of the East India Company. 'See Mr Brummell as soon as you can,' Warren Hastings urged a friend in London, 'for he is active and intelligent, and has more influence than any man with Lord North.' He had a hand in Macpherson's much-criticised appointment to a seat on the Governor-General's Council at Calcutta in 1781, which resulted in Macpherson's temporarily taking over the Governor-Generalship when Hastings returned to England to face impeachment.

Macpherson came back the following year to a baronetcy and to regain his former seat as MP for Cricklade (where he was shortly unseated for bribery). He became so close a friend of the Prince of Wales that 'he was admitted to Carlton House at almost all hours, frequently when the heir-apparent was in bed. Few individuals enjoyed more distinguishing marks of His Royal Highness's favour.' Proof of his close friendship with William

Brummell exists in his letters. 'I am with our friend Mr Brummell at Donnington Grove,' he wrote to Jack Payne in July 1789, when George was just eleven years old. Later the same year he was urging him again to' meet my friends Col North [Lord North's second son, Francis, later fourth Earl of Guilford], Brummell, Anstruther [the Prince's Solicitor-General], Adam–and drink my Madeira'.

He was the first-named of Brummell's executors, and on 14 March 1794 he had the melancholy task of assuming his duties. William Brummell died that day 'at his house in Charles Street, Berkeley Square'. *The Gentleman's Magazine* recorded how 'by unremitting attention to business, the strictest integrity, and an amiable disposition, he became the confidential friend of Lord North', and since his retirement to Donnington had exerted his charitable instincts 'particularly in behalf of the infant poor, many of whom, by his benevolent exertions, have been saved from impending destruction, and must now severely feel, and truly lament, his loss. His three children will divide equally among them about £60,000.'

William Brummell's decision to send George to Oxford was probably with an eye to setting him on a political career, where there were plenty of influential friends to help him. But in politics, then as now, a man must crawl before he can run, and this was not a congenial posture for young George. Freed from parental control he decided in favour of the social education he would acquire in the 10th Light Dragoons. Macpherson must have consented to this and almost certainly obtained the commission from the Prince.

George spent the Trinity Term of 1794 at Oriel College, then left in July, a few days after his sixteenth birthday, to join his regiment. It was a burning hard summer, the drought following on a miserable washed-out harvest the previous year and preceding a long bitter winter. In France the excesses of the Revolution were reaching their climax and at home the Habeas Corpus Act was suspended in the hope of keeping the infection under control. 'The Republican spirit is growing dreadfully among all ranks and descriptions of men,' warned an Exchequer judge;

'democracy is taking long and hasty strides.' Mrs Radcliffe published *The Mysteries of Udolpho* and Warren Hastings's trial moved into its seventh year in the House of Lords.

Those Whig males who still supported the Revolution took to wearing pantaloons instead of the skin-tight breeches of the nobility. ('Those damned breeches were the ruin of my poor sister the Queen of France,' as the Archduchess Christine said to her lady-in-waiting.) Whig women had their hair cut short 'à la Guillotine'. Tory ladies, on the other hand, retained long tresses to twist round and through the caps that were now vying with turbans and scarves. All of the younger ones had gone over to lawn and muslin ('as a result of which eighteen fashionable women caught fire and 18,000 caught cold'), high-waisted and padded over the stomach 'by which they are made to appear five or six months gone with child. This dress is accompanied by a complete display of the bosom—which is uncovered and supported and stuck out by the sash immediately below it.'

The news of Admiral Howe's great victory over the French Fleet on the Glorious First of June set Cockney mobs rampaging in celebration through the midnight streets, knocking up house-holders and offering them the usual choice of illuminating their windows or having them smashed. Within three weeks dispatches from Flanders told how the army that the Duke of York had taken there was being driven back by the French; whereupon the Irish rebels adopted a new toast, 'To His Highness and his brave followers'. In the clubs gamblers continued to stake more than they could afford to lose, and witty Richard Tickell, so often a guest at Donnington Grove, threw himself out of the old Brummell apartment at Hampton Court, unable to face his creditors. 'The fall was so violent that there was a hole *a foot deep* made by his head in the gravel walk.'

But not the weather, the testy public mood, the vagaries of fashion, the bad news from the Continent, nor even the unlucky fall of dice and cards, depressed the spirits of the Prince of Wales's Own. When Cornet Brummell joined them they were stationed at Hounslow, where they exercised in the morning, after which the officers went off to London for dining and drinking, quizzing the world at the opera, gaming at White's or Brooks's, or visiting the ladies of the town. They were mostly second and third sons of noble families, with a good allowance (they needed it–a uniform coat alone cost £29) but without hope of any great inheritance. The regiment had been raised nearly eighty years before to deal with the Old Pretender's rebellion–'six troops of one Sergeant, two Corporals, one Drummer, one Hautbois and thirty private Dragoons, including the Widdowsmen' (one non-existent man in each troop whose pay was credited to a pension fund for widows of officers killed on active service). At the end of the Seven Years War the establishment was reduced, but now they were back to six troops again, this time enlarged to three sergeants, three corporals, a trumpeter and forty-seven men, all still wearing the regulation military wigs, with 'stiff curls on each side, and a long tail behind, the whole plastered and powdered'.

In his first year as colonel the Prince had them brought down to Brighton, meeting them at Preston on his birthday, and riding at the head of the great column (the Dragoons were followed by 7000 regulars, militiamen and volunteers, with some heavy artillery) to the tented camp that had been newly erected west of the town. But in 1794 he had fallen out of love with Brighton–or with Mrs Fitzherbert, who was spending the summer there. His eye had been caught by the Countess of Jersey, whose elderly husband had once been known as 'the Prince of Macaronis', and who herself possessed the essential qualities to engage the Prince's affections by being nine years his senior and twice a grandmother. However, his financial position was now so desperate that he was less interested in establishing a new mistress than in finding a suitable wife. Marriage, with the promise of children to bring succession and stability to the throne, would placate his father and encourage Parliament to settle his debts.

On 23 June he sent a letter to Mrs Fitzherbert, telling her that they must never meet again. A month later he went down to Weymouth to see the King, who delightedly informed the Prime Minister of his son's 'desire of entering into a more creditable line of life by marrying; expressing at the same time that his wish is that my niece, the Princess of Brunswick, may be the person'. Pitt agreed that the grateful nation would raise no objection to increasing the Prince's annual allowance from £73,000 to

£138,000, and giving him £52,000 to cover the cost of the wedding and to equip Carlton House suitably for a married couple. Lady Jersey was cosily appointed Lady-of-the-Bedchamber to the prospective bride.

The Prince had never seen Princess Caroline of Brunswick; she had been suggested to him by his brother, William Duke of Clarence, with a view to annoying the Duke and Duchess of York. The Duchess knew Caroline and disliked her, and, as the daughter of the King of Prussia, would be mortified at having to take rank below a daughter of the Duke of Brunswick. James Harris, Earl of Malmesbury, sent to make the proposal by proxy, found that the Princess had 'a pretty face–not expressive of softness–her figure not graceful–fine eyes–good hands–tolerable teeth, but going–fair hair and light eyebrows, good bust–short, with what the French call *des épaules impertinentes*'. Her father, the immoral old rip whose bullying manifesto to the French revolutionaries had become the death warrant for Louis XVI, told him 'she is not stupid, but she lacks judgement–she has been brought up strictly–and needed to be'.

Princess Caroline had heard of Lady Jersey and told Malmesbury, 'I am determined never to appear jealous. I know the Prince is *léger*, and am prepared on this point.' Whether the Prince was equally prepared for what he was getting was a matter that seriously worried Malmesbury. Caroline seemed unlikely to be able to share his interest in the arts nor hold her own in exchanges of wit. Moreover, she was not at all fussy about the cleanliness of her clothes or her person. However, the Prince was impatient for his bride and the money, and Malmesbury's instructions were to sign, not argue. He asked the Princess's lady-in-waiting 'to explain to her that the Prince is very delicate, and that he expects a long and very careful *toilette de propreté*', and then set off with her to England. It was a protracted journey, because of the need to avoid capture by the French. They finally landed at Greenwich at noon on Sunday 5 April 1795, only to discover that the King's carriage that were to take the Princess on to London had not yet arrived.

They appeared an hour later with an escort of the 10th Light Dragoons commanded by Lord Edward Somerset. Carrying the colours was Cornet Brummell: 'Nature had indeed been most liberal to him. He was about the same height as the Apollo, and the just proportions of his form were remarkable; his hand was particularly well-shaped; his face was rather long, and complexion fair; his hair light brown. His head was well-shaped, the forehead being unusually high. His countenance indicated that he possessed considerable intelligence, and his mouth betrayed a strong disposition to indulge in sardonic humour. His eyebrows were equally expressive with his mouth, and while the latter was giving utterance to something very good-humoured or polite, the former, and the eyes themselves, which were gray and full of oddity, could assume an expression that gave additional point to his humorous or satirical remarks. His voice was very pleasing.'

None of this can have made much impact on Princess Caroline, for she was immediately plunged into a confrontation with her Lady-of-the-Bedchamber. Since most of the accounts of their relationship were written by people of rival factions or families, capable of lies and exaggerations not only in their letters but even in their diaries, it is more than possible that Lady Jersey has been traduced by history, but it seems clear that, even if it was not entirely her fault that the carriages were an hour late, she had certainly made up her mind to begin in the way she meant to go on. She found fault with the Princess's clothes, claimed (unsuccessfully) the right to sit beside and not opposite her in the carriage, and got into a snappish argument with Malmesbury.

'There was very little crowd and still less applause' as Lord Edward and Cornet Brummell escorted their disgruntled notabilities to St James's Palace. There Malmesbury introduced the Princess to the Prince. She knelt. He raised her, took her in his arms, turned and walked to the other end of the room and said to Malmesbury, 'Harris, I am not well; pray get me a glass of brandy.' He drank it and walked out. 'Good God!' said Caroline 'is the Prince always like that? He looked very fat to me, and in no way as handsome as his portrait.'

They were married three nights later, by the Archbishop of Canterbury in the Chapel Royal at St James's. Cornet Brummell had the signal honour of being in attendance on the Prince, who 'was certainly unhappy and had manifestly had recourse to wine and spirits'–it was a silly time of day for a wedding in Carlton House circles. He accompanied the royal couple on their honeymoon to Windsor and to the Prince's estate at Kempshot, near Basingstoke. False or true, the story went round that the resourceful Lady Jersey put sedatives in the Prince's wine and purgatives in the Princess's, so that the marriage was still unconsummated when the Prince's attendants found him next morning, snoring with his head among the fire-irons in the bedchamber. But Brummell, who was among the first to see the Prince, always maintained that 'the young couple appeared perfectly satisfied with each other, particularly the Princess; she was then a very handsome and desirable-looking woman'.

She was a lonely one, for at Kempshot there were no women other than Lady Jersey and few men except the 'very blackguard companions of the Prince, who were constantly drunk and sleeping and snoring in boots on the sofas'. The Prince had a playful habit, when drunk, of pretending there were intruders in the room and searching for them with a drawn sword. This so terrified Mrs Fitzherbert that she had been known to take refuge under tables or in cupboards, but Caroline was made of sterner stuff. She sat out, perhaps even enjoyed, the drunken carousals. But she failed in her determination to overlook her husband's *légèreté*: when he paid too open attention to her Lady-of-the-Bedchamber at the dinner table Caroline replied by ogling the men, puffing at their pipes, shrugging her saucy shoulders, and using language of Brunswickian coarseness. It helped to relieve her feelings during an uncomfortable pregnancy, for the Prince had not spent every night in the fireplace.

It was another ill-tempered year. The price of veal went up from sixpence to eightpence a pound, coals doubled to £5 a chaldron. After a hard winter the spring frosts cut the young wheat; the American grain harvest had failed; the usual shipment from the Baltic had to run the French gauntlet. The quartern loaf went up from sixpence to ninepence, and then to a shilling. To economise flour the London Common Council resolved to cease wearing hair powder and the Royal Academy withdrew the free issue of bread to its sculpture students–a rowdy gang who threw it at each other instead of using it to rub out their drawings and were getting through sixteen loaves a week. At Brighton camp thirteen men of the Oxford Militia protested so vigorously against the bad food that they were charged with mutiny. Two were sentenced to be shot; six others, less fortunate, were ordered 1000 lashes. This meant being flogged to death; however, three were reprieved and the medical officer intervened after the other three had each received 300 lashes. In an attempt to prevent this sort of thing spreading to the civilian population, the Government brought in a new Seditious Meetings Bill, presently to be joined by a Treasonable Practices Act.

Confronted with the Prince's marriage and the consolidation of Lady Jersey's position as *maîtresse en titre*, Mrs Fitzherbert moved from St James's Square to Tilney Street, just off Park Lane: no longer close at hand, but not yet out of reach. And the 10th Light Dragoons were able to return to the camp at Brighton, which from this time onwards became the most fashionable in the country–'its tents stretched forth in beauteous uniformity of lines, crowded with the young and gay, and dazzling with scarlet', just as Lydia Bennet imagined it. The soldiers marched and counter-marched. The ladies drove out to admire. An unknown genius composed one of the most famous of military melodies: *Brighton Camp* or *The Girl I Left behind Me*. And George Brummell, now promoted to lieutenant, had the good fortune to fall off his horse and break his nose. When he was a small boy his nose had resembled a long inverted cone, wide-nostrilled and almost porcine, so that one speculated on some close Irish ancestor to account for his second name of Bryan; but time had fined it down, and now his horse's hoof had turned it up at a quizzical, impertinent, disdainful angle that precisely fitted the character he had chosen to play.

George had come down with the Prince and Princess in mid-summer, the royal couple renting a small house on the Steine because the farmhouse that was later to become the Royal Pavilion was still being reconstructed by Henry Holland. The Princess accompanied her husband to several field days. On his birthday his regiment paraded in brand new uniforms that he had designed for them. The officers, according to *The Times*, 'associate with no one but their own corps. Most of them keep their own

blood horses and their girls. At one o'clock they appear on parade
to hear the word of command given to the subaltern guard;
afterwards they toss off their *goes* of brandy, dine about five, and
come about eight to the theatre.'

On 7 January 1796, Princess Caroline gave birth to a daughter
after 'a terrible hard labour for about twelve hours'. At a quarter
to ten that morning the Prince wrote to the Queen: 'The Princess
is this instant brought to bed of an *immense* girl ... Pray have the
goodness to apologise to my dear sisters for my not writing to
them, but I am so fatigued.' At five weeks the baby was christened
Charlotte Augusta in honour of each of her grandmothers. In
April the Prince, who was too sensitive to stand scenes, sent his
wife a message by way of Lord Cholmondeley his Chamberlain,
that he intended never to share the same room with her again.
The Princess told Cholmondeley she preferred to receive that
sort of news directly from her husband, and in writing. The
Prince complied: it was his determination that they should live
apart, and 'even in the event of any accident happening to my
daughter (which I trust Providence in its mercy will avert) I shall
not infringe the terms of the restrictions by proposing, at any
period, a connection of a more particular nature'.

He was plagued with many grievances. After all that he had
gone through–the distasteful marriage to Caroline, the exhausting
birth of the baby, the agonising decision to put aside his wife–
Pitt and the government were welshing on their agreement to
increase his allowance, simply because they had discovered he had
piled up another £600,000 in debts since Parliament had bailed
him out nine years before. They were insisting that part of the
new grant should be earmarked for payment of the old debts.
He was shocked at their dishonesty. And by the vulgar attacks on
him in the press. He sought refuge with his bootmakers and
tailors. One day in July 1798, the sculptor Rossi had to wait three
hours before continuing work on his bust of the Prince because
the Prince was trying on forty pairs of boots and examining
patterns presented by two successive tailors.

This is the first occasion on which Brummell's increasing influence
is clearly apparent. The Prince had always been a stylish dresser,

but not a fastidious one. The costume in which Brummell had first seen him at Windsor five years before, all gaudy stripes and spangles and silver and gold, was a late Macaroni confection. The extreme Whigs had swung the other way, obstinately declaring their earlier admiration for the French revolutionaries by a calculated slovenliness in their dress. So that Fox, who had in his youth paraded in Macaroni velvets and satins and laces, with muff and red-heeled shoes, blue hair powder and feathered hat, now slouched on the benches of the Commons in a shabby blue coat and buff waistcoat (the American colours which the Whigs wore to provoke the King), crumpled linen and a none-too-clean stock. Brummell set his face as much against the vulgar ostentations of the Macaronis as the sleazy affectations of the Whigs, and the drunken farmyard boorishness of the Bucks. He stood simply for moderation and good taste: 'His chief aim was to avoid anything marked; one of his aphorisms being, that the severest mortification a gentleman could incur was to attract observation in the street by his outward appearance.'

The perfection of elegance at which he aimed was to be achieved by the cut of his clothes, the fit of his gloves (he was said to employ two makers, one for the thumbs, the other for the fingers and the rest of the hand) the immaculate gloss on his boots and, most important of all, 'no perfumes, but very fine linen, plenty of it, and country washing', as he once told the courtesan Harriette Wilson, to whom he repeated his dictum that 'if John Bull turns round to look after you, you are not well dressed; but either too stiff, too tight, or too fashionable'. Throughout his life, after cleaning his teeth and shaving, he would spend two hours washing and scrubbing himself with a pig's-bristle brush, then working over his eyebrows and whiskers with a dentist's mirror and tweezers, before beginning the serious business of the day–putting on his clothes.

He was now educating the Prince in the painstaking exactitude, the consideration of endless variable minutiae, the unremitting search for perfection which he practised each morning in his own dressing room. If he did not entirely succeed, the fault lay not in his teaching methods but in his material. Thackeray, in a famous attack on the Prince, wrote: 'There is his coat, his star, his wig, his countenance simpering under it ... I try and take him to pieces, and find silk stockings, padding, stays, a coat with frogs and a fur collar, a star and a blue ribbon, a pocket-handkerchief prodigiously scented, one of Truefitts best nutty brown wigs reeking with oil, a set of teeth and a huge black stock, under-waistcoat, more underwaistcoats, and then nothing.'

But if Brummell had been stripped of all his clothes, an essential Brummell would still have remained.

He had served two years with the dragoons and had been pro-moted yet again, to captain, but since he spent more time in front of a cheval glass than on horseback, and in attendance on the Prince than with his troop, it was not surprising that he was still unfamiliar with most of his men. Fortunately one of his dragoons had a nose which remained bright blue even in the warmest weather; Brummell ordered that this man should be stationed in the front rank and he was thus always able to identify his own troop. And then one day, as he sat immaculate and motionless on his glossily groomed charger, his squadron commander rode up and sharply demanded what he was doing there.

Brummell gazed at him in polite astonishment. 'You are with the wrong troop!' shouted the colonel. Brummell, casting a quick glance over his shoulder, caught a reassuring glimpse of the blue nose. 'No, no, Sir!' he said. 'I know better than that–a pretty thing indeed if I did not know my own troop!' Alas, because of his estrangement from regimental affairs he did not know that he had recently received some recruits and lost blue nose. But it made a good story when one was dining out. And he had not, after all, joined the army to make a career of it. His attention was fixed on the coming year; 1797.

It is the year distinguished for some by the fact that Thomas Lord, groundsman of a cricket club at King's Cross, set up on his own in Dorset Square, thence to hop in two stages to St John's Wood, where his business flourished in a warm compost of heavy betting, widespread corruption of players and umpires, and riots caused by the brutal innovation of over-arm bowling. It was the year in which Fox dined at Carlton House for the first time since the Mrs Fitzherbert affair, the Prince having invited all the Opposition leaders to mark his displeasure at Pitt's continued parsimony. It was the year that Pitt introduced a tax of ten per cent on all incomes above £200 a year and the Bank of England suspended payment in gold. It was the year of mutinies by the Channel Fleet and the North Sea Fleet. And it was the year in which Captain Brummell came of age and into possession of a capital sum which *The Gentleman's Magazine* estimated at £20,000, which his friend Thomas Raikes thought to be £30,000, and which Brummell himself later said was between £40,000 and £50,000. It was, at any rate, a tidy fortune that probably brought him in £2000 a year, not far short of the sum on which his father had kept a family, a town house and a country estate, and saved as well.

This was also the year in which Captain Brummell was involved in a brief burst of serious military activity. One afternoon when the 10th Light Dragoons were quartered at Dorchester and the Prince of Wales was fox-hunting with some of his officers at Crichel House, the estate he had rented five miles north of Wimborne Minster, word came of a French fleet making for the Dorset coast. It was known that the French had constructed barges and shallow craft for an invasion. The warships were no doubt escorting them. The Prince, throwing himself into the saddle anew, and galloping as wildly as his seventeen-and-a-half stone would permit, led his officers through Blandford, where he alerted a squadron of the Bays, and then on another seventeen miles to Dorchester, arriving well after nightfall. To the blare of trumpets and clatter of startled hooves the Prince of Wales's Own readied themselves for battle while their Colonel went off to confer with the General commanding the district. The General, unaware of the impending invasion of his shore, only half-a-dozen miles distant, had gone early to bed. The Prince routed him out, informed him of the perilous situation, and had him despatch scouts in all directions. They returned with confirmation that a fleet was sailing along the coast. Only in one respect was the Prince's information defective–the ships were English, not French.

The Prince continued to yearn and clamour for promotion that would give him at least equal rank with his younger brother. In April 1798 he begged his father to use him on active service, but the King drily responded that 'military command is incompatible with the situation of the Prince of Wales'. There were in fact no British troops in contact with the French at this time, though rebellion was foaming up in Ireland and at home there was industrial unrest. More than two years before, the King's State Coach had been stoned in St James's Park as he returned from Parliament, the angry mob shouting 'No King, no War' and 'Give us Peace and Bread!' But the war continued, and so did the industrial revolution, with work moving from the water-wheel to the steam-boiler, from cottage to factory, leaving behind a recrement of unemployed incapable of producing anything except more and more children. So that the Reverend Thomas Malthus felt impelled to warn the Prime Minister that his amendments to the Poor Laws possessed in a high degree 'the great and radical defect of all systems of the kind, that of tending to increase population without increasing the means for its support'–in others words, enabling people to stay alive without compelling them to work. The rude and idle mechanics, blind to the wisdom of economists and seeking work but not finding it, took to rioting in a half-starved way. Troops were used to put down the disturbances, and one evening the 10th Light Dragoons were warned to be ready to go north on these duties.

The following morning Brummell called upon the Prince who, astonished to see his young friend up and about at so early an hour, asked what urgent business had brought him.

'Why, the fact is, Your Highness,' said Brummell, 'I have heard that we are ordered to Manchester. Now you must be aware how disagreeable that would be to *me*.'

The Prince waited.

'Think, Your Royal Highness,' Brummell continued, 'Manchester!'

While the Prince considered the horrors of provincial garrison life, Brummell clinched his argument: 'Besides–*you* would not be there.' After the briefest of pauses for the gross flattery to sink in: 'I have therefore, with Your Royal Highness's permission, determined to sell out.'

'Oh, by all means, Brummell,' said the Prince. 'Do as you please, do as you please!'

One of Brummell's close friends later described this conversation as 'utterly unworthy of him and impossible'. But this is to
miss the point of what became one of the Beau's favourite
anecdotes. Certainly the sketches of the Prince's character and the
one that Brummell wished to have accepted as his own are so neat
that it sounds like an invention. But if anybody made it up, it was
Brummell himself. On the other hand, in March 1798 there was
'a considerable disturbance at Manchester among the cotton-
spinners, some misunderstanding between them and their masters
having taken place respecting wages', so the story may well have
some basis in fact.

George was not the only Brummell to hob-nob with the royal
family. The King's sixth son, asthmatic Augustus Frederick whose
tutor had flogged him for failing to stop wheezing, had been
sent to Italy to find a cure in the Mediterranean sun on a diet of
nothing but potatoes and water. At Rome in April 1793 he
married a daughter of the fourth Earl of Dunmore: Lady Augusta
Murray, described by a contemporary as 'a coarse and confident
woman with a very singular-shaped face–the lower part from the
Nose falling as if shaved off'. The wedding was discreet but not
by any means secret, and within the month the London know-alls
were gossiping about this foolish but rather charming affair
between 'Gus and Gussie'. By December, however, both had
returned to England where they repeated the ceremony at St
George's, Hanover Square. Six weeks later Lady Augusta gave
birth to a son who was christened Augustus Frederick and later
surnamed d'Este. A Privy Council promptly sat to consider this
flagrant breach of the Royal Marriage Act, and declared the
marriage void. The twenty-one-year-old Prince was exiled to
Naples in the charge of a Hanoverian, Count Munster, who tired
of his task and was replaced by a steward-cum-warder named
Livingston whose orders were to control Augustus's spending as
well as to keep him away from Augusta.

Livingston disapproved of the 'set of very improper society'
in which the Prince moved (it included the Neapolitan Royal
Family and the British ambassador's wife, Emma Hamilton).
He took him off to Vienna, then Dresden and finally Berlin, where

they arrived in October, the Prince so fatigued by the travelling that
he was quite unable to go to bed for four weeks, spending every
night sitting up in a chair. The relative peacefulness of life at the
Prussian capital restored his health but played havoc with Livingston's. The latter was given permission in the summer of 1799
to return to England and take the waters at Bath in the hope of
relieving his 'very violent rheumatism and flying gout'; he left his
friend Captain Robert Arbuthnot in charge of the Prince.

Meanwhile George Brummell's brother William became involved in one of the many plots to bring the young lovers
together again. Lady Augusta was under constant observation in
England and, though her movements were not as restricted as
Augustus's, it was made clear to her that he would not be permitted to return to England and she would be prevented from
joining him in Prussia. She decided to go to Lisbon in the hope
that they might meet there. About the time that Livingston was
applying for leave, William Brummell and Lord Graves's eldest
son, Thomas, who had known the Brummell boys at Eton, arrived
in Berlin and put up at the hotel where Augustus was staying.
Their mission was evidently connected with the proposed
rendezvous in Lisbon and they presumably found unexpected
difficulties, for when they returned to London Lady Augusta
herself came back from Lisbon to consult with them. On 13
August 1799 Arbuthnot sent agitated letters to Livingston and
the King, warning them that 'Lady Augusta Murray arrived here
on Saturday under the borrowed name of Mrs Ford. She pretends
that her motive for taking such an imprudent step was to see her
husband for the last time, as she had heard from Lady Strafford
that he was dangerously ill and dying. I do not believe a word of
this, as I know that she had seen Brummell in London, who
certainly must have told her that the Prince's health was by no
means in a dangerous situation. She is lodged in the same hotel in
the apartment occupied formerly by Graves and Brummell.'

The Prince renewed his appeals to his father to be allowed home
and for his marriage to be recognised. He begged his brother, the
Prince of Wales, to support him. His father flatly replied no; his
brother sent him a long letter, referring him to the Royal Marriage
Act. 'Our lot by birth and station, my dearest brother, makes us

all amenable to it. Since fate has rendered it inevitable, 'tis our duty to submit, and the more grace and cheerfulness with which we do so, the more dignified and amiable we appear.'

In the early summer of 1800, Augustus decided on defiance. He gave Arbuthnot the slip, returned to London, and settled down with his wife and child in Hertford Street. From there he wrote to William Brummell on 17 July, asking for the loan of £100 for a fortnight: 'Ever since my arrival in England my Relations have never allowed me money, saying that as Arbuthnot had the only Power to draw I could not have any till his arrival. At this moment I am forced to leave my House which I cannot do without paying a hundred pounds. My Wife begs her compliments and I sign myself most sincerely . . .'

William presumably paid, for he remained a close friend of the Prince throughout their lives; and Graves was appointed comp-troller of the Prince's household a few years later. By then the great romance of Gus and Gussie was over, leaving the chinless bride with two children (Ellen Augusta was born in August 1801) and a sense of grievance which she took to the courts without success.

George's resignation from the dragoons did little to lessen his connection with the officers of the regiment. He was constantly calling in to see them, and one of the typical Brummell anecdotes dates from this period. He drove into the barracks at Canterbury in a four-horse carriage and one of his friends, surprised at the extravagance, shouted from the messroom window: 'Hallo, George! When did you take to four horses?' 'Only since my valet gave me warning for making him travel with a pair,' George shouted back. This belongs with another favourite story of how he offered employment to the valet of Colonel Kelly, who had recently been burnt to death. The valet asked for £150 a year. 'Make it £200,' said Brummell, 'and *I'll* work for *you.*'

As for his former colonel-in-chief, he saw more of him than ever, and made a point of advertising the fact. When asked how he caught a cold, he replied: 'Why, do you know, I left my carriage yesterday evening, on my way to town from the Pavilion, and the infidel of a landlord put me into a room with a damp stranger.' Though any traveller in those days was fortunate if damp strangers were the only things he had to share a room with –most of them were infested with bugs and fleas.

In January 1799 George spent three weeks at Belvoir Castle in the party that the Prince took up to celebrate the twenty-first birthday of the Duke of Rutland, 'Cheerful Charlie'–a confusing nickname, since he was John Henry and in fact had a brother, Charles Manners, who, with another brother, Robert Manners, had joined the 10th Dragoons in the year before Brummell left and were among his closest friends. In April he was elected to Brooks's which, with White's, was to be the centre of his existence. With these two clubs in St James's Street as his base, he set out on the career which he now knew could not fail to be dazzling.

His mission was to establish himself as the arbiter of the art of graceful living in which 'wit and taste hold festival, and the associations of reality are exchanged for the associations of imagination', as Amiel described it; so that 'society is a form of poetry'. It was not easy. Even among the fashionable set to whom he carried his gospel of fastidious elegance there were many who still considered it manly to be uncouth and effeminate to be too clean. The task of converting them demanded confidence and character; but beneath his flippant exterior young Brummell had both. There was a very firm hand in the so-carefully tailored glove.

Brooks's, when Brummell joined, had a five guinea entrance fee, an annual subscription of ten guineas, and a limit of 450 members. Among them were most of the wits and gamblers and many of the leading politicians of the time. There was Sir Charles Bunbury, who had won the first Derby Stakes in 1780 with Diomed; Old Q, veteran of hundreds of scandals, at seventy-five still seated at the notorious bow-window of his house in Piccadilly with a mounted servant posted below to be sent after any passing woman who caught the reprobate's rheumy eye; Sheridan; his friend and rival Fox, now slovenly, squat, fat, pasty-cheeked, with tired dark eyes beneath thick black startled eyebrows, living on excessive doses of laudanum to soothe his abused stomach and vast quantities of alcohol to revive his depressed spirits. 'Charles', said his friend Frederick Byng, 'loved only three things, women, play and politics. Yet at no period did he ever form a creditable connexion with a woman; he lost his whole fortune at the gaming-table; and, with the exception of about eleven months, he has remained always in opposition.'

The club was still mourning the death of one of its most famous wits, George Selwyn, whose interest in the dead so exceeded that in the living that he 'professed never to have had connection with a woman but seven times in the whole course of his life, and that the last time was with a maid at the inn at Andover when he was twenty-nine', yet he would go to any lengths to witness a public execution and made a journey to Paris solely to see the regicide Damiens torn to pieces by horses. Filling his place as a wit, though not in other respects, was the amiable General Fitzpatrick, Fox's uncle, former Secretary of State for Ireland and for War, ardent no less against the American rebels than in the boudoirs of his friends' wives, one of whom, Lady Anne Foley, once wrote to him, 'Dear Richard, I give you joy. I have just made you the father of a beautiful boy. P.S. this is not a circular.' It was Fitzpatrick who said of the repetitious reminiscences of the club bore, 'It is not every man who can be trusted with a good memory.' Like Brummell he was a stickler for the proprieties, so that on his death bed he chose his last words in French–*la pièce est finie*–'there being servants in the room'.

Other members included men of learning such as Thomas Grenville who bequeathed his fine library to the British Museum, and Richard Payne Knight, numismatist and poetaster; men of compassion such as William Wilberforce; men of immense riches such as the Duke of Devonshire, who entertained as many as 180 visitors and their servants at Chatsworth simultaneously and fed them on sixteen sheep a week and five bullocks a fortnight, yet could never give a large enough allowance to his wife Georgiana to keep her out of debt. The Duchess, who owed her spirit and carroty hair to her great-great-grandmother, Sarah Jennings, the wife of Malborough, was a compulsive gambler. When she and her sister, Lady Bessborough, could neither honour their debts nor ask their husbands for more 'they would go to a tradesman's shop and order a hundred pounds' worth of goods upon condition of the tradesman advancing them £50, to be also made a debt'. When she died it was calculated that the Duke had already paid out £200,000 for her debts–and she still left many unsettled.

Apart from his clubs and his friends' dining tables, Brummell was mostly to be seen at the opera–the theatre in the Haymarket which eventually achieved supremacy over the Pantheon in Oxford Street and was claimed to be 'one of the most superb in Europe–a circular vestibule, almost lined with looking-glass, and furnished with sophas, in which female loveliness is not only seen but reflected'. Other places of entertainment included the large theatres at Covent Garden and Drury Lane; Sadler's Wells, which specialised in pantomimes, and the Sans-Souci, where Charles Dibdin gave a one-man show of music, comedy and melodrama; Astley's Equestrian Exhibition at the Amphitheatre of Arts on the south side of the Thames and the two best-known pleasure gardens at Ranelagh and Vauxhall, where an average of a thousand visitors a night (entrance fee, two shillings) was needed to make a profit on the three-and-a-half month season. These, however, were seldom visited by the gentry of Mayfair and St James's except as a joke or for the pursuit of frail females.

The Prince's callous treatment of his wife brought him into universal disgrace with the people, the press and his father. When the King reviewed the 10th Light Dragoons he refused to allow his son to appear on parade with them. When he discovered William Beechey, the Queen's official portrait painter, inserting the Prince's figure in the painting he made of the review, he strode across shouting, 'Hey! What, what, what! Beechey! The Prince? Damn the Prince!' and ordered the canvas to be thrown out of the window. The Prince changed tack. He invited Caroline to dine with him at Carlton House–she refused. He wrote his admonitory letter to Augustus Frederick and made sure his father knew of it. He also let it be known that he had parted from Lady Jersey–though this was only in order to return to the unreluctant Mrs Fitzherbert, to whom he sent a copy of a will leaving all his property to her, which he claimed to have made in January 1796, three days after the birth of his daughter, proof that his love had never waned. Whether she believed this or not, it was a useful document to have at her bankers. Within six months they were being seen at the opera together. In June Mrs Fitzherbert gave what was virtually a second, and this time public, wedding breakfast, for 400 guests who assembled in Tilney Street at two in the afternoon, dined in three marquees in the gardens at seven and kept up the junketings until five o'clock the next morning.

Nuptial celebrations were in the air. In May the Beau's brother William had taken advantage of the Brummell and Macpherson connections with the East India Company by marrying Miss Anne Daniell whose father, James, had held a seat on the Governor-General's Council and controlled the district of Masulipatam. They settled down on an estate that William bought at Wivenhoe. Neither William nor his sister Maria had much in common with George. Maria is said by family tradition to have made a runaway marriage with a Captain Blackshaw of the Rifle Brigade. William evidently became an old-fashioned Tory squire. When George was asked if he intended to bring him to Brooks's, he replied: 'Yes, in a day or two; but I thought he had better walk the back streets till his new clothes came home.' More than forty years later William was seen on holiday in Hastings driving a four-in-hand and wearing one of the heavy caped coachman's greatcoats that George condemned from his very first days as a dictator of men's fashions.

Brummell, despite his reputation for having an acid tongue, was in fact endowed with such imperturbable amiability that he could maintain a simultaneous friendship with people who were bitterly at odds with each other. Thus he never ceased visiting the neglected Lady Jersey while continuing his close association with the Prince. For the latter, a martyr to chronic insecurity, it was manna and unction to have a deferent and amusing companion who was so supremely sure of himself. He fell into the habit of calling on Brummell in the morning to hear him gossip and watch him dress, and even on occasions lingered on to share dinner with him.

They had the same tailors–Schweitzer and Davidson, and later Guthrie, in Cork Street, Weston and Meyer in Conduit Street–and it was not long before Brummell was setting the style instead of the Prince. A customer who asked Schweitzer what cloth he recommended for a coat was told: 'Why, Sir, the Prince wears

superfine, and Mr Brummell the Bath coating; but it is immaterial
which you choose. Suppose, Sir, we say the Bath coating–I think
Mr Brummell has a trifle the preference.' So much the preference,
in fact, that his treatment of the nobility had a great deal more
princely authority than the Prince's. Having had the Duke of
Bedford rotate slowly in front of his disapproving gaze, he finally
demanded, 'Bedford, do you call this thing a coat?' And to another
member of the peerage whom he had stopped in St James's Street
to inquire what he had on his feet: 'Shoes, are they? I thought
they were slippers!'

Another remarkable example of Brummell's ability to get on
well with sworn enemies was the way in which, for some years
at any rate, he managed to ride the waves of envy and bile that
surrounded and separated the royal brothers. He met the Duke
of York at Devonshire House and was soon on excellent terms
with this 'big, burly, loud, jolly, cursing, courageous man'. York
was 'affectionate and lovable, noble and generous to a fault, never
known to break a promise', totally unlike his elder brother except
for the round head, scarlet cheeks and watery blue eyes that made
so many of the Hanoverian males look like choleric whitebait.
He took his duties seriously enough to spend most of the week
at his house in Piccadilly (later converted into apartments under
the Duke's second title, Albany). At weekends he went to Oatlands Park, his estate in Surrey famous for the three-roomed
grotto decorated with seashells and artificial stalactites that looked
out over a pretty prospect of pond and woodland. Here the
Duchess, 'pretty little Fred', breakfasted and dined during the
week and the Duke played interminable games of whist on
Saturdays and Sundays.

Brummell was one of the most frequent guests at Oatlands. He
shared with the Duchess a passionate love of animals. When
Oatlands caught fire while the Duke was in Flanders, her guests
noticed that the Duchess 'seemed more anxious about her animals
than about the house' and persuaded the King, who had spent
the day there, to take one of her dogs home with him for safety.
Besides the scores of dogs whose burial mounds and graves spread
farther and farther around the ornamental basin that faced the
grotto, she kept eagles and macaws in the flower garden, monkeys

on the lawn in front of her bedroom, and ostriches and kangaroos in the paddock.

She was the child of a broken home. Her mother, divorced by the Prince Royal of Prussia, was said to have commented, on learning of her daughter's marriage to the Duke of York, that it was 'a good enough match for the daughter of Müller the Musician'. Frederica disliked the females of the human species and was happiest when there were none around. She was much neglected by her husband in the early days of their marriage, but she did not complain and they eventually settled down happily. With Brummell she was immediately on the best and easiest of terms; if he can be said to have ever truly fallen in love with a woman, she was the one.

Certainly he felt more at home at Oatlands than in any other of the great houses he visited. There were no activities more violent than a stroll from the house to the grotto. The company, apart from his hostess the Duchess, her lady-of-the-bedchamber Lady Anne Culling Smith and Lady Anne's three daughters, was almost exclusively masculine and therefore more appreciative of his elegant schoolboyish quips. It was here that Brummell, when asked if he *never* ate green vegetables, replied: 'Yes, Madam, I once ate a pea.' He made great play with this affectation that kitchen garden produce was fit only for common people; years later, when it surprisingly appeared that he was about to get married but the affair was equally unexpectedly broken off, he explained, 'My dear fellow, what could I do? It was impossible, for I found that she actually ate cabbage.' His appetite in other respects, for meat and fruit and his beloved bread and cheese, was large enough by modern standards to make it astonishing that he managed to keep his slim figure–though by comparison with many of his fellows he was almost abstemious.

The amount of food consumed at this period by those who could afford it was marvellously disgusting. The Duchess of Devonshire's daughter, staying at the house of her brother-in-law, Lord Stafford, wrote: 'The dinner for us two was soup, fish, fricassee of chicken, cutlets, venison, veal, hare, vegetables of all kinds, tart, melon, pineapple, grapes, peaches, nectarines, with wine in proportion. Six servants to wait upon us, whom we did not dare dispense with, a gentleman-in-waiting and a fat old housekeeper hovering round the door to listen, I suppose, if we should express a wish. Before this sumptuous repast was well digested, about four hours later, the doors opened, and in was pushed a supper in the same proportion, in itself enough to have fed me for a week. I did not know whether to laugh or cry . . . God bless you. I am summoned to an immense cold collation. We breakfasted two hours ago.' In the big houses, there were so many servants on duty that they often got in each other's way. Each guest at a house-party would be expected to bring his own man to stand behind his chair throughout dinner and to help him to bed when he tumbled drunk to the floor.

Most well-to-do people were hypochondriacally concerned with their bellies, simply because they stuffed them too full for peace of mind or body. And when they at last staggered to their bedrooms they consumed vast quantities of the calomel pills which, with Godbold's Vegetable Balsam (for Consumption and Asthma) and Velno's Vegetable Syrup (for almost everything else) were the staple remedies in every household. In summer dinner was often an afternoon meal; after two or three hours at table, the company would stroll in the garden and grounds or go for a ride in the countryside and then return to drink tea before retiring. With the meats, claret was offered by most hosts, champagne by the vulgar; tokay with the pudding; often hock, sherry–even port or port and water–throughout the meal; the latter custom Brummell did much to change, insisting that this 'hot, intoxicating liquor so much drunk by the lower orders, should wait for the cheese. Statesmen as brilliant as Pitt kept themselves going on continual glasses of port throughout the day; women as beautiful and vivacious as the Duchess of Devonshire were sipping themselves headlong to cirrhosis; the bulk of the aristocracy were, to put no fine a point on it, boozers. During one period of stress Brummell and Harriette Wilson are said to have drunk four bottles of champagne at a sitting, but usually he was as moderate and discriminating in drink as he was in dress.

The Duchess of York, a small amiable woman with bad teeth and tiny feet, was described by Brummell's friend the banker

Thomas Raikes as 'not only a *très grande dame* in the fullest sense
of the word, but a woman of the most admirable sound sense and
charity'. She attracted the young as well as the middle-aged and
eagerly received any who offered high spirits and good conversation. On Saturday afternoons about five o'clock the chaises
gathered in St James's Street to carry the weekend guests down to
Oaklands: Henry de Ros, the Premier Baron of England; Lord
Foley, whom the others called 'No. 11' because of his skinny legs;
Lord Yarmouth, the young polished roué whose mother, the
Marchioness of Hertford, was shortly to join the band of the
Prince of Wales's matronly mistresses and who was himself to
become the model for Thackeray's Lord Steyne and Disraeli's
Lord Monmouth; William Spencer, 'The Poet of Society'; the
young officers, Herbert Taylor, Arthur Upton, James Armstrong
and 'Kangaroo' Cooke–the last two aides-de-camp to the Duke of
York; Matthew Lewis, who had recently shocked society with his
Gothic romance, *Ambrosio, or the Monk*. Like so many authors of
bold bad books, 'Monk' Lewis was not an imposing figure–an odd
little chap with tiny protuberant eyes and a tendency to tears. At
Oatlands on one occasion he was asked why he was crying after
dinner, and he replied: 'Oh, the Duchess spoke so *very* kindly to me!'

'My dear fellow,' said Armstrong, 'pray don't cry; I dare say
she didn't mean it.'

He managed not only to be a butt himself but also to have a
Negro servant who provided endless opportunities for the very
simple word-play that so delighted Brummell and the Prince and
their friends. One of the Beau's most successful stories was of his
calling at Lewis's to ask after a young woman who had sprained
her ankle. Lewis was not in, but had said in his servant's presence
that 'The doctor has seen her, put her leg straight, and the poor
chicken is doing well.' This, Brummell claimed, was relayed to
him by the Negro as, 'The doctor has been here; she has laid
eggs; and she and the chickens are doing well.' Gales of laughter
swept St James's Street.

At Christmas the Duchess brought a lavish German touch to
the festivities. The great dining room was decorated like a fair
ground; a table at one end bore the presents brought by the guests
for the Duchess; on another at the opposite end were displayed

the Duchess's presents to her guests. In the middle stood a Christmas tree loaded with oranges, sweetmeats and gingerbread. The servants were brought in, and after them the orphans and various charity children under the Duchess's patronage who were let loose on the Christmas tree. Before the guests sat down to dinner, there was a great distribution and reception of gifts. The Duchess would sometimes add little touches of embroidery to the presents that she gave; they were frequently of fine leather and semi-precious stones. 'The original intention,' recalled one of the Oatlands set, 'was that the presents should be of moderate cost on both sides; but Brummell once brought down a Brussels lace gown as his offering which cost 150 guineas.' It was one of his rare excesses, explained if not excused by his great affection for the Duchess, who loyally returned it in later years.

A dress for ordinary occasions would have been considered quite expensive at twelve guineas. But this was evidently a special party gown, like the one the Duchess wore at Queen Charlotte's birthday ball that year: 'a petticoat richly embroidered in purple and gold wheat ears, terminating at the bottom with a border of geranium leaves entwined with gold. Over the petticoat was a magnificent Indian sash, looped up at the left side by a rich cord and tassels, whilst the body and train were of white satin embroidered with gold and ornamented with purple to correspond.' Formal court dress was simple and severe–black muslin over pink sarsenet with a few discreet antique jewels or gold chains.

The new century marched warily along. Times grew harder, highwaymen on the roads bolder, footpads in the streets more frequent. Food became scarcer, particularly in London, where the population, despite Malthus's disapproval, now exceeded a million. In November 1800 Lady Malmesbury recorded the rumour that 'there is to be a compulsory law about the quantity of bread to be consumed by each person, and you are to be obliged when eating in other persons' houses *to carry your bread with you*'. Some society hostesses no longer served bread at dinner, offering potatoes or rice instead. This, said Lady Malmesbury, 'is absurd. The summer has been one of the hottest ever known, and the harvest magnificent. The real cause is the immense consumption and still greater waste from fleets and armies and expeditions which float about and do nothing.'

That summer Bonaparte had defeated the Austrians at Marengo, and in December Moreau finally crushed them at Hohenlinden. Britain, in the not unfamiliar situation of being deserted by her Continental allies, fought on alone. The restive, over-conscientious King took refuge in a bout of madness which lasted from February to May 1801. In August the French army that Bonaparte had deserted in Egypt surrendered to the British, and in October he proposed a peace which would enable him to regain breath for more aggression. English tourists flocked across the Channel to view the little monster at close quarters and discover what ravages his military dictatorship was inflicting on Paris. They observed that 'he smiles with his mouth but his eyes never have a corresponding expression' but the Parisians who 'were a few years ago gloomy, savage, without regard to dress or cleanliness, are now coming fast round to cheerfulness and civility'.

Much the same, in a milder sort of way, could have been said of the Prince of Wales, who spent the autumn of 1802 and the winter very quietly at Brighton, decorating the Pavilion in the old-fashioned Chinese style that he favoured at Carlton House, riding and walking with his aides, Admiral 'Jacko' Payne and Colonel Conyngham, and basking in the joy of his reunion with Mrs Fitzherbert. 'My neighbours here go on most lovingly,' wrote a Brighton resident in February 1803. 'The affection seems to grow with their growth and fatten with their fat.'

Love was rife in Surrey as well as Sussex. In that same week Lord Glenbervie recorded in his diary that Charles Culling Smith, Lady Anne's husband, 'has been long supposed to be, *au dernier point*, in the good graces of the Duchess of York . . . The other day the Duke of York, having returned to Oatlands suddenly and unexpectedly, actually surprised the Duchess and Mr Smith in the very fact.' The Duke was said to have protested in a forthright military manner, but the King ordered there should be no fuss. Since the Duke was at the time beginning a liaison with the beautiful Mrs Clarke–who was later to cause him so much embarrassment–he decided to regard the affair as settled on what a later generation was to call a knock-for-knock basis.

It could have had a very serious outcome. Duelling was a scourge of the time and had grown more lethal with the fashion of using pistols, discharged at twelve paces, instead of swords. The Duke himself, when Colonel of the Coldstream Guards in 1789, had faced one of his company commanders, Charles Lennox, on the field of honour–in this case Wimbledon Common–and had come near to death. Lennox's bullet clipped a side-curl off the Duke's wig; the Duke did not return fire. Lennox's son, Lord William, later calculated that during the reigns of George III and George IV one hundred and fifty duels took place among what were termed distinguished people. Ninety-seven occurred during the former and fifty-five during the latter reign. Seventy men were killed and forty-five wounded. Among the combatants were forty noblemen, including a royal duke, three common dukes, two marquesses, two earls, two viscounts, two lords by courtesy, seventy-nine officers of the army, eight naval officers, forty-two gentlemen, twenty-eight Irishmen, thirteen lawyers, twelve members of the House of Commons, five actors, two students of Dublin University, eleven Americans, thirty foreigners, the rest Scottish and Welsh.

The pretexts for fighting ranged from adultery to political disagreements, from drunken insults to an uncomplicated delight in killing. In April 1803 a young army officer named Montgomery was riding in Hyde Park, followed by his Newfoundland dog, when he encountered a naval officer named Macnamara, similarly accompanied. The dogs fought; their masters challenged each other. They met at Chalk Farm that evening. Colonel Montgomery was shot in the heart and died instantly; Captain Macnamara was also wounded in the chest but lived to rise to admiral. Montgomery was an expert shot and practised bully who had called out and killed several men before. Another military fire-eater, Major Campbell, who deliberately provoked and shot dead a fellow officer, was successfully convicted of killing him 'with malice aforethought' and hanged at Armagh in 1808. This did not have a great deterrent effect, but for a time the bullies took to sparing their victims' lives in favour of maiming them–by shooting them in the knee-cap, for instance.

Brummell derived no pleasure from such affairs. He seems to

have been involved in at least three difficult situations. In the first, according to his own typical self-mocking account, the other man's second called upon him and demanded that Brummell should name a time and a place for the duel—or apologise within five minutes. 'In five minutes, sir?' said Brummell. 'In five seconds, or in less time, if you prefer it!'

'Perhaps you are not aware of the circumstance,' he told a friend on another occasion,

but I am not naturally of an heroic turn. Nevertheless, I once had an affair at Chalk Farm, and a dreadful state I was in, I can tell you. Never in my life shall I forget the horrors of the previous night! Sleep was out of the question, and I passed it in pacing my room. The dawn was to me the harbinger of death, not of another day, and yet I almost hailed it with pleasure. But my second's step upon the stairs soon neutralized the feeling; and the horrid details, which he carefully explained to me, annihilated the little courage that had survived the anxieties of the night. We left the house, and no accident of any kind, no fortunate upset, occurred on our way to the place of rendezvous.

There was nobody on the ground, and each minute seemed an age. At length the clock of a neighbouring church announced that the hour of appointment had come, but there was no appearance of my antagonist. My military friend kindly hinted that clocks and watches varied, a fact I was well aware of, and which I thought he might have spared me the pleasure of hearing him remark upon; but a second is always such a 'damned good-natured friend'.

The next quarter of an hour passed in awful silence; still no one appeared, not even on the horizon. My companion whistled and, confound him, looked much disappointed. The half-hour struck–still no one; the third quarter and at length the hour. My centurion of the Coldstream now came up, this time in *truth* my friend, and said to me–and I can tell you they were the sweetest accents that ever fell upon my ear–'Well, George, I think we may go.' 'My dear M——', I replied, 'you have taken a load off my mind, let us go *immediately!*'

Brummell certainly exaggerated his timidity. On one occasion Harriette Wilson repeated to one of her lovers an uncomplimentary remark that Brummell had made about him. The lover, a military man, stormed round to Brummell's house and demanded satisfaction. Brummell ordered him to leave and, when he refused to go, chased him out with a red-hot poker. Harriette, her rival Julia Johnstone said, never forgave Brummell for failing to fight the duel she had planned for him.

*   *   *

By May 1803 Bonaparte was ready to go to war again. The English visitors who had flocked to stare at the romantic little Corsican found themselves interned in his unromantic fortresses; the menacing barges were assembled at Calais and Boulogne; the Martello Towers rose on the opposing coasts. The invasion scare spread. Newly-formed volunteer corps were marching in the streets, drilling in the squares, manoeuvring in the parks and firing at Chalk Farm butts. The King reviewed the combined corps of London and Westminster in Hyde Park—upwards of 27,000 men, and yet only a tenth of the total raised throughout the country. In the course of the martial exercises, demonstration volleys and *feux de joie*, a musket ball whisked very close to the royal wig. It was a foggy late October day, so the marksman could not be identified and his motive remained obscure.

With the exception of two of their units the metropolitan volunteers were all infantrymen; but in rural areas there was a great raising of mounted troops. The young Duke of Rutland, forming his Belvoir Volunteers, hit upon the felicitous idea of appointing the well-known cavalryman George Brummell, Capt. (Retd), to command it with the rank of major, thus contributing to the defence of the realm and at the same time ensuring a measure of witty elegant companionship for himself as honorary colonel. There was less enthusiasm locally when it turned out that the Duke, one of the nation's wealthiest citizens with an income of £40,000 a year, had with one hand contributed £500 to the County Volunteer Fund and with the other withdrawn £800 to set up his own unit.

In the course of time, a general was sent by the War Office to see how Brummell was progressing in the preparation of his troops for war. He found them drawn up for inspection in the meadow below the castle, but with no commanding officer to greet him. When he could wait no longer without loss of dignity, he began to review them. Presently Brummell came galloping up, wearing hunting pink. He assured the general that it was only by the most atrocious and unforeseeable mischance that he had been prevented from arriving in time. The meet had found early but his horse had failed at a fence. Both horse and rider had been winded; they had needed time to recover; it was then no longer possible to return to the castle and change into uniform.

The general was not to be placated. According to Brummell, who was an excellent mimic, he raised himself in his stirrups and barked: 'Sir, this conduct is wholly inexcusable; if I remember right, Sir, you once had the honour of holding a Captain's commission under his Royal Highness the Prince of Wales, the Heir Apparent himself, Sir! Now, Sir, I tell you, I tell you, Sir, that I should be wanting in a proper zeal for the honour of the service, I should be wanting in my duty, Sir, if I did not, this very evening, report this disgraceful neglect of orders to the Commander-in-Chief, as well as the state in which you present yourself in front of your regiment; and this shall be done, Sir! You may retire, Sir!'

Brummell bowed, began to walk his horse away, then turned back. 'Excuse me,' he said, 'but in my anxiety to explain this most unfortunate business I forgot to deliver a message which the Duke of Rutland desired me to give you when I left Belvoir this morning: it was to request the honour of your company at dinner.'

The general, who had expected to take pot-luck at some wretched inn on his way back to London, was delighted at the opportunity to dine at one of the richest tables in England. 'Why, really, I feel, and am, very much obliged to his Grace; pray, Major Brummell, tell the Duke I should be most happy–and, Major Brummell, as to this little affair, I am sure no man can regret it more than you do.'

Brummell bowed again, then found an excuse to hurry off to the castle, where he warned the Duke that there would be an extra guest for dinner.

rederica, Duchess of York, with some of her dogs, by Stroehling

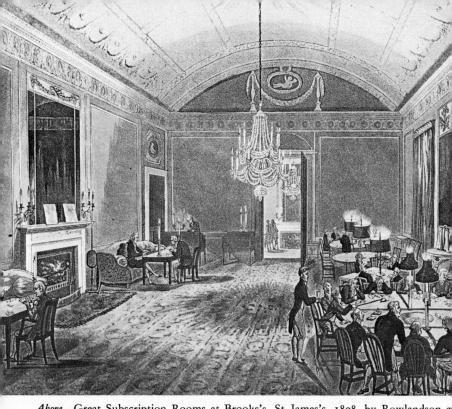

Above   Great Subscription Rooms at Brooks's, St James's, 1808, by Rowlandson a Pugin

Below   A game of whist: illustration by Cruikshank

CHAPTER THREE

The Dandy Club

It was a golden age for all those animals who delight in being hunted and torn to death. During the winter months the *beau monde* deserted London to join the squires and richer farmers in pursuing the fox in the morning, eating and drinking themselves stupid in the afternoon and evening. At other times and places they chased the stag, a rarer animal, which was put back into a cage at the end of the run and carted off to the stables, not to be hunted again until its wounds were healed. The otter was the prey of bumpkins and rustic gentry who, having dug him out of his river-bank refuge, stabbed and beat him with spears and bludgeons through the shallows until the dogs could sink their teeth into him.

But the most popular of outdoor sports was shooting. Squire Osbaldestone, a five-foot-six-inch giant of the coverts and the butts, was credited with having brought down 20 brace of partridge with 40 shots, 97 grouse with 97 shots and 100 pheasants with 100 shots, yet remained a modest and unassuming person— perhaps because fate had cast him in the same generation as the five-foot-six-inch Corsican giant who, admittedly using superior fire arms, brought down more than one and a half million men.

Autumn opened with battues of such vast proportions that members of house-parties became physically and emotionally exhausted by the slaughter of thousands of birds: a catharsis that may not have beaten cockfighting (which was available without stirring from London, or even the West End of town, at Tothill

Fields, together with such other spectator sports as dog-fighting or the baiting of badgers and bulls) but was agreed to be more manly than lady-killing and widely recognised as a cure for the after-effects of late nights and heavy drinking.

As soon as the season opened, Fox would set out for Norfolk with 'Comical Bob'–Lord Robert Spencer, a son of the Duke of Marlborough. Lord Robert was famed for having taken the Hon. Mrs Bouverie as his mistress shortly after she gave birth to her eighth child in 1786. The pair lived in devoted adultery until 1811 when, her husband having died, they got married: he aged sixty-four and she sixty-two. Both were well-known to Brummell, since Spencer was a fellow-member of Brooks's, and it was Mrs Bouverie's father who proposed Brummell for membership in 1799. Fox and Spencer hired a house at Thetford, where they 'rose at an early hour and passed the whole day with a fowling-piece in their hands, among the coveys of partridges and pheasants, for successive weeks during the autumn. These salutary occupations never failed of restoring the health that Fox had lost in the clubs of St James's Street and in the House of Commons.'

It was one of the heavier burdens of Brummell's life that, to maintain and consolidate his position in society, he had to conform to these annual rituals. He was soft-hearted about animals and he deeply disliked the filthy conditions out of doors and the chilly inconveniences indoors at the great draughty noble mansions. With the result that he was not always the most easy of guests to please.

During his visit to Belvoir with the Prince in January 1799, Brummell was not forced into any outdoor exercise more strenuous than skating, the weather having been so cold that the bullocks roasted whole as part of the celebrations were said to have frozen on one side while they were being cooked on the other. As his visits became more and more frequent, he took to keeping a stud of hunters at the Peacock Inn below the castle, but these were more for show than for use. If his valet managed to get him up and dressed in time for the meet, he would ride a few fields, curse his companions for bespattering his clothes, and then jog back to the castle to join the ladies and chatter about the elegant arts. He wrote society verses in an old-fashioned style and was a careful water-colourist, though he could not paint from nature. At Cheveley, another of the Rutlands' country mansions, which they opened up for the October Newmarket races, he had his own set of rooms always at his disposal, as did the Duke of York, who on one occasion distinguished himself by shooting his host's favourite liver-coloured pointer in mistake for a hare.

Life, in Brummell's view as in Samuel Johnson's, could be enjoyed only when its setting was urban and metropolitan, not rural or provincial. When the rites of high society compelled him to leave London in August he was back again as soon as possible for the little season before Christmas and again in the spring. And during the rest of the time he at least insisted on making himself as comfortable as possible. There are many stories of his high-handed treatment of his hosts, particularly in the early days when he was establishing himself. At one stately home a servant was conducting him to the chilly upper rooms where bachelor guests were usually bedded. Brummell halted and said, 'Stop! I cannot go up and down these infernal stairs! Is there no room lower? Here, for example?' He opened a door into what proved to be a very comfortable bedroom. The servant explained that this part of the house was reserved for married couples, and this particular room for an earl. 'The single gentlemen's apartments are–.' 'I know! I know,' said Brummell. 'So put the earl in one of them–he is a bachelor. There–bring in my portmanteau and dressing case.'

He was getting ready for dinner when there was a knock on the door and the earl called angrily.

'Mr Brummell! Mr Brummell!'

'My lord!' Brummell shouted back, 'I am dressing and cannot be disturbed. I am in my buffs, *in naturalibus*.'

'But this is my room, Sir!' yelled the earl.

'Possession, my lord! Possession!' Brummell replied. 'You know the rest! You are single, my lord. I am a married man–married to the gout.'

The earl had to be satisfied with a room elsewhere.

Some of the guests' bedrooms in Belvoir Castle were served by a gallery in which hung the rope of the fire bell. One night about half an hour after the duke and his friends had retired, they were awakened by the clanging of the bell. They scurried down to the hall, which was soon full of agitated lords, ladies and lesser personages in various forms of undress. While the servants were still searching for the fire, Brummell appeared at the balcony. 'Really, my good people,' he said, 'I regret having disturbed you, but the fact is my valet forgot to bring my hot water.'

Earls and marquesses and even dukes were put down by that sort of arrogance. And duchesses too. That very sharp-witted woman Lady Hester Stanhope used to tell–with considerable admiration–a score of Brummell anecdotes, all illustrating his audacity. At a very grand ball, for instance, he said to his friend the Duchess of Rutland, 'In Heaven's name, my dear Duchess, what is the meaning of this extraordinary back of yours? I declare I must put you on a backboard; you must positively walk out of the room backwards, that I mayn't see it.'

At another he 'cruised round the room asking everybody where he could find a partner who would not throw him into a perspiration, and at last crying out "Ah! there she is!–yes, Catherine will do; I think I may venture with her."–And this was the Duchess of Rutland's sister.'

And at another he walked up to Lady Hester herself–who was noted for the elegant lines of her cheek and the way she held her head–'and coolly took out her earrings, telling her that she should not wear such things: meaning that they hid the best part of her face'.

Despite impertinences of this kind, he had a great deal of respect for Lady Hester, and she for him. One day when they were both riding in Bond Street–he 'with his bridle between his forefinger and thumb, as if he held a pinch of snuff'–Brummell said to her, 'Dear creature! Who *is* that man you were talking to just now?' Lady Hester told him it was a Colonel So-and-So.

'Colonel what?' asked Brummell, 'whoever heard of his father?'

'And whoever heard of George Brummell's father?' she replied in her sharp forthright way.

'Ah, Lady Hester,' he said 'who, indeed, ever heard of George B's father, and who would have ever heard of George B himself, if he had been anything but what he is? But you know, my dear Lady Hester, it is my folly that is the making of me. If I did not impertinently stare duchesses out of countenance, and nod over my shoulder to a prince, I should be forgotten in a week: and, if the world is so silly as to admire my absurdities, you and I may know better, but what does that signify?'

The Prince of Wales, piqued that he should have made no military progress while even Brummell had been advanced to the rank of major, resumed his demands on the King, the Duke of York and Addington the Prime Minister, for 'a military command', though it soon appeared from the correspondence that wrangled on into the following year that what he wanted was simply promotion: 'The Duke of York commands the army; the younger branches of my family are either generals or lieutenant-generals; and I, who am Prince of Wales, am to remain colonel of dragoons!' He particularly blamed the Duke of York, who, when he called at Carlton House, 'was left a good while waiting in the hall, and at last a message came, that after what had passed, the Prince could not think of seeing him'.

The open quarrel still had no effect on Brummell's attitude to the Duke and Duchess. It was one of the finest of his characteristics, and a source of indignation to his contemporaries, that in an age of toadies he insisted on putting loyalty first–and thus gathered round himself a set of friends who were equally loyal to him. He continued, for instance, on the friendliest terms with Lady Hester Stanhope, although she was the niece and housekeeper of William Pitt whom the Prince hated. 'If you are as conceited as formerly,' Lady Hester wrote to Brummell from Cheltenham in August 1803, 'I shall stand accused of taking your groom to give me the opportunity of writing to you for his character.' Besides asking for the reference she sent him news of some of their friends whom she had met on her recent tour of Italy: the Duchess of Devonshire's nephew Lord Althorp, the Earl of Essex's son Thomas Capel, and 'a rival of yours in affectation', William Hill, the future Lord Berwick.

That same summer season Lady Jersey came face to face with the Prince on the staircase at the opera. She apologised for not making way for him quickly enough; he passed on without a word. Next morning he sent Colonel MacMahon, the Keeper of his Privy Purse, to tell her 'it was the desire of the Prince that she would not speak to him'. The snub was widely known within a week, but Brummell refused to desert Lady Jersey and a little later gave her daughter, Lady Harriet Villiers, a desk-pad inlaid with ivory, cornelian, gold and mother-of-pearl which was sold at auction one hundred and seventy years later for £15,000.

True to his habits, he put in an appearance on the country house circuit that autumn but was promptly back in London by the end of October. 'The whole set of *Petit Maîtres* are flocking to town,' the Duchess of Devonshire's eighteen-year-old daughter Lady Harriet Cavendish informed her sister. 'Henry Pierrepont, Dick Bagot, Mr Brummell and Pagets without end, are already here, and Charles Bagot expected in a day or two.' A few days afterwards she reported that 'Mr Brummell has been seen at the play' and before the end of November, 'Lord Granville, Mr Brummell and C. Bagot in our box'. It is significant that, even ten years later, he was still 'Mr Brummell' even in her letters. It was not that she did not know him well enough to give him his Christian name, nor that she considered him inferior, in which case he would have been just 'Brummell'. The fact was that already at twenty-five he was the sort of person that ladies, as well as gentlemen, hesitate to get too familiar with.

In January 1804 a false alarm set the invasion beacons aflame along the Scottish border, and in February the Prince's physician and apothecary were hurriedly summoned to deal with his inflamed stomach, brought on by a week's drinking with the Duke of Norfolk. That month the King's wits went wandering again, not to return until June. There was reconciliation on all sides: the Prince of Wales shook hands with the Duke of York; Lady Bessborough reported that Lady Hester Stanhope said Princess Caroline wanted to get in touch with the Prince and 'the Prince's Fat Friend [Mrs Fitzherbert—the first use of the fateful phrase in this connection] was all anxiety to send a message to the Princess.'

The fear of invasion increased during 1805 as Bonaparte (now Napoleon, Emperor of the French) assembled his army and vast fleet of transports at Boulogne; then suddenly collapsed when Nelson scored his great victory at Trafalgar. At Brighton the Prince was trying out the waltz, finding that 'once round the table made him giddy', and giving the Duke of York a very cool reception again when he came down to review the troops on the downs. Brummell joined a party at Colwick Hall, Nottinghamshire, where his host was Jack Musters, 'King of Gentlemen Huntsmen'.

Musters had been in the same house as Brummell at Eton, where he was long remembered for a famous fight with Tom Assheton-Smith. 'The battle lasted an hour and a half, and both were so punished at the close that in the last round they could not distinguish each other.' Musters, whose father presented him with a pack of hounds when he came of age in 1798, was reputed to be able to 'ride, fence, fight, play at tennis, swim, shoot and play at cricket with any man in Europe'. He had recently married Mary Chaworth, who had the distinction of having received advances from Lord Byron, two years her junior, when he was a schoolboy at Harrow—and the good sense to have rejected them. She appeared in his poem *The Dream*.

> The Maid was on the eve of Womanhood;
> The Boy had fewer summers, but his heart
> Had far outgrown his years, and to his eye
> There was but one belovèd face on earth . . .
> He had no breath, no being, but in hers;
> She was his voice; he did not speak to her,
> But trembled on her words; she was his sight,
> For his eye followed her, and saw with hers,
> Which coloured all his objects: he had ceased
> To live within himself; she was his life.

Brummell, on the other hand, thoroughly disliked her. He admitted the genuineness of Byron's passion—'I have frequently heard him romanticise for hours about her'—but said he was quite unable to understand why it was aroused. 'She appeared to me to be always vigilant for admiration, coarse in her manners, and far from resembling what I should have conceived the *beau idéal* of Byron.'

Most women got on very well with Brummell. It is clear that he had no strong sexual passions. The ladies could enjoy his elegance and caustic chatter without fear of physical or emotional involvement. 'Everyone from the highest to the lowest conspired to spoil him,' wrote his friend Thomas Raikes, 'and who that knew him well could deny that with all his faults he was still the most gentlemanlike, the most agreeable of companions? Never was there a man who during his career had such unbounded influence and, what is seldom the case, such general popularity in society. Without being a man of intrigue, for I never knew him engaged in what is called a *liaison* in society, he was the idol of the women. Happy was she in whose opera-box he would pass an hour, at whose table he would dine, or whose assembly he would honour. And why? Not only because he was a host of amusement in himself with his jokes and his jeers, but because he was such a favourite with the men that all were anxious to join the party.' Yet he certainly had no overt homosexual tendency, otherwise public opinion, even in the loosely moralled upper layers of society, would not have allowed him to become the leader and dictator of taste and conduct.

Some of Brummell's acquaintances tried to credit him with sundry love affairs but there is nothing in his record to support the belief that he ever indulged in anything more serious than polite dalliance, though he may have tried to find himself a rich heiress when he was hard up for money. After his death a miniature of the Duchess of York's eye was found among his possessions. The Prince of Wales and Mrs Fitzherbert had popularised the custom of lovers exchanging these rather unattractive keepsakes. It no doubt marked the depth of his affection for little Princess Fred, but there is no evidence of a more intimate relationship.

Many of the Dandies, as the later generation of his followers were called, married only well on in life or not at all: they were too preoccupied with their pursuit of elegance to have time to fall in love with other people, just as the younger Pitt was too taken up with politics even to pay attention to the many women eager to capture him (and too crippled with debt to win the one he chose). Brummell frequented the fashionable courtesans, such as Harriette Wilson, because his friends did, and it was, after all, part of the social round, like race meetings and the opera and the summer show at the Royal Academy. Harriette, for her own aggrandisement, made much in her *Memoirs* of her acquaintance

with Brummell. There was the occasion when she was entertaining
Lord Frederick Bentinck, a bold military man who eventually
commanded the Grenadier Guards.

Brummell at this moment was announced. 'How very apropos you are
arrived,' I remarked. 'Lord Frederick wants your opinion on his new
leather breeches.'

'My dear fellow, take them off directly!' said Brummell.

'I beg I may hear of no such thing,' said I, hastily–'else where would he
go to, I wonder, without his small-clothes?'

Fred Bentinck put himself into attitudes, looking anxiously and very
innocently from George Brummell to his leather breeches, and from his
leather breeches to the looking-glass.

'They only came home this morning,' proceeded Fred, 'and I thought
they were rather neat.'

'Bad knees, my good fellow! Bad knees!' said Brummell shrugging up his
shoulders.

A little later, Harriette is 'interrupted by my servant, who
brought me a letter from George Brummell, full of nonsensical
vows and professions. "When," he wrote, "beautiful Harriette,
will you admit me to your house? Why so obstinately refuse my
visits? Tell me, I do entreat you, when I may but throw myself at
your feet without fear of derision from a public homage on the
pavement, or dislocation from the passing hackney-coaches!" '
Though Harriette is never to be believed without corroboration,
this is not a bad imitation of Brummell's style–sufficiently
pompous–facetious to avoid the risk of being taken seriously.
She says that, in fact, it was not to her but to another noted
woman of the town, Julia Johnstone, that Brummell was 'making
strong love' at this time–1806.

A more recognisable portrait of him comes from the diary of
Lady Shelley, a very distant cousin of the poet. They met as
fellow-guests at Lord Cholmondeley's house at Houghton. George
was supposed to be copying a miniature of his friend the Prince
of Wales. 'But he made so little progress that we declared he
never touched it. He then began to make an album which contained many *vers de société* and led to much banter and fun, so the
days passed very agreeably.'

A frequent contributor to this celebrated quarto vellum album,
bound in blue velvet with corners and clasps of heavy embossed
silver gilt, was the Duchess of Devonshire. One of her earliest

pieces lamented the death of James Hare, wit of an earlier age and close friend of Fox.

> Hark! 'twas the knell of death–what spirit fled,
> And burst the shackles Man is doom'd to bear?
> Can it be true, and 'midst the senseless dead,
> Must sorrowing thousands count the loss of Hare?

Since it was not written for publication it would be unfair to print the remaining four verses. More in keeping with the spirit of the album were Fox's *On the Death of Faddle, a Favourite Spaniel of Georgiana, Duchess of Devonshire's, who died an Early Victim to Love: his Father, Faddle Senior, having perished by a Similar Fate.* Or Brummell's own *Butterfly's Funeral*, a thirty-six-line mock elegy, inspired by a popular piece of children's verse, *The Butterfly's Ball.*

> Oh ye! who so lately were blythesome and gay,
> At the Butterfly's banquet carousing away;
> Your feasts and your revels of pleasure are fled,
> For the soul of the banquet, the Butterfly's dead.
>
> No longer the Flies and the Emmets advance,
> To join with their friend in the Grasshopper's dance;
> For see his thin form o'er the favourite bend,
> And the Grasshopper mourns for the loss of his friend.
>
> And hark! to the funeral dirge of the Bee,
> And the Beetle, who follows as solemn as he;
> And see where so mournful the green rushes wave,
> The Mole is preparing the Butterfly's grave.
>
> The Dormouse attended, but cold and forlorn,
> And the Gnat slowly winded his shrill little horn;
> And the Moth, who was grieved for the loss of a sister,
> Bent over the body and silently kiss'd her.
>
> The corse was embalm'd at the set of the sun,
> And enclosed in a case which the Silk-worm had spun;
> By the help of the Hornet the coffin was laid
> On a bier out of myrtle and jessamine made.
>
> In weepers and scarves came the Butterflies all,
> And six of their number supported the pall;
> And the Spider came there, in his mourning so black,
> But the fire of the Glowworm soon frighten'd him back.

The Grub left his nutshell, to join in the throng,
And slowly led with him the Bookworm along!
Who wept his poor neighbour's unfortunate doom,
And wrote these few lines to be placed on her tomb:—

Epitaph

At this solemn spot, where the green rushes wave,
Here sadly we bent o'er the Butterfly's grave;
'Twas here we to beauty our obsequies paid,
And hallowed the mound which her ashes had made.

And here shall the daisy and violet blow,
And the lily discover her bosom of snow;
While under the leaf, in the evenings of spring,
Still mourning his friend, shall the Grasshopper sing.

The year was one of mourning for both Whigs and Tories. In January the forty-six-year-old Prime Minister, William Pitt, died of drink at his villa in Putney. In the new Ministry of All the Talents formed by Lord Grenville, Fox, his complexion now 'the colour that yellow crape would have, stretched over black', was given one of his rare spells in the Cabinet as Foreign Secretary. When the Duchess of Devonshire applied to the Archbishop of Canterbury for seats at Pitt's funeral service, His Grace uncharitably misconstrued her motive and tartly replied that 'Westminster Abbey was not a place of public amusement'; but within two months the charming Duchess herself was dead 'her liver decayed'–a few weeks short of her forty-ninth birthday. And in September her much-admired Fox died, aged fifty-seven.

For a time it almost seemed as if the Prince of Wales would follow him. Weighed on the scales that Brummell also patronised at the Old Coffee Mill in St James's Street, he had shrunk to less than twelve stone. At Lady Salisbury's assembly he was observed to look 'shockingly' and at Lady Darnley's 'wretchedly'. His tailor Weston reported that 'Cloaths which he formerly wore hang like great coats upon him, and are obliged to be taken in greatly. The Prince looks very old and wrinkled. He eats now at dinner only Fish and Salad, and drinks no wine. Since the death of Mr Fox he has worn Black Cloaths only.' He had lost ten or twelve inches round the waist. 'It is certain that he cannot live, at least so says an Eminent Medical Man. That he can never recover from the state he is in. He has now the *strongest tea* made for him, which stands until it is cold, and it is then *iced* before he drinks it to allay an internal heat.'

But it gradually became clear that it was neither grief for Fox nor some mysterious malady that was reducing the Prince to a shadow of his former self. The truth was simple–he was in love again. The summer of 1806 saw the end of a long dispute between members of the Seymour family and Mrs Fitzherbert over the seven-year-old Mary Georgiana Seymour, whom Mrs Fitzherbert had brought up since 1799, when the child was left motherless. Minney, as she was known in the family, called Mrs Fitzherbert 'Mama' (she was perhaps the first to call the Prince of Wales 'Prinny') and was evidently very happy in her foster home. But other members of the family disapproved of Mrs Fitzherbert's influence, whether because of her religion or her morals, and decided to take Minney away. Mrs Fitzherbert resisted and applied to her friend Lady Hertford–mother of Brummell's friend Lord Yarmouth–for help. When the dispute eventually went to the House of Lords, Lady Hertford's husband, the senior member of this branch of the Seymour family, asked to be appointed as Minney's guardian. No sooner was the request granted than the sixty-three-year-old Marquess restored his niece to the ample bosom of the delighted Mrs Fitzherbert.

The Prince had taken part in the long negotiations and found himself frequently in the company of the helpful Lady Hertford. She was all that he admired in a woman–large, stately and older than himself (though four years younger than Mrs Fitzherbert) So–he aged forty-four and she forty-six–another royal romance began; and the Marquess of Hertford became a Knight of the Garter.

Earlier in the year, a Commission had been appointed to make a 'delicate investigation' into the Prince of Wales's allegations that Princess Caroline had given birth to an illegitimate child. Although they conducted the proceedings with as much discretion as possible, the news that the Commissioners were taking evidence from the Princess's servants created a scandal that increased when it was known that the Prince was making advances to Lady

Hertford. Prayers for the King's health became more fervent and the wits invented a new toast: 'The Prince of Wales *for ever*!'

On the other side of Europe, where Austria had been vanquished by Napoleon the year before, Prussia was now crushed at Jena and Austerlitz.

> Another year!–another deadly blow!
> Another mighty Empire overthrown!
> And We are left, or shall be left, alone;
> The last that dare to struggle with the Foe,

wrote Wordsworth.

For George Brummell the year was more memorable because it saw the foundation of the fraternity of gay, reckless, brilliant, dissipated, witty men about town which he was to dominate and which was to be known as the Dandy Club.

Men had been using clubs as a refuge from their lodgings or their wives ever since the reign of Queen Anne, under the cover of a common interest in literature, or a political cause, or food, or other entertainment. Many met only on certain days of the week or month, and usually in public places–coffee houses or taverns. Of the few who set themselves up in their own premises and restricted admission to formally elected members, the two best known were Brooks's and White's, facing each other across St James's Street. Brooks's was regarded as a Whig Club, White's as Tory, but these labels had never meant much and in practice Brummell and the Prince and most of their friends belonged to both. As Harriette Wilson remarked, the custom at each 'is and ever has been, never to blackball any man who ties a good knot in his handkerchief, keeps his hands out of his breeches pockets, and says nothing'. Which club the member preferred to use often depended on the whim of the moment, the stakes currently played for, or the quality of the dinner; though the Prince, who once preferred Brooks's because Pitt preferred White's, had transferred his patronage entirely to White's since Brooks's blackballed 'Jacko' Payne.

Food was the foundation of the Dandy Club. A group of the musically inclined rented a house at the corner of Bolton Street and Piccadilly where they met to sing catches and glees. The catering was put in the charge of Jean-Baptiste Watier, formerly chef to the Prince of Wales. He provided the club with its official name and such excellent meals that Brummell and his friends joined simply for the pleasure of eating there. 'The catches and glees were then superseded by cards and dice; the most luxurious dinners were furnished at any price, as the deep play at night rendered all charges a matter of indifference. Macao was the constant game, and thousands passed from one to another with as much facility as marbles.' Brummell was the supreme dictator, 'their club's perpetual president', laying down the law in 'dress, in manners, and in those magnificent snuff-boxes for which there was a rage'.

It was Byron who, a few years after, gave Watier's the nickname of the Dandy's Club. 'I liked the Dandies, they were always very civil to me,' he said. Indeed, if his friend and biographer Medwin is to be believed, 'Lord Byron frequently spoke, and with almost envy, of Brummell and prided himself much on his intimacy with him. There was a time when he would have wished to be Brummell.' He was later to say that the three great men of his time all came to grief in the same year–Brummell, Napoleon and himself.

Brummell had by now introduced one of the two innovations in dress for which he is best remembered: the use of starch, so that thereafter the well-dressed man's neck was encircled not by a loose, sagging, baggy circle of often grubby cloth, but by the finest and cleanest muslin standing stiffly under his chin, meticulously tied and symmetrically creased. It was, even for the master, a difficult perfection to achieve, and the story soon got around of his valet descending the stairs with an armful of discarded ties, remarking 'our failures!' to the ascending visitors (for Brummell held a daily levee in his dressing-room).

Harriette Wilson's publisher, Stockdale, brought out a half-serious, half-satirical pamphlet *Neckclothitania, or Tietania: Being an Essay on Starches*, with a frontispiece showing examples of the Oriental, the Mathematical, the Osbaldestone, the Napoleon, the American, the Mail Coach, the Trône d'Amour, the Irish, the Ball Room, the Horse Collar, the Hunting, the Maharatta and the Barrell knot.

'The Oriental is made with a *very* stiff and rigid cloth. Not a single indenture or crease should be visible. The Mathematical is far less severe. There are three creases in it. The colour best suited to it, is that called *couleur de la cuisse d'une nymphe émue*.' The Trône d'Amour was well starched, with one single horizontal dent in the middle: colour, *Yeux de fille en extase*. The Ballroom united 'the qualities of the Mathematical and Irish, having two collateral dents and two horizontal ones. This should never of course be made with colours but with the purest and most brilliant *blanc d'innocence virginale*.' While the Mail Coach, best made out of a Cashmere Shawl and 'worn by all stage-coachmen, guards, the *swells* of the *fancy* and Ruffians', had one end brought over the knot, spread out and tucked into the waist.

This style was particularly popular among members of the Four-in-Hand Club, founded in the rackety days of the notorious Barrymores but now become respectable. They delighted in travelling by stage-coach, preferably on the box, and replacing the driver. 'They touched their hats to their passengers, and some among them did not disdain even the tip of a shilling or half-crown with which it was the custom to remunerate the coachman.' One of them 'was so determined to be looked upon as a regular coachman, that he had his front teeth so filed that a division between them might enable him to expel his spittle in the true fashion of some of the most known stage-coach drivers'. It was not the sort of thing to appeal to Brummell, though he enjoyed the periodic grand parades of the club, when they drove in their own carriages from George Street, Hanover Square, to the Windmill at Salt Hill, just outside Slough on the Maidenhead Road, an inn famous for its food.

After dinner, 'in high spirits and not infrequently overcome by the quantity of sound port wine for which that inn was celebrated', they returned to London. Happily, the escapades of the Barrymores were a thing of the past. 'The driving was never of such a character as to cause any accidents; it was steady and well-regulated; one of the rules of the club being that no coach should pass another, and that the pace should never exceed a trot.'

A description of Brummell's own method of tying his neckcloth has been left by one of his friends who frequently attended the morning ceremony. 'The collar, which was always fixed to his shirt, was so large that, before being folded down, it completely hid his head and face, and the white neckcloth was at least a foot in height.' The neckcloth, which was outside the upturned collar, was tied first, and the collar was turned down; and 'Brummell then, standing before the glass with his chin poked up to the ceiling, by the gentle and gradual declension of his lower jaw creased the cravat to reasonable dimensions', dabbing it with a piece of linen to keep each crease perfect.

In this, as in everything else, Brummell deplored excess, particularly anything which inhibited free movement and a graceful carriage. Sometimes the neckcloth was worn so high and stiffened with so much starch that the wearer could not turn his head. As with the young man at dinner who 'when he wanted to speak to a footman, bent his head back until his face became horizontal'. There were many such stories: of the man who 'cut his ear with the corner of his shirt collar, it was starched so stiff, when he attempted to turn his head' or the other who 'burnt his chin by ironing the bows of his neckcloth after it was tied'. There were rumours, quite without foundation, 'that Brummell had a large dressing room and kept two valets who each laid hold of one end of his neckcloth and walked round his chair while they wound it round his neck'.

Brummell's second sartorial invention was at the other extremity. Top boots, because of their association with the French revolutionaries, were replaced in fashion by the tasselled Hessians, respectably German in origin like the Royal Family, and bought by the wealthy from Hoby, the bootmaker on the corner of St James's Street and Piccadilly who was said to employ three hundred workmen and to have died worth £120,000. With the Hessians came pantaloons, and soon trousers were replacing the former 'small clothes'–knee-breeches–which had at first been retained for their aristocratic associations but then discarded because Napoleon and his upstarts adopted them. Here the problem of the neckcloth repeated itself: pantaloons grew baggy, developed unsightly creases, distorted the purity of line of the male nether limbs. Brummell spent anxious hours with his tailors and eventually appeared as the first man in London to wear permanently unwrinkled pantaloons; the bottoms of the trousers were held down by buttons and straps which passed under the arch of the foot.

Knee-breeches were retained for evening wear, accompanied by a swallow-tail coat. By day it was usual to prefer a frock-coat to the swallow-tail, frogged with silk and trimmed or even lined with fur in winter. Brummell had by now managed to discourage the excess of satin and silk, gold lace and multi-coloured embroidery that the Prince of Wales and his set had formerly carried to such an extreme that 'an assemblage of both sexes became as rich as a bed of flowers'–though he still permitted the wearing of a fancy waistcoat. For riding boots he introduced white leather tops instead of brown.

Carlyle defined the Dandy as 'a Clothes-wearing Man, a Man whose trade, office and existence consists in the wearing of Clothes. Every faculty of his soul, spirit, purse and person is heroically consecrated to this one object, the wearing of clothes wisely and well; so that as others dress to live, he lives to dress... Understand his mystic significance, or altogether miss and misinterpret it; do but look at him, and he is contented.'

This cumbersome clowning is very far from the Brummell mark. Baudelaire came closer.

Dandyism is not an exaggerated taste for fine clothes and material comfort. These things are merely symbols of the Dandy's spiritual refinement. It is primarily a desire to be original as a person, but within the limits of social conventions. It is a kind of self-worship, which can dispense with the need to find happiness in others–in women, for example. It is the love of astonishing others and the delight of being astonished oneself. Dandyism appears at times of transition. At such times some men–dissatisfied but rich in energy–may toy with the notion of founding a new sort of aristocracy that will be more difficult to destroy because it will be based on qualities which cannot be acquired with either work or money. Dandyism is the last heroic gesture amid decadence. It is a setting sun, glorious but without warmth and full of melancholy.

All of which is perhaps a little too philosophical and pretentious for Brummell and his disciples. It is evident that he intended to establish a superiority not of birth or money but of character and taste–to become the most elegant figure in this Age of Elegance. But he did it with the active cooperation of his fellow

men and chosen friends, and would have been very wary of all
that talk about astonishing people. He was no lonely *poseur* but a
member of a lighthearted, ultimately civilising group; grasshoppers, indeed, but grasshoppers of grace and personality and,
in an odd way, of purpose. As a friend of Raikes remarked: 'The
manners of the Dandies were themselves a charm. Their speech
was pleasant, their language thoroughbred. Many among them
were highly-gifted, doing all that they did well; the less apt,
always to the point, letting it alone; without enthusiasm, without
illusions–a school of gentlemen, liberal and openhanded; ephem-
eral as youth and spirits, yet marked with this endearing quality,
that they remained, with few exceptions, true and loyal friends,
tested through years of later adversity.'

Nor must they be thought of as effete; many of them served
in the army with great gallantry. The stocky, round-faced Lord
Alvanley, for example, who was ultimately to inherit Brummell's
reputation for wit though not for elegance, was at this time a
young officer in the Coldstream Guards, shortly to take part in
the disastrous expedition to Walcheren, but first coming to public
notice as an athlete.

It was a great time for contests in walking and running and
riding. In September 1807, an officer won 1000 guineas by riding
his horse from Ipswich to London, 70 miles in 4 hours 50 minutes.
In October, Captain Barclay walked 40 miles in 6 hours 20
minutes at Newmarket for a wager of 600 guineas and various
side bets. In March 1808 a hatter's apprentice ran nineteen times
round the railings of St Paul's Cathedral within an hour to
win 20 guineas. And three months later Alvanley ran a mile in
less than 6 minutes in the Edgware Road for a bet of 50 guineas.

The following year Captain Agar, a specialist at the mile, did it
in 4 minutes 51 seconds. Captain Barclay walked 1000 miles in
1000 hours, at one mile every hour for 43 days–with bets totalling
£100,000 at stake. And a clergyman ran one of his horses over
50 miles at 15 miles an hour.

Though he was as ready as anybody to wager on sporting
events, Brummell was not noted for high play at cards in his
early years as Perpetual President of Watier's. One of the most
popular games there was Macao, a form of vingt-et-un, calling

for no particular skills but a steady nerve, of which Brummell had plenty. Tom Raikes recalled him 'coming in one night after the opera to Watier's and, finding the Macao table full, one place of which was occupied by Tom Sheridan, who was never in the habits of play but, having dined freely, had dropped into the Club and was trying to catch the smiles of fortune by risking a few pounds which he could ill afford to lose'. Tom, the only son of the playwright and politician, had in 1805 married the beautiful Caroline Callander, who eventually bore him four sons and three daughters. At this time he was trying to find the money to pay off £1000 damages for 'Crim-Con' awarded against him in an Edinburgh Court for an offence committed a year before his marriage. These charges of Criminal Conversation (a common law offence in which the adulterer was accused of Assault and Trespass on the husband's property) frequently brought the plaintiff very heavy damages and the defendant, if he could not meet the bill, was faced with the choice of a debtor's prison or escaping abroad.

'Brummell proposed to him to give up his place and go shares in his deal; and, adding to the £10 in counters which Tom had before him £2000 for himself, took the cards. He dealt with his usual success, and in less than ten minutes won £1500. He then stopped, made a fair division and, giving £750 to Sheridan, said to him, "There, Tom, go home and give your wife and brats a supper, and never play again."' The gesture was, as Raikes commented, 'characteristic of the times, the set, and of a spirit of liberality in Brummell which was shown towards an old friend in a way that left no pretext for refusal'.

1808 was a year of climatic extremes. It was to reach some of the highest summer temperatures ever recorded in England–from 11 to 19 July the thermometer only once dropped below 80° Fahrenheit and on the famous Hot Wednesday it climbed to 99°– but it began with 17 degrees of frost in January, bringing woeful complaints from George Brummell.

The winter was never his favourite time of year. Like Byron he felt the cold more acutely than most men–probably because of the many hours he spent in the company of the Prince of Wales, who always kept his houses uncomfortably overheated. When

Mrs Creevey accompanied Mrs Fitzherbert to a ball given by the Prince at the Pavilion, she reported that 'We were sick of the heat and stink.' Yet Brummell basked in the warmth, and had been known to sit through the opera at the Haymarket Theatre in high summer in a fur-collared greatcoat.

It was indeed often difficult to keep warm even in the houses of the rich. When Albinia Countess of Buckinghamshire, one of the founders of the Pic-nic Club, gave a house-warming in honour of the Princess of Wales at her villa in the King's Road ('an inconvenient distance from town, without being exactly in the country'), one of her male guests complained that 'We could very well have borne a little more squeezing for the sake of additional warmth. If Venus herself had been present, I could not have admired her for the first half-hour, during which most of the poor scantily-clothed women then present had very blue noses, and shoulders of the fairest *peau satinée* were puckered up into goose flesh; the sight of which nearly froze my already chilled blood.'

Brummell disliked the winter not only because of the temperature but also because of the difficulty of avoiding the crudities of country amusements, the smell of sweat and muddy leather, the 'excessive devotion to stables, drunkenness and coachmanship', with, as often as not, the heavy scent of the ladies of the town who came to be close to their protectors or to fish for new ones. Harriette Wilson was particularly scathing about the loose women who infested Melton Mowbray, though it is clear that she tried her luck there herself. So did her friend and rival Julia Johnstone, whose acquaintance with Brummell went back to childhood. According to Harriette, Julia described the Beau as 'an old flame of mine, who was violently in love with me, when I was a girl at Hampton Court'. Julia's own account was: 'This is a piece with all that lady's falsehoods concerning me, I never had the honour to refuse George's hand, for he never offered it to me.'

They almost certainly did know each other at Hampton Court. Julia's mother, the Hon. Mrs Storer, was a member of Queen Charlotte's household and is usually described as the sister-in-law of Lord Carysfort. She was more probably his sister, Elizabeth Proby, wife of Thomas James Storer. She was also a friend of

Colonel Cotton, whom Brummell knew when they were captain and cornet respectively in the 10th Light Dragoons. In March 1771, the same month that William Brummell moved into Hampton Court Palace, Mrs Storer took over Suite Nineteen, with the Chocolate Room on the Coffee Room Staircase as a kitchen, and Suite Twenty-seven in the Queen's Half-Storey. She held these rooms until 1808. They looked on to Fountain Court–the centre of the 'New Palace' built by Wren for William III–from the south and east, and were entered from the Gold Staff Gallery where William Brummell held Suite Seventeen until he handed it over to Richard Tickell. The other rooms which William Brummell had up to the time of his death were in the opposite corner of Fountain Court but on the same floor. It would have been difficult for the Brummell and Storer families not to make each other's acquaintance.

The Cottons or Cottins do not appear in the Hampton Court Palace records before 1797, when they took over Suite Twenty-one, almost adjoining the Storers on the top-floor east side of Fountain Court, and held by Colonel Cotton until his death in 1843. They were probably living elsewhere when Cotton suggested to Mrs Storer that her daughter Julia, not yet in her teens, should live with his family and complete her education with his young children. He was a tall, dark man in his thirties; she an attractive child of inquiring disposition. When she reached the age of sixteen the colonel seduced her.

'It was not without many compunctious visitings of conscience that I fell from the eminence of virtue.' But fall she did. 'And when I discovered myself to be in a peculiar situation, the Colonel removed me to a cottage near Primrose Hill.' They lived there as Mr and Mrs Johnstone. Brummell marked the birth of one of the several children that she bore the colonel by copying into his album a set of verses beginning:

> Unhappy child of indiscretion,
>   Poor slumberer on a breast forlorn!
> Pledge and reproof of past transgression,
>   Dear, though unwelcome to be born.

He claimed to have composed them himself.

Julia did not reserve all her charms for the colonel, and was for

a time mistress of Sir Henry Mildmay. It is quite possible that
Brummell introduced her to Mildmay, as he did Charlotte
Bouverie, a niece of the Earl of Radnor, whom Mildmay married
in 1809. It was an ideal marriage, the young couple so in love
with each other that, as Lady Granville said, 'They go about in
attitudes–but they match so well and look so handsome that one
forgives them for it.'

Mildmay, a rich Hampshire squire, soon to be Member of
Parliament for Winchester, member of White's, charmer of ladies
with his sweet light baritone and soulful expression, a gay spark
in the hunting field and in the gaming rooms as well as in the
boudoir, was typical of the new set that Brummell was gathering
around him. From being a young though dominating member of
the Prince of Wales's clique he had now, at thirty, established
himself as the unchallenged leader and arbiter of his own.

Much of his civilising mission was already accomplished. The
gentry frequenting St James's were restrained, immaculate. It was
Brummell who had made them so, and it was his intention that
they should so remain. The women as well as the men accepted
his sway. He extended his authority from the privacies of the club
and the country house to the great public gatherings at the opera
house and the ballrooms. 'No party was complete without him;
and the morning papers in giving the details of a rout, always
placed his name first on the list of untitled guests' (though it must
be admitted that he had always had an alphabetical advantage
here). At Almack's, now converted from a gaming club to smart
assembly rooms in King Street, St James's, one duchess was heard
to say to her daughter, appearing for the first time, 'Do you see
that gentleman near the door? He will probably come and speak
to us; and if he enters into conversation be careful to give him a
favourable impression of you, for he is the celebrated Mr
Brummell.'

The year 1809 had begun sadly for George's dear friend the
Duchess of York. In January, Colonel Wardle informed Parlia-
ment that he had cause to demand an investigation into the
Duke's conduct at the War Office. Lord Grey, the Duchess of
Devonshire's former lover, was shocked 'to see the time of the

House of Commons and the attention of the public, occupied by such matters at the present moment. It is impossible to believe that anything more can be imputable to the Duke than might have happened to any man who has the misfortune to keep a mistress.' But on 20 March the newspapers announced the Duke's resignation. It was clear that the mistress in question, pretty, witty and brazen Mrs Clarke, had been selling commissions and promotions, though it was highly probable that the Duke knew nothing about it.

That January too, had brought sorrow to another of Brummell's friends–Lady Hester Stanhope–with the news that Sir John Moore, whom she was believed to be in love with, had died at Corunna. She shortly afterwards left England and settled in the Lebanon where, twenty years later, a small masculine figure in Arab dress, puffing away at her chibouk, she still enjoyed talking about Brummell to English visitors.

It was a fidgety, bad-tempered year. The British reverses in Spain were followed by a disastrous expedition to the Low Countries in which the troops sent to capture Antwerp found themselves cooped up on the island of Walcheren, where they died in hundreds from fever. Drury Lane Theatre was burnt down in February (as Covent Garden had been the previous year) and when it reopened in September the rise in prices by one shilling for the boxes and sixpence for the pit was greeted with rioting by indignant theatregoers.

Castlereagh fought a duel on Wimbledon Common with Canning, who criticised him for mismanagement of the Walcheren affair. Napoleon trounced the Austrian Emperor as a prelude to marrying his daughter. Ladies had taken to wearing newfangled undergarments in addition to petticoats; these, because they resembled the knee-breeches sketched by George Cruikshank for Washington Irving's newly-published *History of New York by Diedrich Knickerbocker*, were christened knickers. Mrs Fitzherbert refused to set foot again in the Pavilion until the Prince got rid of Lady Hertford: 'I owe it to myself not to be insulted under your roof with impunity. The influence you are under renders my situation in your house impossible any longer to submit to.'

The rioting over the Drury Lane prices ended in December

1809 and was followed in April 1810 by rioting over Sir Francis Burdett. Sir Francis, a popular reformer, had put forward the theory that the House of Commons had no right to imprison people. The House proved him wrong by shutting him up in the Tower of London, whereupon the streets were subjected to four days of mob terrorism. The Duke of Cumberland, George III's fifth son, was attacked with a sword by his valet, who in turn was found with his throat cut. The coroner said suicide, but rumour preferred murder by the Duke following on homosexual advances to the valet and seduction of the valet's wife. Byron swam the Hellespont; nearer at home informed and nervous circles were once again gripped by fears of invasion, predicting that 'we shall, at no distant date, have to do battle with Bonaparte on our own soil'.

And Brummell began to fall out with the Prince of Wales.

CHAPTER FOUR

Who's Your Fat Friend?

It is not clear exactly when, or for what reasons, the relationship between the Prince and his protégé, and the protégé who had made a disciple of the Prince, began to deteriorate. Resentment at Brummell's assumption of the leadership of the fashionable set may have played a large part in it, but the Prince's march through life was so orchestrated with the clash and clangour and dull bass thump of broken promises, fractured principles and dropped friends that any pretext–or none–would have sufficed. As one of the members of Princess Charlotte's household once said: 'He hates without a cause, and never forgives.' For Brummell, ascendancy in society, achievement of the ambition that had been with him since his schooldays, would have encouraged him to be less careful in concealing his contempt for his royal crony. Himself scrupulously loyal to friends, he was not the man to observe without wincing the Prince's shabby treatment of the Princess of Wales, of Mrs Fitzherbert and of Lady Jersey. Arch-apostle of disciplined elegance, he watched with mounting distaste as the Prince, basking in the elderly charms of Lady Hertford, grew grosser and more swag-bellied day by day, so that by August 1810 an astonished observer reported him to be 'enormously large: a figure like Henry 8th'.

The King, still wandering in wit, weeping for the recent death of his favourite daughter Amelia, blind to the extent that he could no longer distinguish faces and had to be led by a groom when he was allowed out riding, was so clearly beyond recovery that in February 1811 Parliament reluctantly agreed that the Prince should become Regent, though carefully restricting his powers for a probationary year. The Whigs, so long in opposition, believed that their great moment had come. But the Prince left the Tories in control, hinting that until he had full powers he dared not risk a change in the administration. The Whigs were to wait in vain, for he was a Tory at heart and had played the Whig throughout the years only to torment his father. To Brummell it was just another example of the Prince's appalling lack of loyalty.

This was the year that the bow window was built at White's (soon to become even more famous than Old Q's window in Piccadilly) and promptly taken over by Brummell and his friends. From here they launched their flight of puns and satires on the passing scene and on absent friends and enemies. From now onwards almost any smart remark or slick story was attributed to Brummell, no matter how much it was out of character. During his lifetime an enterprising publisher put out a collection of anecdotes whose authenticity can be judged by the fact that he even got Brummell's name wrong: *The Book of Fashion; being a digest of the axioms of the celebrated Joseph Brummell.* Among the apocrypha can be included the story that he gate-crashed a ball given by a Mrs Thompson and, on being challenged, produced an invitation to a party given by a Mrs Johnson, saying 'Johnson and Thompson are really so much the same kind of thing.' Or, having been invited to dine with Mr Hoare, the banker, and to bring any friends that he wished, recounting the next day: 'The affair turned out quite unique. There was every delicacy in or out of season; but my dear fellow, conceive my astonishment when I tell you that Mr Hoare had the assurance to sit down and dine with us!' Another version was that, having dined at one house and needing to continue to a party given by Lady Jersey at another, Brummell asked if anybody would give him a lift in their carriage. His host immediately offered to take him, and Brummell replied, 'Very kind of you indeed! But pray how are you to go? You surely would not like to get up behind? And yet it will scarcely do for *me* to be seen in the same carriage with *you*.'

Brummell himself denied many such stories. He had always drawn the line between amusing impudence and gross rudeness;

now that he was established he was increasingly gentle and whimsical unless irked by what he considered to be anti-social behaviour. A typical Brummell witticism was, on being commiserated for having gout, 'Oh, I should not mind so much, but it is in my favourite leg.' Or, on being asked if he had ever seen such an unseasonable summer: 'Yes, last winter.' Or, on seeing Frederick Byng, once the curly-haired page-of-honour who stood beside George at the Prince of Wales's wedding, driving in the park with a poodle beside him: 'Ah! a family vehicle I see!' From that moment Frederick, still inordinately proud of his light wavy hair, was always known as 'Poodle' Byng.

One set of stories intended to explain the quarrel with the Prince is based on the premise that Brummell, in friendship to Lady Jersey, attacked the favourite whom she displaced at Carlton House–Mrs Fitzherbert; that he once at Lady Jersey's house called loudly for *Mistress* Fitzherbert's carriage; and that arriving shortly after at Claremont, Lord Seaford's house, he was met at the door by the Prince who told him 'that his presence was offensive to Mrs Fitzherbert, and that the party would be destroyed if he did not return to London'. Back to town went Brummell, and from that moment 'all intercourse with the Prince of Wales ceased'.

This is quite out of character. More plausible is the story that one of the porters at Carlton House was a very fat man named Ben; that Brummell facetiously nicknamed the Prince and Mrs Fitzherbert 'Ben and Benina'; that the Prince took offence when this was repeated to him. But the Ben and Benina joke was in circulation long before the split came.

On another occasion Brummell is said to have called on Mrs Fitzherbert when the Prince was there. In the course of the conversation, George put his snuff-box down beside him, whereupon the Prince snapped, 'Mr Brummell, the place for your box is in your pocket, not on the table.' But since there was nothing ill-mannered in what Brummell did, this does not explain the bad feeling but merely confirms that it existed. In any event Brummell was more often defending Mrs Fitzherbert than attacking her, and later became a close friend of her son-in-law, George Dawson-Damer.

One of the most popular legends current at the time was that one evening at Carlton House when the Prince was entertaining a few friends, Brummell roused his anger by saying to him: 'Wales, ring the bell!' Brummell himself denied this with some indignation: 'I was on such intimate terms with the Prince that if we had been alone I could have asked him to ring the bell without offence; but with a third person in the room I should never have done so–I knew the Regent too well.' Another version of the same myth is that it was the Prince who asked Brummell to ring the bell and Brummell replied, 'Your Royal Highness is close to it.' At this the Prince rang the bell and ordered Brummell's carriage. Both of them are variants of a probably true story that a nephew of 'Jacko' Payne bet his fellow midshipmen that he would use the impertinent words to the Prince next time his uncle took him to Carlton House; and that when he did so, the Prince rang the bell and said: 'Put the drunken boy to bed.'

The true explanation of why the split occurred is probably quite simple. They had never been well-suited in temperament. The Prince was a gross sensualist; Brummell, in an odd way, an ascetic. The Prince was fascinated by Brummell's self-assurance but lacked the self-discipline to emulate it. Brummell was snob enough to enjoy the Prince's patronage but very soon ceased to need it. When neither had anything more to offer the other they inevitably began to drift apart, Brummell forming a coterie of his own. Most of the Prince's friends disgusted Brummell; most of Brummell's friends were disgusted by the Prince. The rival circles touched but barely overlapped. Brummell's increasing prominence and dominance in smart society aroused the Prince's resentment as surely as it turned the Beau's head. With peevish sensitivity on one side and disdainful wit on the other, the former warm relationship cooled, turned sour, grew bitter.

There is no doubt that Brummell made remarks in private which, when carried back to the Prince as he knew they would be, infuriated him. As when he said to Colonel MacMahon, ' I made him what he is, and I can unmake him.' Or, in a similarly arro-gant vein, that if the Regent did not behave, 'I shall bring the old King back into fashion.' The laughter echoed down to Carlton House and the gossips invented still more impertinences.

Brummell was deeply addicted to snuff. There is a story, true or false, that he once went into Fribourg and Treyer's when a hogshead of Martinique–his favourite–had just arrived and found that it had been entirely taken up in advance by his friends. He asked to try it and pronounced it abominable. The other purchasers cancelled their orders, whereupon Brummell asked the proprietors for three jars of it, assuring them that they would sell the rest as soon as it became known that he had bought some. It sounds like a fiction made up by George for his own amusement and aggrandisement, but it is an indication of his standing as a connoisseur. As early as 1799 he bought one pound of Bureau and Canister for the Prince of Wales, price seven shillings and sixpence. By the second decade of the nineteenth century he had changed to Martinique which he bought in jars, twenty or thirty pounds at a time, with an occasional pound or two of marino.

The Prince was less of a snuff-taker than a snuff-box manipulator. He prided himself on the elegance of the motions with which he opened the box, pretended to convey the dust to his nose, and flicked away the imaginary residue with his handkerchief. This made another bond with Brummell, who is credited with having introduced the left-hand-only style of manipulating the box–pushing the lid up with the thumb, closing it with the indexfinger, and using the right hand only to put a pinch of snuff on the back of the left. Brummell also had a rare collection of expensive and curious boxes, including one called a 'Lawrence Kirk' which had an invisible hinge. He passed this round the dinner table at Carlton House one day. The Prince soon said he was damned if he could open it. The Prime Minister, Lord Liverpool (son of grandfather Brummell's lodger Charles Jenkinson), picked up a knife to prise it open and Brummell cried out: 'My Lord! Allow me to observe that's not an oyster but a snuff-box!'

The Prince was examining this collection one day, when he suddenly said: 'Brummell, this box must be mine; go to Gray's and order any box you like in lieu of it.' George, who knew how to flatter, asked to be allowed one with the Prince's miniature on it–a proposal that was immediately agreed to. As the work progressed it was shown to the Prince, who suggested alterations and took a great interest in it. Then came another tiff and, when Brummell next called at Gray's, he was told that the Prince had sent explicit instructions that the box should not be handed over to him. It never was–and his own box was never returned. 'It was this, more than anything else,' according to one of his friends, 'which induced Brummell to bear himself with such unbending hostility towards the Prince of Wales. He felt that he had treated him unworthily and, from this moment, he indulged himself by saying the bitterest things.'

The Prince's infatuation with Lady Hertford continued. She was now popularly known as Madame de Maintenon (whom Louis XIV had married when she was fifty-one) but was supposed to be a sensible woman who was having a good influence on the Regent. Others claimed that she had 'infused some Methodistical notions into the Prince's mind', an alarming prospect since doctors in the West Country had recently traced an increase of insanity to 'Methodism and drinking. The cases in which religion of this character has been the cause are found to be the most difficult to cure.' Perhaps under this religious influence, the Prince at a public dinner proposed the toast of 'The Duke of York and the Army' thus indicating a temporary reconciliation with his brother and the Duke's approaching reinstatement as commander-in-chief. Brummell went down to Oatlands in May to celebrate this, and the Duchess's forty-fifth birthday. The King was in a sufficiently quiet mood to be allowed over from Windsor with the Princesses, the local peasantry were plied with pies and beer, and the Duchess led off the dancing which continued far into the night.

The following month the Regent gave a vast reception, nominally in honour of the exiled French royal family, but in fact to mark his appointment as Regent. By eight o'clock in the evening the string of carriages waiting to enter Carlton House stretched all the way to St James's Street, and by nine, when the gates opened, they reached the top of Bond Street. The two thousand guests supped in a tent in the grounds while the Prince, heavily bediamonded, starred, badged and aigretted, and wearing 'a very rich scarlet uniform, of not very good taste or very well made', entertained the visiting royalty in the cathedral-like conservatory. The Princess of Wales was not invited. Mrs Fitzherbert returned her invitation on finding that she was not to have her usual seat on the top table, and protested to the Prince that he was 'excluding the person who is not unjustly suspected by the world of possessing in silence unassumed and unsustained a Rank given her by yourself above that of any other present.' Or, as one of the guests remarked, while the Prince so lavishly celebrated, 'the two wives sat at home by themselves'.

They were far from being the only aggrieved parties. When the wife of one of the Lords of the Bedchamber complained of not receiving an invitation somebody jokingly suggested they must have been sent out alphabetically and the number of places ran out before they reached the letter W, with which her name began. 'That can't be,' said her ladyship, 'for half the Whores in town were invited.' The gossipy Mr Creevey was even more outspoken: 'The folly and villainy of this Prinny is beyond anything,' he wrote to his wife. Mrs Fitzherbert never spoke to the Prince again.

This may also have been the last time that Brummell was invited to Carlton House, although his path was to cross the Prince's many times later. When it did Brummell's carefree impertinence often compounded his offence. An eyewitness describes one occasion when the Prince was being driven to a picture gallery in Pall Mall:

Brummell, who was walking with some other man about ten yards in front of me, was exactly opposite the door of the exhibition as the low dark-red carriage stopped. Brummell evidently saw it, and saw who was in it, though he pretended not to do so, and when the two sentries presented arms, he, with an air of affected surprise and mock dignity, which was most amusing, gravely raised his hat, as if the salute had been to him; as he did this he paused, turning his head very graciously towards the sentries and his back to the carriage window, which he was quite close to. I saw, as I passed, the Regent's angry look, but he said nothing.

Brummell's fortunes were changing in other directions. Baudelaire was right in saying that 'The dandy regards neither love nor money as an end in itself.' And until now money had been for

George something that one distributed to the lower classes in return for their services, or that one used as counters at play, or that one raised by putting one's signature to pieces of paper. It was an attitude that must have caused continual anguish to the late William Brummell of Donnington Grove, gazing down from his stool in some celestial Office of Angelic Corruption. It was also an attitude that was becoming more and more difficult to preserve.

The war had wreaked havoc with trade, particularly from the American continent. Some produce could not be got over because of the blockade and counter-blockade at sea; the rest could not be sold in the European markets that had been sealed off by Bonaparte. There were great failures in the City of London in the summer of 1810. A year later, City merchants reported that 'West Indian produce is a drug, scarcely producing more than pays the freight.' George had some of his capital invested in the West Indies and was beginning to feel the pinch.

He could, of course, have lived in great comfort on the income that remained to him. He had once facetiously informed a rich country gentleman who asked him how much it would cost to dress his son when he entered the London scene that 'with the strictest economy—mind, I say the strictest economy—it may be done for £1000 a year'. But in fact about this time the painter Lawrence–another great spendthrift–calculated that he needed £800 a year for all his expenses, including four servants; and Brummell must still have had twice this.

There were indeed others with considerably less. Farmworkers averaged not more than two shillings a day, except for harvest time, when labour was short and wages two or three times higher. Children of ten and eleven employed at one of Mr Arkwright's manufactories in Derbyshire worked from seven in the morning to seven in the evening (with a forty-minute break for dinner at noon) for three and sixpence a week for boys and two and three-pence for girls. They were excused work on Sundays, when they went alternately to chapel or to school. 'The whole plan,' as one visitor observed, 'appears to be such as to do Mr Arkwright great credit.'

But unlike the Derbyshire children, or the farmworkers, or

Left Full dresses for May 1808

Below Dandies and dandiyettes in Hyde Park, 1818

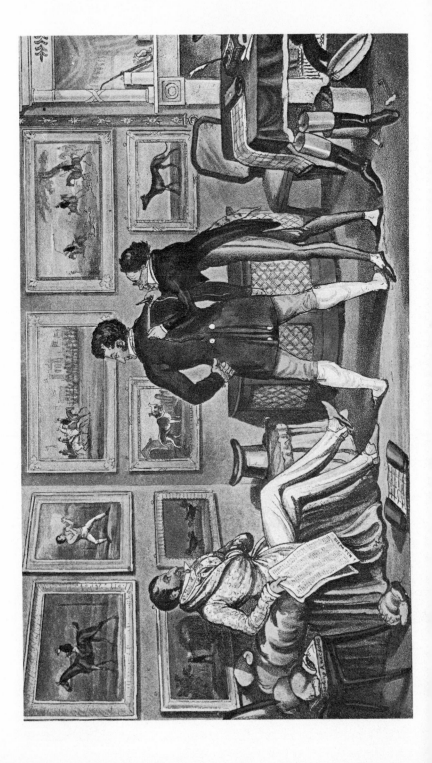

even the popular portrait painter, Brummell had a special position to maintain. He had ceased to be the reformer of fashionable society, and was now the leader of the society he had reformed. His companions were almost all much richer than he. In order not merely to keep up with them but to stay ahead, he began to gamble. It was a vice to which he had never before been addicted and which he adopted now from necessity, not passion. It was not as foolish a decision as it would be nowadays, for he played only in his clubs, where the bank passed from hand to hand and the odds were even. He had, too, a winning gambler's temperament—an equable disposition and a cool nerve.

Nevertheless, there were bound to be downs as well as ups. There could be long periods between winning spells, moments of some embarrassment. As the Beau's disciple, Lord Alvanley, just arrived at his majority, confessed: 'My damned duns made such a noise every morning I couldn't get a moment's rest, till I ordered the knocker to be taken off my street door.' About the same time, Harriette Wilson was writing to her sister Fanny, 'Brummell, they say, is entirely ruined. In short, everybody is astonished and puzzled to guess how he has gone on so long.' The rumour was better founded than most of Harriette's malicious gossip. In the summer of 1810 Brummell's financial situation was so tight that the Duke of Rutland wrote to the Prime Minister, Spencer Perceval, asking that a vacant post as Commissioner of Excise should be given to the Beau. It was typical of Brummell that he never asked for a favour while he was a close friend of the Prince of Wales; it was inevitable that it would be refused now that they were falling out and the Prince was about to become Regent. Perceval replied that the Board of Excise was in need of legally-trained members and appointed a lawyer. Brummell returned to piquet and macao.

The manufacture of cotton and woollen goods had suffered almost as much as the sugar trade from the mutual French/English blockade. And in February 1811 the Americans, irked by the keenness of the British anti-contraband patrols, renewed the Non-Intercourse Act, cutting off the supply of raw cotton. It was not the best time to introduce new systems, such as more efficient frames requiring fewer weavers. The owners insisted on following

BB—D

the march of progress; the workers, faced with receiving lower
wages for cottage work, or moving from country to town, or
more often losing their employment entirely, took axes and
sledgehammers and broke up the frames. The trouble was
intense for two years, from early 1811 to 1813, and grumbled on
for five years more.

The attacks, at first confined to the winter months when the
longer nights helped the raiders to avoid recognition, were
accompanied by coercion of both fellow-workers and employers.
The magistrates and the militiamen who were called out to deal
with the disturbances had their hayricks burned and their horses
and cattle maimed by the unseen followers of the unknown
'General Ludd'. Others were menaced into contributing to the
General's funds. 'Gentlemen all: Ned Ludd's Compliments and
hopes you will give a trifle towards supporting his Army as he
well understands the Art of breaking obnoxious Frames. If you
comply with this it will be well; if not, I shall call upon you myself. Edward Ludd.' Ned's army presently took to firearms as well
as axes and hammers; factories were besieged in military fashion,
with volleys of fire exchanged from both sides. By 1812 there were
more than 12,000 troops in the field against the Luddites, but it
was the skilful use of spies and informers that brought the worst
of the troubles to an end in January 1813 when seventeen men
were tried and hanged at York.

The Beau's old regimental comrades were not among those
sent to hunt down the miscreants. For years they had fretted under
the nickname of the China Tenth—handled like precious porcelain
because the Prince was their colonel. Now that the Prince was
Regent and evidently could not be expected to accompany them,
they were available for active service. Renamed and re-equipped
as Hussars they had taken part in the campaign that ended at
Corunna. In the summer of 1811 they were brigaded with the
15th and 18th and shipped back to Spain to reinforce Wellington.
Many of Brummell's young disciples were now at war, in
cluding the nineteen-year-old Marquess of Worcester, who had
become deeply involved with Harriette Wilson and, to the con-
sternation of his father, the Duke of Beaufort, looked like being
tricked into marrying her—just as William Hill's brother, Lord

Berwick, married Harriette's younger sister, Sophia, in February 1812.

On his return, Worcester was to join Brummell in several hare-brained schemes to raise money; but for the moment the Beau's partners were the Duke of Rutland's younger brothers, Lord Robert and Lord Charles Manners. With one or the other of them in turn he entered into the risky business of contracting to pay annuities in return for single cash payments. The interest seems to have averaged more than fifteen per cent–and the capital was, almost certainly, used to cover gambling losses. It afforded a way of paying debts of honour when no more loans could be obtained from the banks or other usurers, but there was nothing else to recommend it. Except, perhaps, that it was itself another gamble. And life could continue its elegant course, outwardly unruffled whatever inward doubts might plague the small hours between a late retirement and a tardy rising.

By 1812 Brummell had moved into new quarters–No. 13 Chapel Street (now Aldford Street). The book-lined downstairs parlour, next to the dining room, served as a waiting room for those not granted the privilege of attending his levee. Close friends were invited up to the first floor where they could sit in the chintz-upholstered, Brussels-carpeted drawing room, chatting with the Beau through the open door that led to his dressing room. Here, wearing a muslin dressing-gown and facing a mahogany-framed cheval glass with two brass arms for candles, he would sit in a low armchair while his *coiffeur* attended to his hair, which was rather light and thin and, for evening appearances, was often waved with curling tongs by his valet, Robinson. The furniture and ornaments, throughout the house, were carefully chosen and costly: in addition to his collection of snuff-boxes he had some fine pieces of boulle furniture and Sèvres porcelain. His book-shelves revealed an orthodox taste in literature. Eton had put him on easy terms with the classics; he had a smattering of Italian, a very little German, and enough French to read if not to speak the language (the Duchess of York habitually wrote to him in French; he replied in English). In his cellar he kept several dozens of mature port and claret, and for the rare occasions when he entertained he had a dinner service of twelve oval dishes, twenty soup plates and seventy-eight meat plates, as well as nine wine-coolers, three claret jugs, a dozen hock glasses and forty others. Usually he dined out, at friends' houses, at Watier's and at White's.

The gossip at White's in the spring and summer of 1812 returned again and again to the Prince of Wales, whose twelve-month probationary period as Regent ended in February and who had finally disillusioned his few remaining Whig supporters by doing nothing to let them take a turn at government. In the previous November he had injured his ankle while attempting a Highland fling at a ball at Oatlands in honour of his daughter, Princess Charlotte; a horse trod on his foot, breaking a tendon; his hands became gouty and palsied; and he developed strange pains in his head. His brother, the Duke of Cambridge, hopefully spread a rumour that he was going the same way as his father—which, since his father's disease was probably hereditary, may well have been true.

By March, just about the time that Brummell was awaiting delivery of a fifteen-guinea embroidered waistcoat from Guthrie in Cork Street, the Prince had 'fallen into a habit which excited the grave foreboding of his friends–viz. of abusing anyone he disliked in the most open way'. He was also prone to fits of weeping. When Lord Moira, his old friend and champion whom he had betrayed like the rest, said farewell to him he 'began to blubber (as he once did when he was told that Brummell did not like the cut of his coat)'. The King, on the other hand, though now judged to be beyond all hope of recovery, was reported to be very cheerful. 'He passes his time talking, sometimes to himself and sometimes to those about him, and in playing upon a Harpsichord in an irregular manner.'

The estrangement between Brummell and the Prince presented problems for their common friends, which Brummell did his best to ease. In 1812, when the Duke of Rutland issued his usual invitations to Belvoir Castle, Brummell realised that his presence might lead to a lot of pouting and petulance from the Regent and deep embarrassment for their host. He asked the Duke of York to take soundings at Carlton House, and the Duke reported that 'his answer to me was that he could never think of making any exceptions whatever, but should be happy to meet any company there the Duke of Rutland might wish to invite. I look forward with pleasure to seeing you there ... God bless you, and believe me, Ever Yours sincerely, Frederick.'

Whether Brummell went is not known; in any event there seems to have been no improvement in his relationship with the Regent. But others were as eager as ever for his company. Byron for one, back in England after three years of travelling in southern Europe, was delighted to be patronised by the Beau. 'I received everywhere a marked attention, was courted in all societies, made much of by Lady Jersey, had the entrée at Devonshire House, was in favour with Brummell (and that was alone enough to make a man of fashion at that time).'

From Europe the news grew brighter. In January 1812 Wellington's army stormed and captured Ciudad Rodrigo; in April Badajoz; and on 22 July he defeated Marmont at Salamanca. Just four weeks before, Napoleon had crossed the Neimen with an enormous but ill-prepared army, heading for the parched plains of Poland and the agonising destruction of the myth of his invincibility. The horrors of the Russian winter, and Bonaparte's cowardly desertion of his harassed army, lay only a few months in the future. In London the mob was out once more, terrorising the town with three nights of rejoicing for the victories in Spain, discharging firearms in the street, overturning coaches and setting them alight, and attacking any houses that did not have lamps and candles shining in celebration; for there was still a war party and an anti-war party at Westminster and easy money to be earned in proving the righteousness of the one by hurling stones or poking poles through the windows of the other.

Autumn saw Brummell embarking on another outwardly unruffled round of the country houses, and two letters that he wrote to Sir Stephen Glynne, a fellow-member of White's and future father-in-law of W. E. Gladstone, probably belong to this period. (The paper is watermarked 1808, the address is Chapel Street. Brummell lived at 22 South Street at least until 1810, and before that at 18 Bruton Street.) Whatever the exact date, the correspondence reveals the kindness of heart and deep loyalty that were concealed beneath his cynical hedonistic exterior.

In the first letter, dated 7 August, he told Glynne that

the situation of our friend Horace Beckford is so immediately exigent that I am confident you will forgive the abruptness of my application.

To provide for those losses to which he has so imprudently exposed himself at Play during the present summer, he has involved himself in engagements to a set of rascally moneylenders who are now urgently pressing him for payment, and whose menaces, in the event of his inability to satisfy their claims, I fear, will be put in execution.

Any endeavour to defend or extenuate these recent follies which have placed him in this unfortunate predicament, would be almost an insult to the most common judgement, however partial, when the remembrance of his former imprudence, and the liberal manner by which he was extricated from its consequent embarrassment by his Uncle, is yet fresh in our minds. I would therefore, for the moment beg of you to forget the fact in feeling for the misery of his present situation, and should it be conveniently in your power, I will earnestly solicit your assistance.

Horace Beckford, a handsome young man who had for a time been Julia Johnstone's lover, was the nephew and heir of the childless Lord Rivers. In 1807 he had run up gambling debts believed to amount to £30,000. His father, Peter Beckford, a well-known fox-hunter, refused to help him. His uncle Lord Rivers agreed to advance the money on condition that 'You are to take your name out of all Clubs. To give the most binding Promises never more to play—you are not to keep Hunters, whereby is meant Horses *merely for that purpose*: you must part with your Post-Chaise, and travel as becomes your circumstances, *not Post*: I expect you will be careful not to incur Debts with Tradesmen, but to Pay for everything as you have it.'

Horace gratefully accepted. Shortly afterward he married and gave the impression of settling down; but the old habits died hard. He forgot his promises and went back to the tables. Now, therefore, as Brummell continued: 'It is impossible to repeat any application to Ld Rivers on his behalf and any intercourse with his Father and himself has been long closed. The only method that remains open and promises success, is to appeal to those who are best known to him, and may possess the inclination and means to extend their temporary aid.'

He enclosed a list of his friends who had already promised to lend £1000 each. They were Lord Foley, Lord Gwydir, husband of Lady Willoughby d'Eresby who succeeded Lady Jersey in

Princess Caroline's household, Gwydir's son Peter Burrell, Lord Sackville the future Duke of Dorset and Nicholas Vansittart. Glynne agreed to make a loan; Beckford was saved and this time kept his promise to give up gambling–until, many years later, he relapsed, fell into debt again and, in a fit of remorse, drowned himself in the Serpentine.

Brummell had rightly judged his man. On 19 August Brummell wrote again to Glynne, to thank him and ask him to send the money to Beckford's solicitors in Stratton Street, and to accept Glynne's invitation to visit Hawarden. The letter, besides providing an example of Brummell's rather heavily facetious style, gives an insight into the pattern of the Beau's bachelor progress around the country house parties now that autumn was at hand.

I propose being at Foley's the day after tomorrow and shall proceed from there to Forrester's. As I am at present almost ignorant of the geography of my country beyond Salt Hill I cannot yet decide upon the best plan for the navigation of my course from Ross Hall; Wynstay, Vale Royal (if such a place still remains) or Hawarden. I will leave the direction of my travel to Forrester, and if his old age has not interfered with his former meritorious talents of getting over a country, he will point out the nearest route–at all events I will be with you within the period of three weeks, for I assure you a visit to your domains is one of the most prominent features of my itinerant progress.

Salt Hill was the village on the Bath Road to which the Four-in-Hand Club drove to dine and wine. Lord Foley, the skinny 'No. 11', lived at Whitley Court in Worcestershire. His spendthrift wife, Cecilia, was a Fitzgerald, daughter of the Duke of Leinster, sister-in-law of another of Brummell's friends Lord Kinnaird, and cousin to Charles James Fox. Cecil Forester (as his surname is usually spelt) was in his early forties. He had married the Duke of Rutland's sister, Katherine, and was later created Lord Forester of Willey Park.

I have ordered a good comfortable Parasol for my morning promenade about the grounds at Vale Royal [Brummell continued], as I understand there is little umbrageous protection to be expected within ten miles of the House, from the noonday sun. I do not know how I shall get on with the natives at Wynstay, not being in the least conversant with the Cambrian dialect, and bearing the most inveterate prejudice against toasted cheese and ale. I suppose, however, Sir Hurricane will have the humanity to extend some considerations upon the fastidious palate of a metropolitan, and allow

some more refined beverages after dinner than his Welch Laudanum.
Should the road to Hawarden be difficult to find out, I wish you would
detain John Talbot with you, and send him out as an obelisk for my direction.
One could see him at any distance, even at night, with a little gas upon his
toupee.

Wynstay, the seat of Sir 'Hurricane' Watkyn Williams-Wynn, was
close to Ruabon in Denbighshire; his daughter Henrietta had
recently married Thomas Cholmondeley, later Lord Delamare,
who lived at Vale Royal, close to Northwich. Hawarden, the
home of Sir Stephen Glynne, lay back westward again in Flint-
shire, an indication that Brummell had indeed not studied a map
very carefully before drawing up his itinerary. John Talbot, a tall
Guardee, was the son of the second Baron Talbot of Malahide.

If the journey was made in 1812, then Brummell returned from
Hawarden to Tixal Hall in Staffordshire, as the guest of the former
Lady Harriet Cavendish, now Lady Granville Leveson Gower.
'Mr Brummell *se fait plutôt attendre que désirer*' [keeps us waiting,
rather than wishing, for him], she wrote on 11 September. 'I feel
it a matter of perfect indifference whether he arrives at any
moment or not at all.' But as usual he enchanted her and the rest
of the company when he finally appeared.

They were a moderately strange collection. Lady Harriet,
plain but vivacious, kindhearted and sharp-tongued, had been a
reluctant bride for the tall, handsome Lord Granville, well knowing that her aunt, the beautiful Lady Bessborough, was Granville's mistress and had borne him two illegitimate children. This
did not prevent Lady Bessborough from being the guest of
honour, accompanied by her only daughter Caroline, who was
married to William Lamb, the future Lord Melbourne. The Lambs
were a hopelessly ill-matched couple, he jovial, hearty, eating
'like a trooper', she, on the eve of her scandalous infatuation for
Byron, 'in a sad way, alternately in tearing spirits and in tears'.
The other guests included two of Brummell's close friends, the
dark, beautiful-complexioned Lady Harriet Villiers and her husband, Richard Bagot, who on getting married had entered holy
orders so as to take advantage of family preferments and was
presently to be appointed Bishop of Oxford.

Brummell had no conventional artistic gifts, but the neatness and attention to detail which he displayed in his dress was reflected in a talent for copying. He copied other people's verses into his famous album. He copied other people's paintings and gave them as presents to his friends. In earlier days he had made considerable play with the miniature on ivory of the Prince of Wales which he was making from Cosway's original, though he proceeded so slowly that when he was at last goaded into producing the finished article there were many ladies who claimed to believe that he had paid Cosway to do it for him. During his stay at Tixal, he endeared himself to his hostess by making a copy of Sir Joshua Reynolds's portrait of her beautiful mother, the Duchess Georgiana–and Lady Harriet gave him in return some verses she had written for her mother, titled *The Voice of Praise*–seven octets of impeccable sentiment, concluding

> There is a lip, there is an eye,
> Where most I love to see it shine;
> To hear it speak, to feel it sigh,
> My Mother! need I say 'tis thine?

Brummell gratefully transferred it to his album; where he already had a lot more like it.

It was on this occasion too, that an elderly recluse named Lister was invited to dine and, before the meal, was shown some of Brummell's drawings. 'At last dinner was announced, and the Beau rose to offer his arm to a lady of high rank, his intimate friend, as did also Mr Lister to the same lady; but observing the old gentleman's intentions he immediately withdrew; when Mr L., mistaking him for an artist, said, to the infinite amusement of the lady, "I'm glad to see the young man understands his place"; and it was only towards the close of dinner that he discovered who the modest young man really was.'

He spent Christmas as usual with the Yorks at Oatland's a particularly light-hearted occasion because of the news that had been coming out of Russia for the past three weeks of the French retreat, rumours at first but, by 17 December, firm details that set the guns at the Tower and Hyde Park booming salvoes of relief and celebration. Many of the party, including Brummell, stayed on to welcome in the New Year. Lord Erskine, the brilliant

advocate, composed a great length of verse describing his fellows
guests at the Duchess's table: Colonel Armstrong, the Duke'-
aide-de-camp, the poetic William Spencer, 'Monk' Lewis, Lt-Col
'Kangaroo' Cooke.

> By this Colonel sat one, in gay circles well known,
> Yet, who see him in rounds of amusement alone,
> Know little about him–they see him at ease,
> A high man of fashion, with talents to please;
> But believe me, in London to rise to the top,
> Like Brummell (since London discarded the fop)
> You must know all that's known to the highest in place,
> And possess the rare gift to give knowledge a grace.

Well, it was Christmas, and Erskine was an inexorable rhymer,
and Brummell once more considered the lines worth including
in his album, together with those describing all the others at the
table; his neighbour Lady Anne Culling Smith, Colonel de Lancey
Barclay of the Royal Corsican Rangers, Lady Anne Fitzroy,
daughter of Lady Anne Smith by her first marriage, and Culling
Smith himself, 'so sprightly, so gay, as airy and light as a bird on
the spray'. The company was choice, friendly, witty, polite: the
atmosphere in which Brummell blossomed best.

The season of 1813 brought to London the famous Madame
de Staël and a fashionable craze for the waltz, which had been
introduced some years before but without much success.

Old and young returned to school, and the mornings which had been dedi-
cated to lounging in the park were now absorbed at home in...whirling a
chair round the room, to learn the steps and measure of the German waltz.
Lame and impotent were the first efforts, but the inspiring airs of the music,
and the not less inspiring airs of the foreigners, soon rendered the English
ladies enthusiastic performers. What scenes have we witnessed in those days
at Almacks! What fear and trembling in the débutantes at the commencement
of a waltz, what giddiness and confusion at the end! It was perhaps owing to
this latter circumstance that so violent an opposition soon arose to this new
recreation on the score of morality.

Brummell could not be expected to approve the boisterous-
ness of this 'riotous and indecent' dance; he equally resisted the
aggressive charms of Madame de Staël, whom his friend Lady
Jersey introduced to London society at a reception on 20 June.

Germaine de Staël was a plain woman who could not bring
herself to recognise the fact, an unflagging intellectual and one of

history's great monopolisers of conversations. She had fled to London once before–from the Revolution, and a shrewd observer had noted then that: 'She is one of those women who are greedy of admiration, and lay themselves out for it in all ways, purchasing any quantity of anybody at any price, and among other prices by a traffic of mutual flattery. She is also to have the whole conversation to herself, and to be the centre of every company she is in.'

After twenty years she had not changed, though she was now better known and better considered for having been sent into exile by Bonaparte. Someone who met her at an evening exhibition of Reynolds's pictures at the Academy ten days later described her as 'of the middle size in height at most. Her face very much of the Swiss form and character, her hair and eyes black, the latter animated. Her mouth wide and disfigured by two very projecting upper teeth; her complexion tending to swarthy; her person rather broad and apparently strong.' She had two immediate aims: to establish a fashionable coterie and to marry her daughter.

'The Dandies,' as Byron remarked, 'in general disliked literary people.' He was proud of being an exception to the rule. 'They made me a member of Watier's (a superb club at that time) being, as I take it, the only literary man, except two others, (both men of the world) Moore and Spencer, in it.' And he was not in the least surprised when 'the Dandies took an invincible dislike to the de Staël's, mother and daughter. Brummell was her aversion, she his ... they persecuted and mystified Mme de Staël most damnably.' They persuaded her that the stocky, ugly Alvanley (who certainly threw his money about like a very rich man) had an income of £100,000 a year. Whereupon she 'praised him to his *face* for his *beauty*! and made a set at him for Albertine (Libertine, as Brummell baptised her, though the poor girl was and is as correct as maid and wife can be, and very amiable withal), and a hundred fooleries besides'.

For a while, wherever Alvanley went Mme de Staël and Albertine were sure to go, with Albertine, on Mama's instructions, playing up to him outrageously. One of Alvanley's favourite stories for years after was how, dancing with Albertine at Almack's, he saw Lord Jersey enter (the widowed Lady Jersey's son) and said to her, 'What a handsome man Jersey is!'

Whereupon Albertine, 'obeying her instructions, immediately replied with a tender look, "He shall not be so pretty than you." '

Byron was himself having trouble with an unwanted admirer.
The week before Mme de Staël's arrival he encountered the
flirtatious and unpredictable Lady Caroline Lamb at Lady
Heathcote's ball. They quarrelled and Lady Caroline 'stabbed
herself with a knife at supper, so that the blood flew about her
neighbours. She was taken away and, as it was supposed she was
faint, a glass of water was brought, when she broke the glass and
struck herself with the pieces.' The unfeeling Byron put it about
that 'he is haunted by a Spectre (she being very thin) and treats
her with the utmost disregard'.

The Dandies were all experiencing a revival in fortune.
Brummell, after a run of bad luck at Macao, was walking home up
Berkeley Street with Tom Raikes at five o'clock one fine summer's
morning when he 'suddenly stopped on seeing something glitter-
ing in the kennel; he stooped down and picked up a crooked
sixpence. His countenance immediately brightened. "This," said
he, "is the harbinger of good luck." ' Its previous owner evidently
believed so, for the coin had a hole drilled in it.

The charm worked. He at once began to win large sums. So
much so that in July 1813, after he and Alvanley, Henry Pierrepont and Henry Mildmay had won a great amount at Hazard, the
four of them decided to give a fancy dress ball for their friends at
the Argyle Rooms. On Brummell's insistence, no invitation was
sent to the Prince Regent, but the Prince was not the man to take a
hint gracefully. When somebody told him of the ban, he simply
wrote to say that he intended to be present. There was clearly
nothing to be done except to receive him as politely as possible.
An invitation was sent, signed by all four.

On the evening of the masquerade the hosts lined up at the
door to receive the Prince. He bowed to Pierrepont, turned to
the other side, saw Brummell standing there, and at once turned
back to Alvanley, who was next to Pierrepont. In the shocked
silence that followed this deliberate cut and atrocious piece of
ill-manners, Brummell's voice, clear, cool and penetrating, was
heard asking, 'Ah, Alvanley, who is your fat friend?'

Pierrepont said later: 'We were dismayed, but in those days

Brummell could do no wrong.' Others regarded it as 'a witty retort to a provocation, rather than an unmannerly insult'. Those who were still waiting to receive the Prince, and had a good view of his face, saw that 'he was cut to the quick by the aptness of the satire'.

The Prince, who passed into the ballroom visibly shaken, sent back a message saying that he wished to speak to Sir Henry Mildmay. Mildmay, with Dandy loyalty, replied that it must be a mistake, because 'his Royal Highness had seen him and took no notice of him whatsoever'. His Royal Highness was, indeed, being much misunderstood at this time. Public sentiment, though fickle, still remained largely on the side of his sad, grotesque wife, turned out of his home, deprived of her daughter and her rank, and guiltless of anything except, as she rather wittily said in reference to her sad honeymoon, 'one act of adultery with the husband of Mrs Fitzherbert'. She seemed resigned to the fact that she would never find justice or happiness except by his death or her own. 'After dinner,' one of her attendants revealed, 'she made a wax figure as usual, and gave it an amiable addition of large horns; then took three pins out of her garment and stuck them through and through, and put the figure to roast and melt in the fire.' It was no secret which fat gentleman the wax figure represented.

While his wife roasted him at her house in Blackheath others did the same in print. Thomas Moore published a collection of satirical verses, which contained advice to those seeking to provide mistresses for the Regent:

> Include those only, plump and sage,
> Who've reached the regulation age;
> That is–as near as one can fix
> From Peerage dates–full fifty-six!

This injustice to Lady Hertford, who was only fifty-three, was followed by an imaginary soliloquy in which the Prince repeated Brummell's famous quip.

> Neither have I resentments, nor wish there should come ill
> To mortal–except (now I think on't) Beau Br-mm-l,
> Who threatened last year, in a superfine Passion,
> To cut *me*, and bring the old K-ng into fashion.

Leigh Hunt was beginning a two-year prison sentence for libelling him in *The Examiner* as 'a violater of his word, a libertine over head and heels in disgrace, a despiser of domestic ties, the companion of gamblers and demireps, a man who has just closed half a century without one single claim on the gratitude of his country or the respect of posterity.'

Charles Lamb, a more timid soul, was writing but not as yet publishing his verses on *The Triumph of the Whale*)

> By his bulk and by his size,
> By his oily qualities,
> This (or else my eyesight fails)
> This should be the Prince of Whales.

To fill his cup of bitterness, before the year was out Lord Thanet, another of the Sackvilles, had nicknamed him 'the *Bourgeois Gentilhomme*' after the vulgarian in Molière's comedy: 'a name which has got about and must inevitably annoy P. more than even "our fat friend" ', as the future Lord Brougham wrote to Creevey.

There is a legend, unsupported and, because the only authority for it is Captain Gronow's reminiscences, probably untrue, that the Prince managed to have his revenge on Brummell. He invited the Beau to Carlton House, with the Duke of York and General Upton, and in the course of dinner made himself so pleasant and plied his guests with so much wine that Brummell became quite overjoyed at the renewal of the old friendship, laughing and joking as in their early days. Whereupon the Prince pretended to take offence, said to the Duke of York, 'I think we had better order Mr Brummell's carriage before he gets drunk,' rang the bell and had Brummell sent home.

In August Brummell went down to Oatlands to join the Yorks for the Egham Races just across the river. He sent his congratulations to the Duke of Rutland, whose son, the Marquess of Granby had just been born at Cheveley, signing himself 'yours without a guinea, George Brummell'. It was a joke; for more than a year, with the aid of his lucky sixpence, he was almost continuously successful. He was estimated by one acquaintance to have won £30,000 on horses, and by another £26,000 at one sitting of cards. Even allowing for exaggeration he evidently did very well, in a

London that was soon filling with heroes returned from the battlefields after the false final victory of 1814, most of them determined to squander their back pay on fast women, slow horses, and the green baize tables of the clubs. Unfortunately Brummell, like the Guardees, did not know when to stop. Some *folie de grandeur*, already showing in his attitude to the Regent, drove him on to new elegant excesses and an entirely reckless disregard of the consequences.

There was one source of money that he had not yet tapped—he could marry a rich heiress. He made some moves in this direction—one of them noted in a letter sent by the Regent's daughter, Princess Charlotte, to her friend Margaret Mercer Elphinstone in September 1813: '...Brummell has of his *own* accord made up his quarrel with Lady Anne [Culling Smith], who is quite good friends with him again, and Georgiana [Fitzroy, her daughter], who has shaken hands with him, as he promised in future never to molest or to talk love again. He went as far as to say that as they were going to Grimthorp and he was *invited* at the *same time*, that he would be *guided* by what they said as to his going there or not. They said it was better for him to keep away, which he has done handsomely enough.' In the following July Georgiana was married to the Marquess of Worcester.

The allied sovereigns arrived in June 1814 to celebrate the defeat of Bonaparte and his exile to Elba. The members of White's gave a magnificent masquerade ball in their honour at Burlington House, attended by the Regent who tried to prevent members giving their tickets to any but their relations—in order to exclude the Princess of Wales. The handsome, disingenuous Alexander of Russia was there, attempting to seduce every pretty woman he met; Frederick William of Prussia, too relieved at being freed from the threats and humiliations of the Corsican tyrant to look for further delights; and four thousand other guests, received by Lady Harriet's brother, now the sixth Duke of Devonshire, and his cousin the Duke of Leinster. All the men who were not in masquerade wore full dress uniforms; Colonel Armstrong came as a dowager of the time of Queen Anne; Julia Johnstone wore boy's clothes, black satin breeches and a light blue silk jacket, and was accompanied by Harriette Wilson as her sister, an unexpected choice of roles, since Julia had a delicately fair complexion and a womanly figure (after at least five children) while Harriette, according to Sir Walter Scott, who dined with her at 'Monk' Lewis's house, was 'a smart saucy girl with good eyes and dark hair, and the manners of a wild schoolboy'. Brummell spent most of the evening chatting in a corner, not competing with the heavy royal guns.

He did not shine at these crowded too-public occasions, but at Almack's he was as prominent and as powerful as the committee of high-born ladies who nominally governed it and among whom were many of his close friends–Lady Jersey, Lady Sefton, Mrs Burrell. These, with support from Brummell, laid down the stringent rules which were accepted without a murmur, for to be excluded from Almack's was to be banished from society. So the men meekly put on their knee breeches and white cravats and carried their three-cornered hats under their arms, and did as the ladies and Brummell bade them. One officer, whose wife had been refused a ticket, challenged Lady Jersey's son to a duel but 'Lord Jersey refused to "go out" on the ground that it would be impossible for him to meet the vast number who could make that a cause of quarrel'. Captain Gronow reckoned that 'out of the three hundred officers of the Foot Guards, not more than half a dozen were honoured with vouchers of admission to this exclusive temple of the *beau monde*'.

On the other hand, there were rare occasions when Brummell himself met defeat–usually by mischance, as when he went to the opera with Alvanley and found himself cheek-by-jowl in the Round Room with a family of happy well-to-do vulgarians–Ma, Pa and their two noisily coy daughters. Alvanley mischievously pretended to recognise them and introduced Brummell.

'Brummell? Brummell?' said the father, a fat man in an advanced state of perspiration, 'I fancy, Sir, I have had the pleasure of meeting you before. I am sure I have. You are the gentleman as sung such a good song at our club.'

The Dandies and their ladies gathered round to enjoy the fun, while Alvanley whispered in the fat man's ear that he must be right, Brummell certainly *did* sing a good song, though he was possibly too shy to admit it.

'Sir!' said the man, vigorously mopping his face with his handkerchief and bowing to Brummell at the same time, 'I shall be most happy to see you at my snug box at Clapham. All my family are fond of a good English song, and I will venture to say I can give you as good a bottle of port wine as any in England.'

Confronted for once with a situation that he had no idea how to deal with, Brummell returned the bow and disappeared into the crowd. If the Thompson-Johnson incident ever did take place, the two ladies were adequately revenged.

A few weeks after the allied sovereigns returned to their thrones even greater and more widespread celebrations were organised in honour of a hundred years of Hanoverian rule, the centenary falling on 1 August 1814. The reflected glory that should have shone on George I's successors was dimmed by the insanity of the King and the unpopularity of the Regent, whose continuing feud with the Princess of Wales had flared up again. But the series of fêtes produced some beneficial side-effects, notably in London, where parks were cleaned up and some permanent improvements made. In St James's Park, then 'a long dirty field, intersected by a wide dirty ditch, thinly planted with rotten lime trees and sur-rounded by a wooden railing', the rank and weedy grass was cut and a wooden bridge built across the canal. This supported a tall wooden pagoda from the top of which a firework display enter-tained the crowds who paid half-a-guinea to stroll about the park and scatter their money at the gaming tents and refreshment booths. On the first night the pagoda caught fire, the top half collapsed, and several of the pyrotechnicians were burned to death or drowned in the canal. But the grand fête continued 'and for three days and nights *Saturnalia* such as London has never witnessed since, and which it is to be hoped it will never witness again, were kept up without intermission. A vast number of the more active participators in the amusements, both male and female, voted themselves on the "free list", managed to effect an entrance every evening about dusk by getting over the railing or between the rails, transgressed very considerably the laws of decorum and got drunk and disorderly with perfect impunity.'

The lavishness of the celebrations prompted Mrs Fitzherbert to remind the Prince that 'when the memorable event of our

Union took place in the year '85' he had settled £10,000 a year on her, but he had been so pressed for money that she never received more than £3000 a year until 1810, when he increased it to £6000. Despite a reminder that she sent him in 1813, she had still not arrived at the promised £10,000. However, as she wrote with heavy menace on 15 August 1814, 'I thank the Almighty that throughout all my bitter trials I have hitherto had forbearance enough never to utter one syllable that could have affected your interests.' The Prince could do very little. He was about to have trouble in Parliament over his Civil List–and he was more than £300,000 in debt.

Brummell had similar problems though smaller in scale. 'Brummell's sun, they say, is setting,' Harriette Wilson's sister Fanny wrote to her from London. 'Which, you'll answer, was the story long ago; but, since that, I am told Brummell won twenty thousand pounds [probably a reference to the evening at White's when he won that amount from George Harley Drummond, a merchant banker] that is too now gone, and he is greatly embarrassed. Poor Lord Alvanley, they say, is just in the same plight.' 'I have no credit with either butcher or poulterer,' Alvanley wrote to a friend, 'but if you can put up with turtle and turbot, I shall be happy to see you.' The Beau himself lightly attributed his change in fortune to the loss of his lucky sixpence. 'I advertised, and twenty people came with sixpences having holes in them to obtain the promised reward, but mine was not amongst them. No doubt that rascal Rothschild, or some of his set, got hold of it.'

One night he lost not only his previous winnings for the season, but also what he described as 'an unfortunate ten thousand pounds'–the whole of his remaining available capital. In mid-October he raised nearly £5000 by underwriting annuities, this time in partnership with Lord Charles Manners. He was now set on a very dangerous course, unable to meet the interest on his debts except by luck at the tables; and, still without his sixpence, he pursued luck in vain.

After a run of five losing nights, he told his friend Pemberton Mills that 'he had lost every shilling and only wished some one would bind him never to play again'. Mills promptly handed him a ten pound note wagering that, if Brummell played again at

White's within a month, the Beau would forfeit one thousand pounds. In less than a fortnight Mills entered the club and found Brummell back at the tables. It was evidently useless to hope for the thousand pounds. 'Well,' said Mills, 'you might at least give me back the ten pounds you had the other night.' To this period belong the stories of his borrowing money and, on being asked to repay, replying that he had paid already. 'When?' 'Why, when I was standing at the window at White's and, when you passed, said: "Ah, how do you do, Jemmy" '; or 'Why–when I gave you my arm all the way down St James's.'

At the time when Brummell and Lord Charles Manners were selling annuities, a great scandal broke around their old regiment. During Wellington's advance across the Pyrenees into Spain, the Tenth Hussars, so long kept out of action because the Prince was their Colonel-in-Chief, and smarting under the sneers of officers in other regiments, developed such a thirst for glory that after the battle of Arthes in February 1814 they accused their commanding officer, Colonel Quintin, of lacking appetite for war. He had not even come out to join the regiment until after they had fought at Vittoria. Some of the officers signed a round robin binding themselves never to speak to him and the dispute grew so bitter and public that in October Colonel Quintin was tried by court-martial, accused by twenty-four of his officers of incompetence and neglect of duty. Quintin was found not guilty–because of the protection of the Prince Regent, said the gossips–and the officers were transferred to other regiments. Among them were two FitzClarences, illegitimate sons of the Prince's brother, the Duke of Clarence, by the actress Mrs Jordan.

Bonaparte returned from Elba and sent a shudder through Europe. At Waterloo Lord Edward Somerset, who twenty years before had led Cornet Brummell and the Princess Caroline's procession from Greenwich to St James's, now commanded the Household Cavalry and had his horse shot from under him. The victorious allies, terrified of the revolutionary ideal that Bonaparte had dishonestly claimed as his inspiration, restored the stupid Bourbons and their rancorous followers, thus ensuring more revolutions for the future. In war-exhausted Britain, laws to keep up the price of corn brought riots and widespread disorders. And in the half-world of Harriette Wilson, her sisters and Julia Johnstone, the Beau and his friends continued to advance, retire and sometimes collide in ragged cotillions of pretended passion and languid lechery.

Harriette's sister Amy had recently picked up a rich young Hampshire squire named Meyler, who had been at Christ Church, Oxford, with Worcester. After Worcester was packed off to Spain Harriette collected ample compensation from his father, the Duke of Beaufort, and then enticed Meyler away from Amy. He gave her an allowance of £300 a year and set her up in lodgings in Somerset Place, off Marylebone Road. His fortune, estimated to bring him in at least £25,000 a year, had been founded by his grandfather Jeremiah, who distilled it from brown sugar and brown sweat in the West Indies, thus qualifying him for Alvanley's favourite disparaging epithet–'damned sugar-baker'. Through the interest of Sir Henry Mildmay he had been elected MP for the city of Winchester in 1812 at the age of twenty-one. He was 'a hard drinker, a very hard rider, and a good tennis and cricket player'. He was credited with features 'so peculiarly voluptuous that when he looks at women after dinner, although his manner is perfectly respectful, they are often observed to blush deeply and hang down their heads'. He was also the man immediately responsible for Brummell's ruin.

Meyler's friendship with Mildmay was badly strained when he burst into a room at the Key, a well-known brothel in Chandos Street, and found Sir Henry and Harriette in bed together. It ended when Mildmay had to flee to the Continent. In August 1810 the graceful Charlotte Mildmay had died after barely a year of marriage and attitudinising. Sir Henry consoled himself for a while with ladies of the town, but was gradually drawn back to the Bouverie family. One of his younger brothers had married Charlotte's youngest sister; Henry fell in love with Harriet, the middle one. And Harriet fell in love with Henry. There was however one impediment to this romance between brother-in-law and sister-in-law: Harriet was already married to the Earl of Rosebery, to whom she had borne two sons and a daughter.

In October 1814, when the family were at their Dalmeny

estate in Scotland, the Earl's mother noticed that Harriet was in the habit of going off for solitary walks. The dowager countess did not yet know that a certain Colonel de Grey who had taken rooms at the local inn was Sir Henry Mildmay, disguised with beard and whiskers, but, as is customary with mothers-in-law, she kept a very sharp and suspicious watch on her daughter-in-law. Her vigilance was rewarded. One evening after dinner she led a posse of servants through the corridors of Dalmeny House to a secluded groundfloor bedroom; the door was locked but, after a good deal of thumping, shouting and handle-rattling, the younger Lady Rosebery opened it from the inside.

Sir Henry Mildmay was revealed standing beside the bed, dressed innocently enough 'in a large blue jacket and trowsers, and a red waistcoat covered with a profusion of pearl buttons'; but armed with a brace of pistols. Harriet's costume was more open to misinterpretation: 'The handkerchief which Lady Rosebery had worn round her neck at dinner was off, and her gown unpinned, though not so as to expose her bosom indecently'; which was just as well, for there were servants present, some of whom had already noticed that 'the bed was indented in the centre as if pressed by an extraordinary weight'.

Sir Henry was ushered out–this time by the front door, not the bedroom window. Harriet was advised by the triumphant dowager to return to her uncle, Lord Radnor, while the family considered their next move. In fact, Harriet travelled down to London next morning with Sir Henry, sharing a bedroom at an inn on the way, and then lived openly with him at his house in Lower Brook Street. The following year Lord Rosebery was awarded a divorce and £15,000 damages against Mildmay for assault and trespass on his wife. To avoid paying, Sir Henry took Harriet to Stuttgart, where they were married. They were never able to return to England; thirty years later the once-gay Mildmay of the sweet singing voice shot himself because he could not face his accumulated mountain of debt.

The London season was in full swing and the hotels were crowded: Fladong's in Oxford Street full of naval officers; Stephen's in Bond Street full of the army; Ibbetson's a-twitter with undergraduates and clergy because it was cheaper than the others; the Clarendon crammed with rich gourmets willing to pay three or four pounds for a genuine French dinner; and grubby, gloomy Limmer's with country squires and racecourse touts on the look-out for plain English cooking, a good bottle of port, and nothing but talk about horses from morning to night. Brummell was still having difficulty in getting out of bed. He used to say that 'whether it was summer or winter, he always liked to have the morning well-aired before he got up'; and, when chided for wasting so many of the daylight hours in bed, he replied: 'Dear me! Don't you know that I am a reformed man? I always begin to rise with the first muffin bell!' (That is, somewhere between four and five o'clock.' The late afternoon he would often spend riding with his friends in Hyde Park clad in brass-buttoned blue coats, leather breeches and dazzlingly polished top boots. It was here that a young man asked Brummell one day where he bought his blacking. 'Ah!' said Brummell. 'My blacking positively ruins me. I will tell you in confidence: it is made with the finest champagne.' The ladies drove about in their *vis-à-vis*, little carriages for two, among the cows and the deer, far from the vulgar gaze; for seldom did one see 'any of the lower or middle classes of London intruding themselves in regions which, with a sort of tacit understanding, were then given up exclusively to persons of rank and fashion'.

After a ride or a drive in the Park there was the opera and more mutual display; this time on foot, perambulating among the boxes that ran in a tiered circle from one wing to the other by way of the back of the pit. The Regent, a regular patron, was in the habit of leaving just before the end of the performance, so that his carriage could be brought round before the others. One evening he mistimed his departure and was still standing in the lower waiting room when the audience began to emerge.

Brummell came out, talking eagerly to some friends [an eyewitness recorded], and, not seeing the Prince or his party, took up a position near the check-taker's bar. As the crowd flowed out, Brummell was gradually pressed backwards until he was almost driven against the Regent, who distinctly saw him but who of course would not move. In order to stop him therefore, and prevent actual collision, one of the Prince's suite tapped him on the back, when Brummell immediately turned sharply round, and saw that there was not much more than a foot between his nose and the Prince of Wales's.

I watched him with intense curiosity and observed that his countenance did not change in the slightest degree, nor did his head move; they looked straight into each other's eyes. The Prince was evidently amazed and annoyed. Brummell, however, did not quail or show the least embarrassment. He receded quite quietly, and backed slowly step by step till the crowd closed between them, never once taking his eyes off those of the Prince. It was impossible to describe the impression made by this scene on the bystanders; There was in his manner nothing insolent, nothing offensive; by retiring with his face to the Regent he recognised his rank, but he offered no apology for his inadvertence (as a mere stranger would have done), no recognition as an acquaintance; as man to man, his bearing was adverse and uncompromising.

This silent skirmish at the opera served to underline Brummell's supremacy in society. About this time Dighton made a sketch of him at Almack's exercising his suave discipline. Gronow described it: 'On the left, the man with the red face, laughing at Brummell, is Charles, Marquis of Queensberry. The great George himself, the admirable Crichton of the age, comes next, in a dégagé attitude, with his fingers in his waistcoat pocket. His neckcloth is inimitable, and must have cost him much time and trouble to arrive at such perfection. . He is talking earnestly to the charming Duchess of Rutland.' Two foreign princesses, a pair of counts and a baron made up the rest of the party.

Nothing could be more select, more civilised. Unhappily there was still the vulgar problem of money. The elation of victory in 1815 gave way to the post-war stringencies of 1816. Bonaparte had drained Europe of cash as well as blood. The workers in the manufactories were unemployed because nobody had the money to buy the goods they made. The workers on the farms were unemployed because the workers in the manufactories could not afford to buy the food they grew. Wages had doubled yet still not kept pace with prices. There were riots in the towns, arson in the countryside. The Prince Regent was in the middle of a new public row over £50,000 of furniture he had ordered for the Royal Pavilion which John Nash had begun to remodel in the oriental style. And some of Brummell's bills were beginning to come home to roost.

He had many commitments now—far more than he could meet

out of immediately available capital. In addition to the annuity
schemes in which he was associated with Robert and Charles
Manners, he had joined Alvanley and Worcester in raising a loan
that amounted to £3000 according to Julia Johnstone and £30,000
according to Harriette Wilson. Whatever it was, he had difficulty
in finding money to pay the interest. With the recklessness that
characterised many of his recent actions he went one evening to
Gordon's, a notorious gambling hell in Jermyn Street, stayed on
and on while his luck grew worse and worse, and ended up losing
£5000. He had to confess to Worcester that he could not meet his
share of the joint debt. Worcester passed the news on to Meyler,
who was one of Brummell's creditors.

Meyler was a spiteful man, and, although he had lent Brummell
money, he probably hated him because of the contempt with
which he was treated by the Beau's close friends. The day after
learning of Brummell's plight, Meyler went to White's and
denounced Brummell as a swindler to every member who entered.
Among them was Tom Raikes, the well-intentioned, tight-fisted
gossip with the pock-marked nose, who hurried round to Chapel
Street to warn Brummell of what was happening.

The Beau suddenly found himself faced with a desperate
situation. Meyler's loud talk would set every one of his other
creditors barking; and if the scandal should really result in his
being forced to resign from White's his social standing would be
damaged beyond repair. He accordingly sent Raikes back to the
club at once with a note to Meyler, 'begging to be informed if
such had really and truly been the expressions made use of'. The
implied threat of legal action or a duel had no effect on Meyler:
it is very difficult to bluff a hot-head. He sent word back that 'not
only had he used the expressions but that he further proposed
returning to the club on the following day for the sole purpose of
repeating them between the hours of two and four, to anybody
who might happen to be present, and if Mr Brummell had anything to say to him in return, he would be sure to find him at
White's during that particular time'.

That night Byron was dining at Charles Street with a few
close friends including Scrope Davies, a dandy and classical
scholar and well-known drunk. Davies was a fellow of King's

College, Cambridge (which he was said to visit only during the Newmarket Races), an intimate friend of Jackson the prize-fighter and other members of the Fancy, and a deep though usually lucky card player. He was a great admirer of Brummell, whom he imitated in his dress and quiet wit. As he sat at table, a servant brought in a letter which Davies read and then passed to Byron. It said: 'My dear Scrope–lend me two hundred pounds; the banks are shut and all my money is in the three per cents. It shall be repaid tomorrow morning. Yours, George Brummell.'

The pretext has a familiar ring and had probably been used too often before. In any case, he was applying to the wrong person. 'My dear George,' Davies replied, ' 'tis very unfortunate, but all *my* money is in three per cents. Yours, S. Davies.' It was the same response everywhere. Now and then a note for fifty guineas, but nothing that came anywhere near solving the problem.

The following day, Thursday 16 May, crowds of notabilities thronged into the Queen's House facing St James's Park–the former residence of the Duke of Buckingham, which nearly ten years later was pulled down to be replaced by Nash's Buckingham Palace. They were there to congratulate Her Majesty on the recent marriage of her granddaughter, Princess Charlotte, to Prince Leopold of Saxe-Coburg-Saalfeld, and they had come in such numbers that it took them two and a half hours to get from the entrance lodge through the colonnade to the grand staircase. The ladies had their dresses torn, the gentlemen lost the hats they carried under their arms and found them retrieved and displayed on tables as they fought their way back again. Brummell stayed clear of White's all day, dined at home off a cold fowl and a bottle of claret sent in from Watier's, and then put in an appearance at the opera.

It was brief. He slipped away and into a chaise that had been ordered for him by a friend, perhaps Raikes to whom he had revealed his intention that morning. In this he drove out beyond the suburbs, where his own carriage was waiting for him. Rattling through the night, changing horses at four post-houses on the way, he arrived at Dover before dawn. There he hired a small ship, had his carriage lifted on board with the few possessions he had managed to get packed into it during the day, and set sail for France.

CHAPTER FIVE

A Man of Fashion, Gone to the Continent

There was only one hotel in Calais for a gentleman of fashion: the celebrated Dessein's, unrivalled throughout Europe except perhaps for Schneider's in Florence. The original Monsieur Dessein, a Gascon whom Sterne had thought to look like a Jew or a Turk when he hired a carriage there for his sentimental journey fifty years before, was dead long since and the business had passed to his granddaughter and her husband, Monsieur Quillac, another Gascon and proprietor of the second-best hotel, the Silver Lion, where Hogarth had stayed. Dessein's amenities included a large court and garden, the room on the first floor 'where Sterne slept' (proudly shown to distinguished visitors as such despite the evidence in Sterne's own account that he arrived in the early afternoon, ate a fricasseed chicken, and departed soon after four), an excellent restaurant, and even a theatre, with an entrance from the hotel garden. Brummell settled himself in and, after only a day for recuperation, set about writing to the friends in London whom he had so unceremoniously and unexpectedly deserted.

Among the first were the Manners brothers, Charles and Robert, who would now be as disastrously involved in his failure as were Worcester and Alvanley. The letter, very long and rather pompous, has a ring of genuine contrition. He began:

'Persecuted to the worst extent by those to whom I was indebted, without resource or even the hope to evade or protract the execution of those menaces which, I was well assured, would have been instantly enforced against my personal liberty, I have been driven to the only alternative yet left me upon earth–that of quitting my country for ever.' He confessed that: 'I am indeed most sensible, most acutely so, of the heavy wrongs which such a step must inflict upon those who from their former friendly regard for me were induced to impose upon themselves a future charge for my immediate assistance. I will not endeavour to palliate the past or the present–such an endeavour would be vain and only justly prove an aggravation of my misconduct.' He pointed out, what was indeed the truth, that if he had remained in England he would have been committed to a debtor's prison, whereas he could at least try to make restitution now that he had fled to France. 'It was the pressure of circumstances which compelled me to adopt so precipitate and, I will say, so disgraceful a measure at the exigence of the moment.'

He concluded: 'The last remaining hope of my broken fortunes consists in a considerable sum of money now vested in the Court of Chancery which must ultimately become mine. This reversion I abandon legally and willingly to you... I abandon my country a beggar and I can look forward to no means of subsistence beyond the year–yet I feel some remote satisfaction in the idea that the slight reparation I am offering is everything that is left to your former friend, George Brummell.'

Brummell was far from being the only English debtor to take refuge across the Channel, a custom hallowed by time though grievously interrupted by Bonaparte. With the franc at twenty-four to the pound, living was at least thirty per cent cheaper and 'with the strictest attention to economy' interest might be returned to capital and the debts eventually paid off. But for Brummell there were two impediments: his capital, apart from the money in Chancery which he mentioned to Charles and Robert Manners, was almost nil; and he had never in his life known what it meant to practise economy. He was within a few weeks of his thirty-eighth birthday, an elderly dog to learn so difficult a trick.

There is no record of how much he managed to take with him in cash, though Sir Robert Peel, then Chief Secretary for Ireland, wrote to Lord Whitworth on 20 May that, 'Mr Brummell has decamped to the confusion of his collaterals and his creditors. He left town with £1.5s., the relic of his broken fortunes, and has conferred the benefit of his countenance upon the Continent. One of those who has severely suffered by his credulity and reliance on Brummell's promising repayment sent him £100 in compassion. What has become of Lord Alvanley, and how far he is implicated in Mr Brummell's misdeed, I know not. I believe some public good as far as the rising generation is concerned, will result from the downfall of such heroes as Sir H. Mildmay and Mr Brummell.'

The Beau seems to have been sincere in believing he was 'quitting my country for ever', and for the moment was full of remorse. As he wrote to Raikes two days later:

'Here I am *restant* for the present, and God knows solitary enough is my existence; of that, however, I should not complain, for I can always employ resources within myself, was there not a worm that will not sleep called *conscience*, which all my endeavours to distract, all the strength of coffee, with which I constantly fumigate my unhappy brains, and all the native gaiety of the fellow who bears it to me, cannot lull to indifference beyond the moment; but I will not trouble you upon that subject.' He boasted of having turned over an entirely new leaf. 'I am punctually off the pillow at half-past seven in the morning. My first object–melancholy indeed it may be in its nature–is to walk to the pier-head, and take my distant look at England. This you may call weakness, but I am not yet sufficiently master of those feelings which may be called indigenous to resist the impulse. The rest of my day is filled up with strolling an hour or two round the ramparts of this dismal town, in reading, and the study of that language which must hereafter be my own, for never more shall I set foot in my own country.'

There was one other change. Advancing years and constant scorching by Robinson's curling tongs had thinned out his hair. He marked the beginning of his new life by buying a wig 'that has divested me of my former respectability of appearance (for what right have I now of such an outward sign?)' but, he assured Raikes, gave him such a youthful appearance that 'if the care and distress of mind which I have lately undergone had not impressed more ravages haggard and lean than my years might justify upon my unfortunate *phiz*, I should certainly pass at a little distance for *five* and *twenty*'.

That morning, Wednesday 22 May, by order of the Sheriff of Middlesex, Mr Christie had begun selling by auction 'on the premises', 13 Chapel Street, Park Lane:

A very choice and valuable assemblage
of
Specimens of the rare old Sèvres Porcelaine,
Articles of Buhl Manufacture,
Curiously Chased Plate,
Library of Books,
Chiefly of French, Italian, and English Literature, the best
Editions, and in fine condition.
The admired Drawing of the Refractory School Boy, and others,
exquisitely finished by Holmes, Christall, de Windt,
and Stephanoff.
Three capital double-barrelled Fowling Pieces,
by Manton.
Ten dozen of capital Old Port, sixteen dozen of
Burgundy, Claret and Still Champagne,
The whole of which have been nine years in bottle in the
Cellar of the Proprietor;
Also, an
Assortment of Table and other Linen, and some Articles of
neat Furniture;
The genuine property of
A MAN OF FASHION,
Gone to the Continent.

It was the smaller pieces that attracted most attention from his friends–the Sèvres vases, the letter-scale on a black plinth with Cupid weighing an ormolu heart, the chocolate cups, above all the snuff-boxes, one of which was opened and revealed, to everybody's delight, a note in Brummell's hand: 'This snuff-box was intended for the Prince Regent, if he had conducted himself with more propriety towards me.' The sale continued into Thursday and raised a total of £1000, which the Sheriff sequestered.

In Calais Brummell sold his carriage to Quillac and applied himself to his French lessons throughout a miserably wet and windy summer. He was still wary of his fellow countrymen. 'The English I have seen here–and many of them known to me–I have avoided,' he told Raikes, though Count Esterhazy called on him and very kindly took some letters back to England. Among the guests at Dessein's in August was Lord Glenbervie, a Scottish politician to whom a lifetime of placehunting had brought more than he deserved but less than he expected–particularly since he had married Lord North's eldest and plainest daughter Katherine. Their son Frederick, MP for Banbury, met Brummell while walking in the hotel garden one damp Saturday evening. Frederick smugly reported that the Beau 'as soon as he perceived him hung his head down and brushed by him' and his father moralised on 'how Brummell had changed since we saw him at Brighton on his first joining the Tenth or Prince of Wales's Dragoons– handsome, ingenuous and clever...Brummell, who has now been twenty-two or twenty-three years on the town, has been nick- named the Dowager Dandy'.

Living in the hotel was expensive as well as laying him open to unwelcome encounters. He moved into a set of rooms that Quillac owned nearby and had his dinner sent in each day. Here, as the months went by, he increasingly received company of his own choosing. His friends were constantly crossing the Channel, visiting Paris, returning from the army of occupation, setting out on grand tours that had been delayed for almost a generation: 'Cupid' Walpole of the Guards, going back to England, Berkeley Craven hurriedly coming out to avoid the bailiffs and bringing news that Raikes was shortly going to Paris by way of Dieppe but would be calling at Calais on his way back. Brummell at once wrote to ask him to get 'an extra 2lb of the *Façon de Paris* you had the kindness to leave with me on your last return to England. It was the best snuff with which my nose was ever nourished; and my brain has been in a state of inanity ever since it was exhausted. I have not either a pinch of any decent tobacco remaining to befriend my sluggish evenings. Do this for me, and accept an infinity of thanks.' It was such a small favour that he could scarcely offer to pay for it. There were many other small favours that he got into the habit of soliciting from friends–particularly cash. But this, after all, was what he would have done for them had the positions been reversed–what indeed he had done many times before.

'No news here,' he concluded in French. 'I live in great seclusion as a rule. I divide my time between reading, painting and walking and I find that the consoling charms of study and the fine arts can, if not heal the wounds of the past, at least assuage their bitterness. To keep continually busy is to fight bravely against sorrow and tedium. Adieu, mon brave. Toujours à toi. George Brummell.'

The maxim sounds as if it may have been borrowed, but he was justified in showing off his French. According to Harriette Wilson, who called on him out of curiosity rather than friendship, as she was eager to make clear, his French tutor was particularly impressed with his accent. 'It is as fortunate as it is surprising that he never learned to speak French in England,' she gleefully reported the language master as saying, though there is no doubt that the Beau could read French quite fluently. He was still receiving those charming little notes in French from the Duchess of York. He sent her small presents from time to time; she replied with small gifts that she often made herself and which almost always contained banknotes or drafts.

'Thank you for the charming presents you were kind enough to send me (and which I wore on the evening of my little fête),' she wrote to him in April 1817, sending 'my regrets that you could no longer be there. Believe me, nobody feels the loss of your company more than I do. I shall never forget the pleasant moments that I owe to you. Nothing can compensate me except the knowledge of your happiness, for which I sincerely pray, and for anything which may contribute to it, flattering myself that you will always preserve the memory of your affectionate friend and servant. F.'

The Duke, too, was loyal to the old friendship. One day at dinner Berkeley Craven made some cutting remarks about Brummell and Alvanley, and the Duke immediately rebuked him: 'I tell you what, Berkeley, all this may be true or not but I cannot bear to hear them abused by one of their oldest friends.'

Harriette was admitted to the Beau's second toilette and found him in a Florentine dressing-gown, lighthearted, 'still shaving himself with characteristic gracefulness and the tiniest razor I have ever seen', in front of a table 'covered with seals, chains, snuff-boxes and watches: presents, as he said, from Lady Jersey and various other ladies of high rank'. Her greatest surprise was to find him attended by a French valet, 'just such a valet as one would have given the Beau in the acme of his glory, *bien poudré, bien cérémonieux et bien mis*'. (Miss Wilson, too, was fond of airing her French which, since her father was Swiss-born, she had had the advantage or disadvantage of learning at home.)

Brummell touched upon both of his retainers in a letter to Raikes that autumn: 'My personal communication at this place is confined to M. Quillac, his waiter, to a domestique upon trial, and to an old abbé who daily instructs me in the French dialect, at three francs an hour.' There was no mention these days of repayment of his debts. He was finding it difficult enough to preserve a semblance of his former style of life on his friends' bounty and whatever income he was still getting from concealed investments in England. But he had regained much of his old imperious manner.

He had been compelled earlier to chide Raikes for sending him muslin triangles instead of squares, but now

the intention you profess of sending me some square pieces assures me you are in such good humour that I shall ask you to add to my obligations by letting me have them immediately, with the snuff, and do not wait for Alvanley's packet (books of which he advised me, and which I have been all impatience to receive); but the circumstance has perhaps already escaped his memory; and, while he is in a state of suspense about his own personal concerns, I cannot in reason expect he should think of such trifles...If you should have a rainy morning, and ten minutes' leisure, do not, I beseech you, forget such an exiled disconsolate devil as yours most truly.

Alvanley's worries were about his rich uncle, who was promisingly ailing but never quite managing to die. Early in November, when Raikes was making another trip to France, Kangaroo Cooke wrote to him from the War Office with the requests and queries now familiar in their circle–'Can you bring me some Houbigant gloves over? How is the Beau?'–and the news that Alvanley's uncle had still not succumbed to apoplexy. 'Drummond Burrell has turned away his cook; but Alvanley has begged he will keep the cook disengaged a month, that he may have him if the event should occur.' It did, and Alvanley honestly settled all his debts before embarking enthusiastically on accumulating new

The dandy's toilette and the dandy in public

Brummell in 1815

ones. It was perhaps at this time that he performed the distasteful feat for which he is best known: winning a wager to concoct a more expensive dish than anybody else could invent, which he did by using the oysters of more than one hundred different birds.

Brummel moved once more, to rooms over a bookshop kept by Monsieur Leleux in the rue Royale, which ran from the place d'Armes to the rue Française, where Emma Hamilton had died in rented rooms in January 1815, and then to the bridge over the inner harbour that led to the new part of the town. The bookshop had formerly been the Hôtel d'Angleterre and the panels above the entrance to the courtyard carried portraits of George III and Queen Charlotte until the mob tore them down during the Revolution. The Beau's dining room and drawing room were on the first floor, facing the street; his bedroom looked out on to the courtyard. He rented a small garden at the foot of the ramparts in which he sometimes amused himself with a little light prodding at the earth or, when the summer sun became too hot, writing his diary in the summerhouse.

News of this activity reached England and rumours grew that he was planning to publish his memoirs, in which, the Duke of Rutland was told 'he sets everything at defiance, discloses to the world every anecdote he has heard, everything that has come to his knowledge in the intimacy of friendship. And those who have thrown him off he shall treat with the utmost severity.' He certainly enjoyed making distant flesh creep with descriptions to his visitors of the revelations that he said were contained in his commonplace book. Unlocking the covers he would turn the pages and say: 'Here is a chapter on Carlton House; here one on Mrs Fitzherbert and the Prince; this is devoted to Lady Hertford.' and so on.

Reports of the existence of the manuscript brought an offer of a thousand pounds from a London publisher–which Brummell refused. A little later, in December 1818, Thomas Moore recorded a rumour that John Murray, the publisher, 'had offered £5000 for the "Memoirs", but that the Regent had sent Brummell £6000 to suppress!' His landlord, Leleux, an amiable educated man, protested to Brummell that it was foolish to turn down so large a sum when he was so short of money. 'I frequently

asked him why he did not accept it. To this he usually made some
frivolous excuse; but on one occasion, when pressed hard for his
real reason, he said: "I promised the Duchess of York that I
would not publish any notes of mine during the lifetime of George
the Fourth [the Regent had by that time succeeded to the throne]
or his brothers; and I am under so many obligations to her, and
have such a deep respect for her generous and amiable conduct
to me in our early friendship, and since, that I would rather go to
jail than forfeit my word. She is the only link that binds me in
this matter." '

Lord Yarmouth spent a couple of days at Oatlands in December 1818 and noted that the Duchess still kept to her very odd
hours. 'She seldom has a female companion, she is read to all
night and falls asleep towards morning, and rises about 3; feeds
her dozens of dogs and her flocks of birds, etc., comes down two
minutes before dinner, and so round again. She sometimes walks
a little, and does some local charities.'

Like the Duchess, Brummell reserved most of his affection for
animals. He was soon on familiar terms with Leleux's parrot,
which used to hop up the stairs and tap on Brummell's door, to
be regaled with wine and biscuits. 'Don't you see a likeness to
somebody?' he used to ask his visitors. 'Well now, how very
obtuse! Don't you see how like he is to Hobhouse?' (John Cam
Hobhouse, a close friend of Byron as well as of the Beau.) His
daily walks were made a misery by the brutal way in which the
French treated their horses. And when Vick, his over-fed ter-
rier bitch, died a little later, he refused to receive visitors for
three days and had her buried in a private plot in Dessein's
garden. He confessed to a friend that he preferred animals to
humans in such a degree that 'were I to see a man and a dog
drowning together in the same pond, and no one was looking
on, I would prefer saving the dog'.

He was leading a very regular life, getting up at nine, break-
fasting in his dining room and reading until noon, when he
strolled back to the bedroom in his long brocade dressing-gown
and velvet beret. He allotted two hours to his toilet, then another
two to receiving in the drawing room whatever visitors might
call. If the weather was dry (he hated rain, which flecked his

beautifully polished boots with mud as he picked his way along the cobbles) he would stroll with his dog–Vick or her several successors–to the garden below the ramparts or to the harbour to see if any friends arrived on the Dover packet. At five he would be back home again, changing for dinner which he had sent in from Dessein's and accompanied with a bottle of Dorchester ale, a glass of brandy, and a bottle of claret–in that order–from his own cellar. Frequently he dined in the hotel itself, invited by friends who had come in that afternoon across the Channel or down from Paris and were not moving on until the morning.

The gossip from England was of fashion and mortality and the continuing fear of social upheaval. Lord Holland reported that, 'The Prince has left off his stays and Royalty, divested of its usual supports, makes a bad figure'; or, as Lord Folkstone more bluntly announced in February 1818, 'Prinny has let loose his belly, which now reaches his knees,' so that by the end of the year 'his great size and weight make him nervous, and he is afraid to ride.' Richard Meyler–'The Dandy Killer', as he had been nicknamed since he drove Brummell into exile–got into a temper while out hunting, fell off his horse, and died on the spot. There was rioting in Manchester and the Tories introduced more repressive legislation.

Brummell, writing during the March storms of 1818 to Lt-Col Hughes of the 18th Dragoons to thank him for sending a copy of *Rob Roy* (which he had in fact already read) revealed that he still stuck to his Whig principles. 'The Indemnity Bill makes me sick; so indeed does everything where Castlereagh is concerned–you may be assured, however, that Parliament will be dissolved at an earlier period than you calculate–they only wished to carry through that infamous bill by way of superficially white-washing themselves in the eyes of the country and are now anxious to form a new Parliament for the purpose of reviving their first-born hope, the income tax–I hope in God these vampires will not be allowed to pluck its carcass from the grave of corruption.' And so from politics to literature, ignoring with all his old self-confidence the fact that he, in Calais, was instructing Hughes in Cleveland Court, St James's: 'Have you read Horace Walpole's letters to Mrs Montagu? If not, I would recommend you to get them; they are much the most pleasant light reading I have had for an age. The climate of Venice, I fear, has sadly impaired my friend Byron's imagination, for I never waded through such a galimatias as "Beppo".'

Hughes had gone to England from the army of occupation without leave in order to take part in a parliamentary election. He failed to win the seat and was ordered to return to France to face a court martial. On the way back he brought in some goods which were impounded by the French customs as contraband. He asked for Brummell's help in getting them released.

'My dear Hughes,' Brummell replied, 'upon my application respecting the delivery of your things [the customs officers] informed me that the effects in question were confiscated but *sans amende*. Your only remaining chance of recovering this detained property is to repurchase it at the time of the public sale by the Douane, and I will take care to inform myself of the period.

A singular circumstance of mutual suicide happened here three days since, a pair of young sentimental lovers walked out together, coolly tied themselves round their waists with a shawl, and more coolly threw themselves into the canal about half a mile from this town, and were drowned before assistance could be given by those who saw the transaction. I was myself strolling near the fatal spot, and saw them taken out of the water, and I confess much of the interest was diminished in finding the young lady extremely ill-looking–it has been ascertained that she was four months gone with child–this mends the catastrophe, making it a triple murder.

He was quite back to his old cynical form; and very happily taking over Hughes's affairs:

There is an affiche stuck up to-day at the Douane here announcing a general sale of all the contraband goods condemned during the last four months, on the 22nd of this month. But the conditions of the sale are, as usual, that the purchases made shall be re-embarked for England within four days, and I understand from the encreased vigilance and severity of the myrmidons in that department that it is almost impossible to elude the stipulation, as they keep possession of them till they are actually on board the exporting vessel. What is to be done under these difficult circumstances? for presuming that I might bribe the Captain of the vessel to whose charge they are consigned, clandestinely to restore them to me, how am I to distinguish your effects from the various bales of confiscated merchandise among which they will be crowded? It is not, I assure you, to save myself the trouble of executing your wishes that I would advise you to abandon the attempt to recover the different articles, but, considering the expense and more particularly the risk to which you would necessarily be exposed in effecting this redemption, I do most certainly recommend you to leave them to their fate.

When he wrote to Hughes again, in September, the ring of authority is clearer than ever:

Your two despatches were safely placed in the Dover post the morning after I received them. I am really obliged to you for having left one of them open for my perusal; and I cannot resist the observation that your defence is excellent; you could not have said more to exculpate yourself in the consideration of every liberal mind; or, in just retaliation, to inculpate those who have so pitifully attempted to injure you. The provocation was sufficiently malignant to have justified a more explicit and, therefore, more severe exposure of their real intentions in keeping back your leave of absence–it is as manifest as day-light that the delay was premeditated, and employed to serve as a dirty political motive–and be assured such will be the construction that every one, both friends and foe, will place upon it.

His relations with the military were not always so cordial. The army of occupation was being withdrawn, and he wrote to Raikes, by now back in London again, 'There is nothing to be seen here but rascals in red coats waiting for embarcation. God speed them to the other side of the water, for on this they are most heartily loathed.' This was part of his current flirtation with all things French. Despite the fact that he had himself set the style for simple unembellished clothing, he now told Raikes: 'Heard of you the other day in a waistcoat that does you indisputable credit, spick and span from Paris, a broad stripe, salmon colour and *cramoisi* [crimson]. Keep it up, my dear fellow, and don't let them laugh you into a relapse so Gothic as that of your former English simplicity.'

He was just old enough to remember the largely mythical elegance of the *ancien régime* (he was in his sixteenth year when Marie-Antoinette went to the guillotine) and, according to Raikes, 'rather piqued himself' on having preserved some of the style of the *Vieille Cour*. With gross, gouty Louis XVIII back on the Bourbon throne France had regained something of its old magic for Brummell, though perhaps not Calais itself, where English refugees continued to arrive and which, as Lady Granville remarked as early as the summer of 1817, 'seems to have become a purgatory for half-condemned souls'. Now that the war was victoriously over the British custom of self-depreciation was revived. Among the Dandies, England again became stolid old Bulldom, the kingdom of John Bull; as they travelled about the Continent they bemoaned the fact that they found themselves constantly bumping into other Bulls, with their attendant Cows. Their own country having saved Europe from tyranny, they professed to be ashamed of it when visiting the defeated nations whom Britain had rescued, or their former oppressor, France, whom Britain had put down. So Brummell was back to his old style yet abreast of the latest fashion when he wrote to Raikes:

I hear you meditate a *petit domicile* at Paris for your children; you cannot do better. English education may be all very well to instruct the hemming of handkerchiefs and the ungainly romp of a country dance, but nothing else; and it would be a poor consolation to your declining years to see your daughters come into the room upon their elbows, and to find their accomplishments limited to broad native phraseology in conversation, or to thumping the 'Woodpecker' upon a discordant spinet. You will do well, then to provide in time against natural deficiencies by a good French formation of manners as well as talents; and you will not have to complain hereafter of your gouty limbs being excruciated by the uncouth movements of a hoyden, or of your ears being distracted by indigenous vulgarism.

Berkeley Craven appeared again–given a month's safe-conduct by his creditors to attend the Newmarket Races on the unlikely premise that he might make enough money to pay them back. 'The Jews' Pass-Over' he called it, purloining a witticism first made by George Selwyn about No. 11's father. And scarcely had he passed over than Scrope Davies was dining out on a story of Craven being involved in a collision in a carriage that he was sharing with Alvanley. 'The former getting out to thrash the footman, saw he was an old fellow, and said "Your *age* protects you", while Alvanley, who had advanced towards the postillion with the same intention, seeing he was an athletic young fellow, turned from him saying, in his waggish way, "Your *youth* protects you." '

There were more reports of deaths of acquaintances, always a comfort in adversity. Baron Tripp had gone within six months of Brummell's flight. He killed himself, but reports varied about the reason. 'One of pecuniary distress; one that he was in love with that pretty little Mrs Fitzherbert, who was a Miss Chichester, and that he sent to her husband to borrow the pistols with which he destroyed himself; and another that upon Mr Capel sending to tell him he no longer would oppose his marrying his daughter, he avowed a secret marriage and said he had a wife and five children, and then, unable to reconcile the difficulties of this situation, shot himself. It was on returning from a party.' And now Monk Lewis, so often a fellow guest at Oatlands, had been killed by a cure for seasickness on the voyage home from his estates in the West Indies. According to Tom Moore:

When he was told all hope was over, he sent his man down below for pen, ink, and paper; asked him to lend him his hat; and upon that, as he lay, wrote a codicil to his will. Few men, once so talked of, have ever produced so little sensation by their death. He was ruining his Negroes in Jamaica, they say, by indulgence, for which they suffered severely as soon as his back was turned; but he has enjoined it to his heirs as one of the conditions of holding his estate, that the Negroes were to have three additional holidays in the year; and has left a sort of programme of the way those holidays are to be celebrated–the hour when the overseer is to sound his shell to summon them together, toasts &c: the first toast to be 'the Lady Frederica, Duchess of York'; so like poor Lewis.

The continuing scare that Bonaparte might escape from St Helena as he had previously done from Elba reached one of its peaks in November 1818. It turned out to be a false alarm, but Lord Yarmouth took the opportunity to wager Lord Glengall, the MP for Tipperary, at White's 'four guineas to receive one hundred guineas if Mr G. Brummell returns to London before Bonaparte returns to Paris'. It certainly seemed unlikely. Far from being able to satisfy his creditors in England he was now running up debts in France: 'his room was again replenished with commodes in old buhl, with specimens of old Sèvres china and old lacquer; and, if he saw a trinket or a curious snuff-box, no reference to his resources would prevent his yielding to the temptation.' And, added the rueful Raikes, in the meantime his applications to his friends were unceasing.

But he had hit upon a new plan for solving his problems. The British Consul at Calais, Captain Samuel Marshall, was in poor health. His post was worth several hundred a year from the Government, plus sundry fees for certification and other services. It provided a certain position in society. And he was growing reconciled to Calais. It was a busy place where one saw a lot of one's friends. As one of them, the British ambassador, Lord Stuart de Rothesay, said jokingly. 'No one can lead a more pleasant life than Brummell, for he passes his time between London and Paris.' So his new project was to use his friends' influence to get him Marshall's job when Marshall died.

Alvanley was frequently backwards and forwards. He had taken a small apartment in Paris and furnished it, partly to econo- mise by living there, partly to let to other English visitors. Among these was Mrs Fitzherbert, who had brought over her disputed foster daughter Minney Seymour to save her from the clutches of George Dawson. Dawson had been with Sir Robert Wilson's military mission that accompanied the Russian armies as they chased Bonaparte on the terrible retreat from Moscow. He had been wounded and had had two horses killed under him at Waterloo; he was an officer of charm and distinction, and Minney loved him dearly. But he was only the younger son of an Irish peer, and Mrs Fitzherbert was determined that they should not marry. She asked the Duke of York to post him as far away as possible—preferably to the Indies, either East or West. Alvanley, with his usual affability, promised Dawson that he would try to restore the balance with the Duke; while Maryanne Smythe, whom Mrs Fitzherbert called her niece but many people believed to be her daughter by the Prince of Wales, acted as go-between for the separated lovers.

So the fourth year of Brummell's exile wore on. The Regent, mocked out of mounting his horse by means of a chair-lift, had taken to driving around in a two-wheeled gig like a common cad. Shelley composed a sonnet on England in 1819, which began:

> An old, mad, blind, despised, and dying king,–
> Princes, the dregs of their dull race, who flow
> Through public scorn–mud from a muddy spring,–
> Rulers who neither see, nor feel, nor know,
> But leech-like to their fainting country cling,
> Till they drop, blind in blood, without a blow.

At Kensington Palace on 24 May the Duchess of Kent gave birth to a daughter, Princess Alexandrina Victoria. Parliament restricted the employment of juveniles to twelve hours a day. The prolific Shelley addressed a *Song to the Men of England*:

> Men of England, wherefore plough
> For the lords who lay ye low?

Wherefore weave with toil and care
The rich robes your tyrants wear?
Wherefore feed, and clothe, and save,
From the cradle to the grave,
Those ungrateful drones who would
Drain your sweat–nay, drink your blood?...

In Manchester on 16 August, a crowd of fifty or sixty thousand workers and their wives gathered in St Peter's Fields to listen to the radical 'Orator' Hunt and were dispersed by the yeomanry, with eleven dead and six hundred wounded. In September the little sweet-voiced insecure Thomas Moore stayed overnight at Dessein's, escaping from his creditors by accompanying Lord John Russell on a tour of Italy. On 29 January 1820, the old blind King died at Windsor. Amid a deafening silence he was succeeded by his unworthy eldest son, aged fifty-nine, 'enormous, and his cheeks white as chalk'.

The Duke of York, who had been appointed his father's guardian, lost the job and the salary of £10,000 a year that went with it. At Oatlands the irrepressible Alvanley told the Duchess that at White's they had been talking 'of forming a new club, and wanted a name for it. I proposed calling it "The Merry Beggars", and we hope His Royal Highness will be our President.' There were times when Alvanley's friends wondered whether he went too far. He still, for instance, read in bed every night and, whether in his own house or somebody's else's, 'extinguished his candle by throwing it on the floor in the middle of the room and taking a shot at it with the pillow, or else quickly placed it, while still lighted, under the bolster.' At Badminton, where he frequently stayed with Worcester, a servant was posted all night in the passage to make sure the place was not set on fire.

He is at length King [Brummell wrote to Raikes, longwinded with anxiety]. Will his past resentments still attach themselves to his crown? An indulgent amnesty of former peccadilloes should be the primary grace influencing newly enthroned sovereignty; at least towards those who were once distinguished by his more intimate protection. From my experience, however, of the personage in question, I must doubt any favourable relaxation of those stubborn prejudices which have during so many years operated to the total exclusion of one of his *élèves* from the royal notice; that unfortunate–I need not particularise.

You ask me how I am going on at Calais? Miserably! I am exposed every hour to all the turmoil and jeopardy that attended my latter days in England. I bear up as well as I can; and when the patience and mercy of my claimants are exhausted, I shall submit without resistance to bread and water and straw. I cannot decamp a second time.

To Lord Sefton he was said to have written in even more pitiful terms, complaining that he was 'lying on straw and grinning through the bars of a gaol; eating bran bread, my good fellow, eating bran bread'. But he could not help hoping that despite the bitterness of recent years, the new King might remember old friendships and do something for him. And to tell the truth, he had improved the amenities of his gaol, moving to larger rooms in Leleux's great barn of an ex-hotel, so that he now had a separate entrance and his visitors did not have to come in through the bookshop.

While he waited he continued with the hobby which, together with talking and reading, occupied most of his indoor leisure hours–pasting pictures on a screen, five feet six inches tall and folded into six two-foot panels of green paper. It was intended as a present for the Duchess of York and consequently had animals as its theme. The upper half of each panel was dominated by a large picture of an elephant, a tiger, a camel and so on; the lower portions had portraits of famous contemporary figures and of the old friends who used to meet at Oatlands. Bonaparte's head was encircled by the elephant's trunk and the elephant was surrounded by trophies of war including the Russian flag. Below, in two caricatures by Dighton, Lord Yarmouth, with his back to General Upton, talked with Lord Sefton against a background of rocks and forests, satyrs, nymphs, shepherds and cupids. Every sort of drawing, chalk, pastel, ink, pencil, mezzotint, some watercoloured by the Beau himself, was carefully stuck on and all the joins and ragged edges (and Sefton's hump) concealed with borders of fruit and flowers, birds and butterflies. The grouping of the subsidiary characters and incidents on this and the other panels was evidently a comment and often a private joke on the principal figures–or a rather heavy allegory on recent history, as on the third panel, where the tiger of the Revolution was flanked by the Dauphin and his small sister at play, and the rest of the

panel decorated with male and female infants experiencing all
sorts of disasters from blizzards and shipwrecks to plain poverty.
On the bear panel, Fox and Nelson, Sheridan, Louis Bonaparte,
Princess Charlotte and Kemble the actor, were surrounded, and
sometimes infested, with dogs and monkeys, cupids and lady-
birds.

This labour of love came to an unhappy halt in the summer of
1820. Throughout the year the Duchess's friends had been increasingly worried about her health. In April one of them wrote
'I am very uncomfortable on account of the dear little Duchess of
York. Incessant bloodletting and that terrible foxglove have so
debilitated her puny frame that she cannot walk five paces.' She
died on 6 August 1820, in her fifty-fourth year. It was possibly
the saddest outside event in Brummell's adult life. He had lost a
loyal benefactor and protector; and one of the few people for
whom he felt profound friendship, perhaps even love.

In England her death passed almost unnoticed. She had never
appeared much in public and in any case the centre of interest was
once more the Prince and his domestic affairs. He had discarded
Lady Hertford for Lady Conyngham, a fat lady in her fifties,
popularly known as the Vice-Queen; and now that he was
George IV he was more than ever determined not to accord
Caroline the titles and privileges of his consort. She was equally
insistent that she should be given her rightful place as Queen. He
spent many hours poring over various editions of the Book of
Common Prayer, searching for a precedent to avoid Caroline
being prayed for in church by her name and title; for, as Croker
commented, 'if she is fit to be introduced to the Almighty, she is
fit to be received by men, and if we are to *pray* for her in church
we may surely *bow* to her at Court.' The Government reluctantly
consented. Caroline was omitted. The King offered her a pension
of £50,000 a year if she would promise to stay out of the country
and renounce all English titles. She refused and insisted on returning from Europe (where she had been touring the Mediterranean and delightfully scandalising the natives with her
amorous indiscretions) to take her place as Queen.

She arrived at Calais from St Omer late in the evening of 3 June,
accompanied by her legal adviser, the wily Brougham, and went

straight aboard the Dover packet which left the following morning. She was sadly changed from the shy young princess whom Cornet Brummell had escorted to her wedding a quarter of a century before. 'Nature had given her light hair, blue eyes, a fair complexion, and a good-humoured expression of countenance; but these characteristics were marred by painted eyebrows, and by a black wig with a profusion of curls, which overshadowed her cheeks and gave a bold defiant air to her features.' Many unbiased people believed her to be mad; but most of the country agreed that she had been abominably treated by her deplorable husband, who now persuaded his ministers to bring in a bill dissolving the marriage because of her misconduct. When the Duke of York arrived at the House of Lords eleven days after his Duchess's death for the opening of the ill-judged inquiry into Caroline's conduct, the crowd yelled 'Long Live Frederick the First!'

Alvanley and Petersham crossed over to Calais that autumn on their way to Paris, accompanied on the boat by the writer Charles Macfarlane, who was going to Italy and who dined with them at Dessein's. 'They were pupils and almost idolaters of Brummell,' he recorded. 'They invited him to dinner, but he was engaged, if I remember right, with Scrope Davies, who had taken refuge in that dull old French town. However, he came in towards the small hours, and sat until long after sunrise. There was a terrible change in other things besides the financial ones; but still he was an elegant, striking man, and became very amusing and rather animated, though he drank but moderately. At times, however, I thought I saw a look of sadness and despondency. There was reason for it. At this moment he was cruelly embarrassed.'

Petersham, who could ill afford it at the time, left some money with the Beau before he travelled on in the morning. Meanwhile Brummell entertained the company with story after story: 'they were all told with admirable humour, and most of them with good nature. I could understand a good deal of the secret of Brummell's extraordinary success and influence in the highest society. He was a vast deal more than a mere dandy; he had wit as well as humour and drollery, and the most perfect coolness and self-possession.'

Macfarlane was surprised to find there was no resentment in

Brummell's tone when he spoke of the new King: 'On the contrary, he related several clever and two or three kind things of him, and gave him credit for a great deal of natural ability and *esprit*. He confirmed what Raikes and others have said of the Prince's extraordinary powers of mimicry. "If his lot had fallen that way," said he, "he would have been the best comic actor in Europe." '

Brummell agreed that he had made the 'fat friend' remark, and that, after he quarrelled with the Prince, he had threatened 'to go down to Windsor and make the old people fashionable.' But, as always, he indignantly denied the 'Wales, ring the bell!' story, which he seemed to regard as a reflection on his intelligence as much as on his manners. 'I knew the Prince too well ever to take any kind of liberty with him! Drunk or sober, he would have resented it, with a vengeance! His vindictive spirit—and he could be vindictive about trifles—was the worst part of him; and where he once took a spite he never forgave. There might have been twenty good reasons for the rupture, but the world always guesses wrong in these matters.' Despite Brummell's insistence on the Prince's vindictiveness, Macfarlane had a strong impression that he was hoping for some sort of favour now that he was King.

Alvanley was not well, looking like 'a Devil new hunted' in spite of his self-prescribed remedy of frequent bottles of champagne which he shook vigorously in both hands before pouring. But his ill-health did not deter him from continuing to act as Brummell's most energetic advocate. On his return to England he wrote to Lord Bathurst, Secretary for the Colonies:

I am aware that I have little right to address you on the following subject, but I trust you will forgive my doing so on the score of old family friendship. Poor Brummell has now been four years at Calais. He has lived upon what those who were most intimate with him have been able to do for him. So precarious an existence, however, is hardly worth having. I have been told that you have expressed yourself kindly with regard to him. Perhaps you might be able to give him some small situation abroad, in order to relieve him from the position in which he now is. I say nothing about the circumstances that occurred previous to his departure from England. I cannot excuse them in any way. They, however, are no longer fresh in the memory of those who were not sufferers, and I know that the greatest sufferer is most

desirous that something should be done for him. The Duke of York, who
has been very kind to him, would gladly assist any effort in his favour. I will
not trouble you more on the subject. If you can do anything for him I am
certain you will. If not, I am certain your reasons will be better than any I
could give.

The inquiry into the Queen's conduct dragged on, splitting
Brummell's friends as it did the rest of the nation. The folly of
having begun the proceedings became more and more clear and
by early October the Archbishop of Canterbury, a downy old
bird with a taste for dining out and dirty jokes, was openly expressing the opinion that 'it is better the bill should be thrown out,
with the moral conviction in the higher orders that she is guilty,
than carried with the moral conviction in the lower orders that
she is innocent'. The lower orders meanwhile had the time of
their lives escorting her carriage with banners and torches as she
progressed back and forth to the House of Lords and loudly
booing every time they passed 'Nero's Palace', as they had
christened Carlton House.

The Bill, accusing the Queen of 'licentious, disgraceful and
adulterous intercourse', had its three readings in the Lords with
ever-decreasing majorities. The Government, deciding there was
little hope of getting it through the Commons, withdrew it. Poor
Caroline, left in a limbo of unproven and unconfuted libel, was
soon deserted by her fickle supporters and declared a bore.

> Most gracious Queen, we thee implore
> To go away and sin no more;
> But, if that effort be too great,
> To go away at any rate.

When she tried to claim her place beside the King at the cor-
onation on 19 July 1821 she was turned away and returned dis-
consolately to her home in Hammersmith, where rumour said
she found solace in her favourite noyau brandy. The mob had this
time rewarded her with more hisses than cheers. Broken in spirit,
she died within three weeks.

Earlier that year, when the news of Napoleon's death on St
Helena reached England, it was communicated to the King in the
words 'Your Majesty's greatest enemy is dead!' and he unwarily
replied, 'Is she, by God!' Well, now she was, and after a light-

hearted tour of Ireland he set off again without a care in the world
to visit his other overseas kingdom of Hanover, crossing from
Ramsgate to Calais on 25 September 1821 in very windy weather.
He was received at the landing stage by the Mayor of Calais, and
at Dessein's, where he was to stay overnight, by the duc d'Angou-
lême, son-in-law of Louis XVI and nephew of Louis XVIII.

At some point between the landing stage and the hotel Brummell and the King came face to face. According to Macfarlane,
the Beau accompanied the mayor (who was his wine merchant)
and, when the royal barge came alongside, 'many of the English
purposely made room for him, sharing in his hope and expectation that His Majesty would at least recognise him with a gracious
smile, which might have had the effect of tranquillising some of
his Calais creditors. The King, who almost touched him as he
passed up the pier, must have seen him. He turned his royal head
another way–and Brummell turned as pale as a ghost.'

On the other hand, according to the Beau's landlord Leleux, a
reliable man and, by his own account, an eye-witness, Brummell
had gone for a stroll on the ramparts and was returning to his
lodgings at the moment when the King drove up the rue Royale
on the way to Dessein's. 'I was standing in my shop door,' said
Leleux, 'and saw Mr Brummell trying to make his way across the
street to my house, but the crowd was so great that he could not
succeed and he was therefore obliged to remain on the opposite
side. All hats were taken off as the carriage approached and, when
it was close to the door, I heard the King say in a loud voice,
"Good God! Brummell!" The latter, who was uncovered at the
time, now crossed over, as pale as death, entered the house by
the private door, and retired to his room, without addressing me.'

Since Brummell had trained his valet to cater for English tastes,
Monsieur Quillac asked for the loan of his services at Dessein's
to make punch for the King. Brummell sent him off with a
bottle of Maraschino, in the hope that his former friend still had a
partiality for it. He inscribed his name in the visitors' book at
Dessein's. There was now nothing more he could do except wait
for a summons to the royal presence.

There was a story current shortly afterwards that Brummell
sent the King a box of snuff and that the King returned it with a

hundred pound note inside and a message that he could not see him. There was another story that Brummell took up a prominent position in the theatre lobby (a possibility, since he rented a small box) and that the King, when he went to the performance after dinner, bowed to him and later sent him a present.

Brummell denied both of these accounts. Leleux, too, was convinced that there was no reaction from the King and certainly no money. Brummell was always prompt to pay his local bills whenever he could lay his hands on cash. It was because he was reliable in settling tradesmen's accounts that he was able to continue keeping up appearances–at the expense of his bankers, the money-lenders and his friends. To the immediate outside world, such as the woman who kept the tobacconist's shop on the opposite side of the rue Royale, he was a man of both charm and substance. 'We used to call him *le roi de Calais*,' she said. 'He was a truly fine man, very elegant, and really well-off–he always paid his bills and was very good to the poor; and every one was very sorry when he left.' The fact that Brummell certainly did not settle any of his bills around this time is a strong indication the King did not give him any money.

Leleux's account of the snuff-box incident was that the consul, Captain Marshall, came to Brummell late in the evening, told him that the King was out of snuff, took up one of the boxes on the Beau's table, and said, 'Give me one of yours.' 'With all my heart,' replied Brummell, 'but not that box, for if the King saw it I should never have it again.' He gave Marshall a box that was less likely to excite the King's cupidity, and the consul returned to the theatre with it. At the first pinch, the King turned to him and said: 'Why, sir, where did you get your snuff? There is only one person that I know who can mix snuff in this way.' 'It is some of Mr Brummell's, Your Majesty,' replied the consul. The King said no more.

The following morning the members of the King's suite called on Brummell. Several of them tried to persuade him to ask that he should be granted an audience with the King when he passed through Calais again on his way back from Hanover. Brummell refused. As the King got into his carriage to drive out of Dessein's courtyard he said to Sir Arthur Paget, commander of the royal yacht, 'I leave Calais, and have not seen Brummell.' When he returned two months later, he drove straight to the landing stage without alighting.

After this, not even Brummell's optimism could persuade him that he had any immediate hope of a consulship or a colonial appointment. Perhaps inspired by the example of Tom Moore, who had called in twice recently, slipping across to England incognito as Mr Dyke to discuss book contracts with John Murray, the Beau embarked on authorship. His subject was well-chosen: *A History of Male and Female Costume from Ancient Greece to Modern Times*. With his name on the title page it should bring a very good price from a popular publisher. Moore meanwhile had continued to Paris where his recent deals with Mr Murray enabled him to live in comfort though he did not yet have enough money to face his creditors at home. (His troubles arose from negligence rather than extravagance. Having obtained a post in the West Indies he engaged a deputy to do the work. The deputy proved to be an embezzler and left Moore with debts of £6000.)

There are two interesting entries in Moore's Paris Diary this winter. On 30 December 1821 he writes, 'Dined at Brummell's having nearly fainted beforehand with the pain of a blow I got on my knee while dressing,' and 15 February 1822, 'Dined at home...company, Villamil, Brummel, Davison, and Mercer. Mrs and the Miss Brummels in the evening.' These look remarkably like George's elder brother, William, his wife, the former Anne Daniell, and their two daughters, Georgiana Anne and Frances Amelia. Whether they called to pay their respects to the disgraced Beau while passing through Calais is doubtful. There seems to have been little contact between the brothers from their late teens onward. They had friends in common–the Burrells, for instance, one of whom had recently married Anne's sister Frances–but there is no mention of William Brummell in any of George's letters, nor in the lists of his benefactors when he was in France. Captain Jesse, who interviewed many of the Beau's acquaintants, seems to have received no help from the family. They no doubt found George difficult to live up to–and put up with–in his days of fame; and a great embarrassment in his days of want.

Moore was still restlessly travelling to and fro, going back to England again in mid-April 1822 and returning on 8 May. It was very likely the ease with which Tom eluded his creditors that encouraged Brummell to venture across the Channel himself that summer. An entry in the register at the Old Coffee Mill shows that he called in to be weighed on 26 July 1822. It was just like the old days, except that the scales revealed the toll that worry had levied on him. Since the time he first went there, in January 1798, a dashing young dragoon of nineteen, until his last visit in July 1815, his weight had always been somewhere between twelve and thirteen stone. Now it was down to ten stone thirteen pounds.

Why he took the risk of coming to London at the end of the season, when he stood a great chance of being recognised, remains a mystery. Moore, much less well known, never ventured out except in a hackney-cab or in the evening. And even after dark he found the gas-lights, which were replacing the tin and glass parish lamps of whale oil and cotton wick, 'very inconvenient for gentlemen *incog*'. Brummell may have had a pressing need to see his attorney about secret funds that he still held in London. There are indications of similar consultations in other years, though these were in France, not England. There is also the possibility that he had visited London once before, taking advantage of the winter dusk. His last purchase of snuff from Fribourg and Treyer before he fled was on 15 April 1816; but the final entry on his account in their ledger is a 2½lb jar of Martinique on 17 December 1818. Did a friend take it over to him? Knowing Brummell's circumstances, a friend would surely put the purchase on his own account. Did Brummell call in personally and with his old assurance order it to be added to the bill which he had last paid in June 1815 and now stood at £14.8s.0d? It seems the more likely explanation.

An alternative or additional reason for this London visit in 1822 may have been to negotiate the publication of his book on *Male and Female Costume*, which he finished during this year. If so, he was disappointed. He failed to find a publisher and the manuscript did not appear in print until 1932. It is easy to see why. As an author Brummell had no more original talent than as a painter. He could copy but not create. And in this instance he did not copy with very exciting results. The text, with illustrations indicated by figures cut from journals, periodicals and books and sometimes handcoloured, is a superficial and pedestrian survey of 'Grecian and Roman Costume, British Costume from the Roman Invasion until 1822, and the Principles of Costume Applied to the Improved Dress of the Present Day.' The style is uneven and often gives the impression that whole sections, like the illustrations, have been taken from other people's work.

There are some spirited sweeping statements: 'The moment the necessary arts take the place of the ornamental ones in a nation–the moment utility supersedes beauty–that nation has passed the true pitch of refinement, and verges towards its fall.' There is an attempt to keep up with new fashions by praising the practice of allowing 'hair to grow on the upper lip. This habit is a manly and noble one. Its abandonment has commonly been accompanied with periods of general effeminacy, and even with the decline and fall of states. They were bearded Romans who conquered the then beardless Greeks; they were bearded Goths who vanquished the then beardless Romans; and they are bearded Tartars [the Russians] who now promise once more to inundate the shaven and effeminate people of Western Europe.' A very odd proposition from one who made a high ritual of shaving and had the good fortune to live through an age when comparatively few men thought it necessary to hide their inadequacies behind whiskers. But there is at least one sentence which has a genuine Brummell ring: 'There is quite as much vanity and coxcombry in slovenliness, as there is in its most extravagant opposite.'

If in fact he took his manuscript to London and failed to place it, he did not lose heart, and if in fact his journey was principally to see his lawyer, then the outcome seems to have been satisfactory, for during the next two years he accepted his exile with much less complaint. In August Castlereagh joined the long list of eminent suicides for which the early nineteenth century was unhappily famous. His rival Canning succeeded him at the Foreign

Office and the Duke of York made approaches to him to find a post for Brummell. But Canning, despite the fact that he was an old acquaintance of the Beau and that their careers had overlapped at Eton, was not prepared to rouse the King's irritation by such a request. He coldly replied that 'if his Royal Highness insisted on it he would do so, but that he could not recommend Mr Brummell's name to his Majesty on his own responsibility'.

His Royal Highness received petitions from other quarters of France at this time in his capacity as Commander-in-Chief. Mrs Fitzherbert was shuttling Minney Seymour from Paris to Brussels and from Brussels to Dresden and from Dresden to Berlin, in an attempt to keep her out of the clutches of the ineligible Dawson. Kangaroo Cooke, embroiled in the affair as the Duke of York's aide-de-camp, told Alvanley that Mrs Fitzherbert's complaints had made the Duke very annoyed with Dawson. Cooke offered to wager Alvanley fifty guineas that the romance would never end in marriage. By October Minney was back with Mrs Fitzherbert in Paris—where Worcester had rented Alvanley's apartments. And in November it looked as though Cooke's bet was a certainty, for the Duke had Dawson posted to St Vincent in the Windward Islands.

That same month the peripatetic Tom Moore crossed over from Calais to Dover again, but this time with his debts cleared and permanent residence in England assured. He paid a parting call on Brummell, who showed him 'his fine toilette (which the King gave him in the days of his favour) set out in a little bedroom 8 feet by 9'. The King himself was showing renewed signs of the wear and tear that he inflicted on his digestion. He was in his sixty-first year, still drinking heavily and, when in his cups, imagining all sorts of martial exploits for himself. One night he gave the Duke of Wellington a graphic description of how he charged at the head of the Household Brigade at Waterloo, thus turning the tide of battle. Through the winter of 1822 and the spring of 1823 there were constant rumours of his imminent death. But, as Creevey recorded in mid-May, 'Our Beloved is better today—that marvellous stomach of his has saved him... Prinney, whose inflammation had reached from his toe nearly to the top of his thigh, and who was already partially affected with

delirium from the great irritability upon his stomach being literally soused with Opium and Bark Brandy and Wine, sucks in his
cordial like mother's milk, recovers his senses, sleeps soundly,
and shakes off his mortal enemy at a blow. His danger was extreme, but I presume he will now do again.'

It was bad news for Brummell, who must have been hoping
very earnestly that George IV would die–for he could be sure of
favour from the Duke of York who was heir to the throne since
Princess Charlotte's death in childbirth in November 1818. Yet he
was in reasonably high spirits when he wrote to Lord Waldegrave on 1 July 1823: 'Your invitation to Boulogne offers me
much flattering temptation, and it will not be my fault if I do not
avail myself of it before you depart for the opposite island–
England, I think it is called, and I have some faint recollection of
having seen it in my earliest years. At the present moment I am
fettered by the leg like a galley-slave, for my former sins, expecting the menaced visit of *mon homme d'affaires*, or in more vulgar
and explicit designation, of my attorney from London. I would
sooner see the devil; but yet it is necessary that I do submit to his
annual apparition, and sell myself as usual to him.'

He would have found little difference between Boulogne and
Calais. It was so full of destitute English, running away from their
past debts and into new ones, that the natives nicknamed the
gaol the *Hôtel d'Angleterre*. Waldegrave, a Waterloo veteran and
husband of Minney Seymour's cousin, was happily well-off, and
able to return to England whenever he wished. Brummell had
obtained for their common dandy friend Van Tuyll 'two of the
most exquisite waistcoats' in *broderie lyonnaise* but regretted that
'I haven't yet encountered a secure hand by which I could pass
them to him in England'. Perhaps the Waldegraves responded
to this heavy hint. 'Has Lady Waldegrave read *Quentin Durward*?'
he asked in a postscript. 'It is perfect.'

He had made a great number of friends by now, French as well
as English. He was back into something like his old authoritative
stride–very much the 'King of Calais' and a familiar sight to all
his subjects, strolling arm-in-arm with his titled visitors along
the rue Royale or around the place d'Armes or walking his poodle
beside the ramparts on an autumn evening as the westering sun

struck a last diagonal gleam of white from the cliffs of Dover. His screen was put aside for ever; he added very little to his album, though there is one entry–some lines by the Reverend J. Mitford on the notorious Elstree murder–which must be later than 24 October 1823, the date when the crime was committed.

His kingdom was small but pleasant. 'A pretty, gay little town,' said Harriet Granville in February 1824, on her way to Paris where her husband had been appointed ambassador. 'Berkeley Craven, who is settled at Calais [for the same reason as Brummell], walked with us this morning. He says Mr Brummell is the happiest of men, lives chiefly with the natives, and enters into all the little gossip and tittle-tattle of the place with exactly the same zest as he was wont to do in England.' After all these years of disgrace he was still 'Mr Brummell'.

There were in fact two royal deaths in London that summer of 1824. The King and Queen of the Sandwich Islands were on a visit and Frederick Byng was given the task of showing them around. They fell victims to a common, but to them unfamiliar, occidental malady and both died at their hotel in the Adelphi. 'The Poodle has buried his measled Majesties,' wrote Joseph Jekyll in July. Byron, too, died far from his native land, in April that year; while in France the bigoted reformed rake Charles X succeeded his brother, fat gouty Louis XVIII, in September. That other bloated Majesty, George IV, continued in tolerable health until the early spring of 1825, when it was said 'there is a general regular declining in strength and flesh, the symptoms in short of a general breaking up'. Others opined that 'he is better than he has been these two years, but his present extreme inactivity is very unfavourable to the continuance of his health'.

One thing at least was comfortingly certain. 'Our York is all alive O! He dined at Sefton's this day week [9 March 1825] as gay as a lark, and gave them a description of a new house he is going to build upon the site of his present one, which is to be pulled down forthwith,' wrote Creevey. 'You may suppose the scale of his operations when I tell you that his principal apartment is to be 82 feet long. This I think for a gentleman in his 62nd year, without a sou in the world, and owing it is said at least a

million of money, is pretty well, but it shews clearly that those
who raise the money are confident he will get the throne.'

Although the Beau was only in his forty-seventh year, many of
the friends of his early days were now leaving the scene: De
Lancey Barclay, who caught a fatal cold while travelling on the
top of a coach; Mrs Bouverie, who had in Fox's words 'made
adultery respectable' by living in sin but above suspicion for more
than twenty years with Lord Robert Spencer; and, most grievous
news of all to Brummell, the beautiful Duchess of Rutland, so
often his hostess at Belvoir and Cheveley in the golden days, who
died on 29 November 1825. For the sake of those old times the
Beau felt he must send his condolences to the Duke, although the
latter had refused to have anything to do with him ever since he
involved the Duke's brother in his collapse. There is the hint of a
whine in the letter, and a great deal of Brummell's usual over-
wordy style, but through both of these comes a note of honest
sorrow.

Calais, Dec.3.1825.

My Lord,

   You will no doubt at the present distressing moment be surprised if not
offended at my taking the liberty to address you. Years have passed away
since I had the honour to be numbered among those who shared your early
friendship and though I have experienced every privation which might, in
common indulgence to faults even the most reprehensible, have in some
degree mitigated the resentment they provoked at the period of my leaving
England, with your Grace I am painfully assured I have gained no favourable
alteration of feeling towards me. In this persuasion I have nothing to solicit
from you but the liberal kindness to receive from a person now estranged
from you for ever, the assurance of the most earnest concern for the loss you
have sustained in your family. The remembrance of former times, the
happiest in my unfortunate life, when during many months of the year I was
received in your Grace's family almost as an inmate, presses deeply upon
my heart at an instant like this and preponderates over every more worldly
feeling or prejudice which might influence either of us. I cannot resist offering you my sincerest condolences, and I do so in unaffected sorrow.

My Lord,

I have the honour to be

Your Grace's most obedient and very humble servant,

George Brummell.

He had been away from England for almost a decade; he had
become a legend; he was the peg on which to hang all the Dandy

jokes, real or invented. Now he made his first appearance as a character in fiction: as Trebeck in T. H. Lister's novel *Granby*.

He wore a dress in no respect distinguishable from that of ten thousand others, he had neither rings nor chains, his head was not fixed at any particular angle, and the quiet and almost careless tie of his cravat plainly showed that he had neither studied 'Neckclothitania' nor believed in the axiom that 'Starch makes the Man.' There was nothing supercilious or affected in his manner, which was totally free from all peculiarity. As for his person, it was neither plain or handsome, but there was an air of intelligence and subdued satire and an intuitive quickness in his eye.

Lister praised

the 'nameless grace of polished ease' which he really possessed in a remarkable degree. He had great powers of entertainment and a keen and lively turn for satire, and could talk down his superiors, whether in rank or talent, with very imposing confidence. He had sounded the gullibility of the world, knew the precise current value of pretension, and soon found himself the acknowledged umpire, the last appeal, of many contented followers. In the art of cutting he shone unrivalled. He could assume that calm but wandering gaze which veers, as if unconsciously, round the proscribed individual, neither fixing nor to be fixed, not looking on vacancy nor on any one object, neither occupied nor abstracted, a look which perhaps excuses you to the person *cut* and, at any rate, prevents him from accosting you. He had considerable tact and a happy hardihood which generally carried him through the difficulties into which his fearless love of originality brought him. Such was the far-famed and redoutable Mr. Trebeck.

The portrait was satirical but sympathetic. Brummell approved of it: 'Lister must have known those who were intimate with me.' (He was the son of the old man Brummell met at Tixal in 1812.)

It was pleasant to be assured that his fame lived on. And indeed he still insisted on the highest standards in dress and deportment and the furnishings of his rooms in the rue Royale. He wrote to Lady Waldegrave in August 1826 about the difficulties he was experiencing in finding the right silk–a *Gros de Naples*–for curtaining his drawing room. Lady Waldegrave, who was in Belgium, had looked for it without success, and now Van Tuyll and another friend were on the same errand. 'If they fail in their *recherches* I must resign myself to the disappointment and submit to the glare of broad daylight, for I am determined not to compromise my antiquated taste by consenting to substitute miserable dowlas.' (Dowlas, a coarse linen or calico, was a favourite

symbol of uncouth poverty to the Beau, like the straw and bran
bread that he so often assured his correspondents he was lying on
or eating.)

Lady Waldegrave's offer to send him some handkerchiefs he
eagerly accepted: 'You will make a sad coxcomb of me again by
all your kindness; but the Indian silk handkerchiefs you mention
are too irresistible for me to affect anything like compunction in
receiving such handsome presents from you.' He again declined
the Waldegraves' invitation to spend some days with them. 'I
would give the world to go to Brussels for ten days; but to effect
such a wish I should be obliged to trudge it on foot with my
bundle on my back [another favourite symbol of penury, which
unfortunately he had already used in his letter to the Waldegraves
three years before] for I cannot afford to travel *en poste*, and I have
always entertained an insurmountable horror of a diligence.' He
offered another reason for his refusing, though he certainly did
not intend it to be taken seriously: '*Mes beaux jours sont passés*, and
it is now so long since I have renounced the vanities of the world,
from circumstances of necessity, that I have no doubt that I
should turn my feet, hang down my head, and, in short, find myself very uncomfortable in a room where thirty people were
assembled.'

As the years passed many predictions turned out to be quite
inaccurate. Kangaroo Cooke's wager that Minney Seymour
would never marry George Dawson, for example. Two years
after George's banishment to the West Indies, his cousin Lady
Caroline Damer settled her considerable estates on him and he
was transformed overnight into an acceptable husband. Mrs
Fitzherbert put Minney's own fortune into trust as a final precaution and married her off to George (soon calling himself
Dawson-Damer out of gratitude to his benefactress) at St
George's, Hanover Square, in August 1825. A less happy outcome, especially for those who had invested money on it,
attended the forecast that the Duke of York would shortly
succeed his brother as King. During the autumn of 1826 he began
to ail visibly, the victim of gout and dropsy. Brummell's friend,
Lord Sefton, obtained information from the Duke's household
through his cook and companion, the famous Ude, who had

formerly worked for Sefton. In November, Sefton informed his friends that Ude was urging him 'not to mind what the Papers say [about the Duke], for that his appetite is returned, and that he will do'. Alas, the symptoms were misleading. The Duke passed away on 5 January 1827, and Ude moved on to St James's Street, as chef of the gambling club newly established opposite White's by the fishmonger's son, William Crockford–'a fairy palace which certainly beats the drop-scene of a pantomime. The lamp in the staircase cost £1,200 and so in proportion.'

The Duke's death was a serious blow to Brummell, who thus lost a powerful patron as well as a friend. The fact that his financial prospects were much less rosy did not escape the notice of the local bankers who had lent him a good deal of money. They kept a close eye on him and it is probable that, even if he could have overcome his dislike of diligences, they would have prevented his accepting Lady Waldegrave's invitation to Brussels for fear that they would never see him again. Now they began to press him for payment of some of the outstanding loans.

Lord William Lennox visited Calais about this time with Adolphus FitzClarence. They attended the Duchess of Gloucester and her suite across the Channel and, when she decided to continue her journey to Hanover that same day, found themselves at Dessein's with room and dinners to spare–'so we at once sent for Brummell to make a third'. When he arrived at seven he 'looked pale and emaciated; his still well-fitting clothes were what is usually termed "seedy"; his boots were not so brilliant as they used to be when he lounged up Bond Street in the days of the fashionable promenade; his hat, though carefully brushed, showed symptoms of decay, and the only remnants of dandyism left were the well-brushed hair, the snow-white linen, and an unexceptionable tie.' (In another account, Lennox described Brummell's appearance as 'old-fashioned clothes, braided coat, well-managed neck-tie, polished boots, French hat, clean gloves, primrose colour, wrinkled face'.)

'At first the ex-king of fashion was dull, but after a few glasses of champagne he revived, and kept us alive until a late hour, telling us anecdotes of his past career–his misunderstanding with the Prince Regent, his support of Mrs Fitzherbert.' They ques-

tioned him about the vast corpus of Brummelliana; he again
denied the story of 'Wales, ring the bell!' and the impertinence
of omitting his host from the list of dinner guests, but confirmed
that he told Colonel Kelly's valet 'make it an extra fifty guineas
and *I* will work for *you*'.

The news from England that spring was of Raikes insulting
Brougham in Brooks's and being challenged to a duel (Kangaroo
Cooke being his second and Sir Robert Wilson acting for
Brougham); of the opening of the Zoological Gardens near Lord
Hertford's villa in Regent's Park; of the creation of a university
in London by Brougham 'and all the enlightened moderns who
are now founding Stinkomiles Colleges at the end of Gower
Street', as Creevey put it; and–by far the most important item
to Brummell–of the death of Canning in August 1827.

Brummell's friends at once renewed their approaches to Lord
Dudley, who continued as Foreign Secretary under the new
Prime Minister, Lord Goderich. Dudley was an eccentric whose
quirks had burgeoned with the years. He was a classical scholar
of repute but very absent-minded; Queen Caroline, whose
standards in this respect were not high, considered that he ate
like a hog; he had the habit of speaking his thoughts aloud,
with frequently startling effect at the dinner table. Recently his
fellow followers of the Brighton Harriers had noticed him holding long conversations with his horse. Alvanley persuaded
Wellington, who seems never to have met Brummell in person, to
raise the matter with Dudley, who had often met Brummell,
notably at Harriette Wilson's; but Dudley 'objected, and at the
last owned that he was afraid the King might not like it'.

This was not the sort of reply that the Duke was accustomed to
accept without question; he went off to put the request directly
to the King. Two years later he told Charles Greville, Clerk to
the Privy Council, that the King 'had made objections, abusing
Brummell–said he was a damned fellow and had behaved very ill
to him (the old story, always himself, *moi, moi, moi*)'. But, 'after
having let him run out his tether of abuse', Wellington extracted
his approval.

There was no doubt about it. 'George Brummell is to be made
Consul at Calais,' Mrs Fitzherbert wrote to Minney in December

1827. 'The King has given his consent.' Unfortunately the creaking gate, Captain Sam Marshall, was not ready to fall. And Dudley, still chattering to himself, was slow to take action: so slow, indeed, that by January 1828, when the Goderich administration collapsed and Dudley was out of a job, nothing conclusive had been done.

Wellington assumed the premiership, with Lord Aberdeen as Foreign Secretary. And it was now that Brummell must bitterly have regretted the loss of his lucky sixpence with the hole in it. For the Duke was quite unpredictably confronted with mutiny: Aberdeen had doubts about appointing Brummell and could not be persuaded. The matter was not of sufficient importance to warrant splitting the Cabinet. It was not one that particularly roused the Duke's sympathy. For though he had been called 'Beau' in his youth and was careful about his appearance his style of life was far from dandyish, rousing himself each morning, brushing his own clothing, generally refusing to allow his time to be wasted by servants–it was his brother William Wellesley-Pole, and his sister, Anne Culling Smith, whom Brummell impressed. So nothing was done about the Beau's consulship. His creditors, their appetites once more whetted and disappointed, snapped around him more persistently each day. His fiftieth birthday was a very sombre occasion.

In July he wrote urgently to George Dawson-Damer, care of Mrs Fitzherbert in Tilney Street:

Will you so far extend your usual kindness as to endeavour to be of *instant* service to me. It is not to yourself particularly that I take the liberty to address myself, for you must be very much changed if you have any money at command; but to three or four of those former friends who you may think willing to stretch a point in my favour at the moment. I am in a serious scrape from my utter inability to provide for a rascally bill which has been long due, and which, if not paid on or before the 26th of this month, will expose me to the worst consequences–the amount is £73.

Would you so essentially oblige me as to endeavour to gather together a few amiable Samaritans who might so kindly bear me and my actual difficulties in remembrance as to advance £25 each to satisfy this urgent demand? One hundred would relieve me and give me a few pounds over to scramble on with.

He mentioned the porcelain and lacquer ware that Dawson-Damer had seen when he visited him in the rue Royale:

Select what you please to the amount of double the sum in question and it shall be faithfully sent to you or to anyone else in payment. I would sell myself if I could raise a shilling upon my worthless body and soul to be extricated from this predicament which really frightens me out of my wits.

I wrote to Alvanley some time since acquainting him with my apprehensions about this bill, but I fear he is as usual without the means of assisting me. I have written also to Worcester ten days since in the same sense as my present request to you, but I should think he is absent from Town, for I have received no answer from him, and time presses sorely upon me.

I am, as you may have heard, expecting employment through the interference of that best of friends, the Duke of Wellington, but before such expectation may be realised I am sadly alarmed lest some overwhelming disaster should fall upon me.

There is a repeated note of panic in the Beau's letters in this second half of 1828. Many of his former friendships had worn thin with excessive use, and he was having to lean heavily on those that still held. He had no sooner received a sympathetic reply from Dawson-Damer than he was at him again: 'You are a very good fellow for answering my letter at all, but a most excellent one during a fit of gout. What business have you to be tormented with gout? It would become me perhaps, for no one deserves it more for former "hard going" and here I am with uninterrupted good health and, I firmly believe, an unimpaired constitution. It is all, indeed, that is left to me, and I ought to be thankful.' Dawson-Damer had evidently sent money, for Brummell confessed that 'for a long time past I have been unaccustomed to even friendly acknowledgements'. He added that he had also received £50 from Alvanley, who was going to speak to others on his behalf. All these, however, would be merely stopgaps; he desperately needed the security of a regular income.

'My dear Dawson, there certainly is a vacancy in the Consular Department at Petersburgh, for though the present incumbent, Sir Something Bailey, is gone back there, I know he has tendered his resignation, and that Marshall, the Consul here, has several times written soliciting that preferment.

'Can you find out *quietly* whether it is the intention to place me here as Consul, or to send me elsewhere?'

To round off this year of misery, his old friend Colonel Armstrong died and the young Edward Bulwer-Lytton published his

second novel, *Pelham*, in which one of the characters–Russelton–
was an obvious portrait of Brummell.

The contemporary and rival of Napoleon–the autocrat of the great world of
fashion and cravats–the mighty genius before whom aristocracy hath been
humbled and *ton* abashed–at whose nod the haughtiest *noblesse* of Europe
had quailed–who had introduced, by a single example, starch into neckcloths, and had fed the pampered appetite of his boot-tops on champagne–
whose coat and whose friend was cut with an equal grace–and whose name
was connected with every triumph that the world's great virtue of audacity
could achieve–the illustrious, the immortal Russelton, stood before me! I
recognised in him a congenial though a superior spirit and I bowed with a
profundity of veneration.

The tone was a great deal more satirical and mocking than in
Lister's novel, and the Beau angrily dismissed it as 'the grossest
of caricatures'.

Prince Pückler-Muskau, a pert condescending German prince-
ling and notorious rake, called on him one crisp bright morning
in the first week of the new year and

found him at his second toilet, in a flowered chintz dressing-gown, velvet
night-cap with gold tassel, and Turkish slippers, shaving, and rubbing the
remains of his teeth with his favourite red root. The furniture of his rooms
was elegant enough, part of it might even be called rich, though faded; and
I cannot deny that the whole man seemed to me to correspond with it.
Though depressed by his present situation, he exhibited a considerable fund
of humour and good-nature. His air was that of good society; simple and
natural, and marked by more urbanity than the dandies of the present race
are capable of. With a smile, he showed me his Paris peruque, which he
extolled at the cost of English ones, and called himself *le ci-devant jeune homme
qui passe sa vie entre Paris et Londres*'.

Having successfully passed off Stuart de Rothesay's joke as his
own, Brummell politely questioned his visitor about the people
he had met in London 'and then took occasion to convince me
that he was still perfectly well informed as to all that was passing
in the English world of fashion, as well as politics'. Brummell
complained that being aware of everything that went on was no
great consolation when 'they are letting me die of hunger here.
However, I hope my old friend the Duke of Wellington will one
day get rid of the Consul here and appoint me in his stead. Then
I shall be saved.'

Creevey recorded during this year that Calais 'is now much

more like itself than when I was there 5 years ago. Boulogne is the great depot of English, and has taken off, I suppose, what settlers there were at Calais.' But there were enough remaining to decide that they needed to build a Church of England chapel. A representative of the organising committee called on the Beau for a subscription and received a reply quite in the old flippant, open-handed style. 'Really,' said Brummell, 'I am very sorry you did not call last week, for it was only yesterday that I became a Catholic–but never mind, put my name down for a hundred francs.' There was, after all, no harm in putting one's name down for these things–though putting the money down was a different matter. When the bishop came and the consul gave a dinner for the supporters of the fund to meet him, Brummell refused the invitation. 'My dear Marshall, you must excuse me not having the pleasure to dine with you and the Trustees of the Church establishment this day. I do not feel myself sufficiently prepared in spirit to meet a bishop, or in pocket to encounter the plate after dinner; moreover, I should be a fish out of water in such a convocation.'

At other times, necessity induced him to dine with people whose hospitality he would have scorned to accept in his early days at Calais–though he snobbishly tried to conceal the fact. He was walking on the ramparts one day, arm-in-arm with Lord Sefton, when they encountered an extremely vulgar-looking Englishman who gave Brummell a very familiar nod. 'Sefton,' said the Beau, 'what can that fellow mean by bowing to you?' 'To me?' asked Sefton. 'He is bowing to you, I suppose. I know no one in Calais.' The man passed again soon afterwards and this time seized Brummell by the arm. 'Don't forget, Brum!' he boomed. 'Don't forget! Goose at four–goose at four!'

Not that he ever neglected or avoided his duties as a host. When Richard Monckton-Milnes arrived in Calais in the summer of 1828, with his parents and his sister, the Beau invited them all to dinner. And to Major Chambre, who brought a letter of introduction in the following year, he was the soul of hospitality. 'He begged I would dine with him whenever I was disengaged, as he always had sufficient for a friend in the portions sent in from the hotel nearby.' Since Chambre stayed in Calais for some time and frequently took advantage of the invitation, either Brummell's pocket or his very hearty appetite must have suffered to some extent, although Dessein's at this time was providing a meal of soup, sole, stewed veal, mutton cutlets, roast chicken, swiss omelet, cheese, peaches, greengages, cakes and biscuits for four francs.

Chambre, too young to have known the Beau in his hey-day, was charmed and impressed by this 'quiet, gentlemanlike man, without pretension and exceedingly agreeable' who sat all the morning in his dressing-gown and gold-lace cap chatting about the past. Brummell praised George IV's tact and quickwittedness during the Calais visit: 'The Royal Barge was manned to take him ashore, and at the same moment the Calais pilot-boat came alongside the Royal yacht. The King immediately gave preference to the latter, much to the delight of the French.'

He confirmed that he sent round a box of snuff to Dessein's for the King, and a bottle of thirty-year-old brandy. His version of the famous non-encounter was that he was standing on the steps of a shoemaker's shop opposite Leleux's when the King, bowing right and left, was driven down the rue Françoise. Suddenly their eyes met, 'His astonishment was so great that, for the moment, he quite forgot his Kingly bearing and, throwing up his hands, he exclaimed, "Damn it! There's old Brummell!"'

It was a long time since the Beau had enjoyed the flattery of an admiring acolyte. He blossomed; showed Chambre how every Monday morning he prepared his snuff for the week, his valet François bringing in a pot of cold tea to moisten the mixture; told him of the famous lucky sixpence that brought him £36,000 at the tables and £8000 at Newmarket and how he lost it in the street one night, taking his gold snuff-box from his waistcoat pocket and unknowingly pulling out the sixpence with it; laughed over his attempts to bully or wheedle Lady Gwydir into inviting him to her parties, and her persistent refusals because he in turn refused to join in the waltzes that she adored; and very seriously assured Chambre of his dog's psychic powers. These were proved to Chambre's satisfaction when Leleux sent his daughter to Paris for medical treatment; Brummell's dog howled 'in the most unaccountable manner' at two o'clock one morning,

Voluptuary under the Horrors of Digestion': The Prince Regent by James Gillray

and later it was learnt that the sick girl died at precisely that time. This talented animal did much the same thing when an Englishman died in lodgings across the road, and the Beau confessed he was 'convinced the animal had seen the spirit of the departed'.

As the days passed the talk got round to the sad story of Brummell's finances. 'Whenever any one of my creditors calls upon me,' he confessed, 'the moment he enters the room I commence an amusing conversation and tell him anecdotes I think will interest him. This has hitherto succeeded very well, for I divert their attention from the subject that brings them to me. We shake hands and part on good terms; but my stock in trade is exhausted, and I am now completely used up. I have nothing left to tell them, and what to do I know not.'

Chambre offered to interest an auctioneer friend, the son of William Crockford, in the Beau's collection of costly knick-knacks and furniture. Crockford came over, gave the Beau an advance, and later shipped the more valuable pieces back to England, where the Sèvres porcelain was advertised as 'the finest and purest ever imported into England'. The Duke of Buccleuch took some; George IV paid two hundred guineas for a tea-set; and a pair of vases went for three hundred pounds.

In September 1829 Brummell had a note from the tempestuous Sir Robert Wilson, hero of Lavalette's escape from a Paris death cell and champion of Queen Caroline, saying that he would soon be passing through Calais. Brummell replied that he would be delighted to see him. 'I am still vegetating, for I will not call it living, with the fat weeds that keep within the stagnant ditches that surround this place. I am indeed comparatively as fat but that can be accounted for by the windy nature of my nourishment, hope long deferred yet still green and promising in the fancy. My dependance is placed upon the good offices of one great man who, as he has always extended every kindness towards me, will not neglect any favourable opportunity to be of service to me.'

Buoyed up by his faith in the Great Duke he drifted into 1830, a year of high events and tasty gossip. An English traveller, visiting Lady Hester Stanhope in her Lebanese retreat, found by an odd coincidence that the first two persons about whom she inquired were Wellington and Brummell. He told her he had seen the Beau once or twice in Calais 'with no appearance of foppery, except when he leaned out of his lodging window in a sort of fine chintz dressing-gown'. It brought back immediate memories to Brummell's old friend in her strange costume as an Arab sheikh and prophetess. 'Ah!' she exclaimed. 'Those are the patterns that the Prince sometimes used to give £100 for, to have them like his!'

In England all the gossip in the first month of the year was of the scandalous conduct of the Duke of Cumberland with Lady Graves, wife of the Comptroller to the Household of his brother, the Duke of Sussex. Lord Graves—William Brummell's companion on the secret trip to Berlin thirty years ago—was at first accused of playing the compliant husband and accepting £30,000 from Cumberland as compensation for being cuckolded. Cumberland's friends then denied there was any guilty association between the Duke and Lady Graves. If this were true, said the wags, it was a pity, for it spoiled the conundrum: 'Why is the Duke like a resurrection man?' 'Because he disturbs the Graves.' The joke ended in February, when the unhappy Graves committed suicide.

On 4 March Charles Greville arrived from Dover at noon and, unable to get transport to Paris until seven that evening, spent a long time talking with Brummell, 'just as gay as ever. I found him in his old lodging, dressing; some pretty pieces of old Furniture in the room, an entire Toilet of Silver, and a large green Macaw perched on the back of a tattered silk Chair with faded gilding, full of gaiety, impudence, and misery.' Greville was so moved by the Beau's plight that he wrote immediately to the Duke of Wellington, begging him to do what he could about the consulship.

At a little before three o'clock in the morning of 26 June George IV died and his brother, the pineapple-headed Duke of Clarence, succeeded as William IV, a 'most abstemious' fellow who never drank more than a bottle of sherry at dinner, and loved the simple family evenings with his Queen knitting by the fireside, the pair of them surrounded by a horde of Fitzclarences (his illegitimate children by Mrs Jordan) quarrelling over preferment, titles and hard cash. Outside the terror by night of workers' riots had moved from north to south. The artisan followers of

General Ned Ludd were succeeded by the agricultural supporters of another mythical military figure, Captain Swing. The tactics were the same, to burn ricks and kill cattle and to destroy the new threshing machines that were putting men out of work. In London, in July, the unfamiliar omnibuses were plying from Paddington to the Bank; while in Paris, where they had first been used, they were being tipped over on to their sides to form barricades against the troops of Charles X. And in August, Louis-Philippe ascended the throne of France, thus literally crowning many generations of treachery by the House of Orleans.

Finally, in the last week of September, a carriage and four drove into Caen, the capital town of the Department of Calvados. It clattered over the Pont de Vaucelles and up the rue St-Jean, traversing the entire length of the old town from the place des Casernes to the Château, with two postillions cracking their whips, a valet perched among the luggage in the rumble, and one English gentleman inside. The gates into the courtyard of the Hôtel de la Victoire swung open, the carriage wheeled in, and down stepped the passenger: George Bryan Brummell. In his wallet he carried a letter from Lord Aberdeen: 'The King having been graciously pleased to nominate and appoint you to be HM's Consul for the Departments of Calvados, La Manche and Ille et Vilaine, to reside at Caen, I have to desire that you will proceed with all convenient speed...'

He beckoned to the first person he saw. 'The best rooms, the best dinner, and the best Lafitte,' he said.

CHAPTER SIX

His Britannic Majesty's Consul

Brummell's first biographer, Captain Jesse, stated that he was appointed to his consulship on 10 September 1830 as a result of the Duke of Wellington's intercession with William IV. His subsequent biographers have followed Jesse in this, as in almost everything else—thus doing an injustice to George IV, a man whose reputation needs all the justice and mercy that it can get. Brummell was in fact appointed, without any doubt, before 20 March 1830, probably as a result of Greville's letter prompting Wellington to take a firmer line with Aberdeen. The delay in his reaching Caen from Calais (on 25 September, not 5 October as Jesse says) is very simply explained—his creditors would not let him go.

When his appointment came through, he was in debt to the tune of about 24,000 francs. Half of this was owed to a local banker, Leveux, and a quarter to his valet, François Sélègue, household expenses. There was almost 3500 francs outstanding for dinners sent in from Dessein's; of the rest, the only bills exceeding 100 francs were to tailors, a draper, a chemist (for oils and cold cream) and the shoemaker across the road. All had been content to let the debts run so long as Brummell was living among them; none was willing to see him depart without first paying up.

The position was desperate, even by nonchalant Brummell standards. With nothing in his pockets, and most of his credit among his friends in England exhausted, he had to find £1000 before he could enter into the consulship that he had so begged and longed for. The money from the Crockford sale had gone to pay earlier debts. He put up the remaining pieces of boulle furniture but they brought no more than £500–only half what he needed.

On 20 March 1830, in the presence of Sam Marshall, he signed a power of attorney: 'Know all Men by These Presents that I, George Bryan Brummell, have made ordained constituted and appointed and do hereby make ordain constitute and appoint Lewis Hertslet and James Hertslet both of the Foreign Office Westminster Esquires my true and lawful Attornies or Attorney jointly or severally for me and in my name to ask demand and receive of and from the Teller of the Exchequer all Sums of Money that now are or hereafter may become due and payable to me at the said Exchequer on any account whatsoever...'

The crippling arrangement that he had been forced to make with Leveux was that Leveux would take over all Brummell's debts in return for Brummell's assigning the whole of his salary to the Hertslets and giving Leveux authority to claim an annual repayment of capital and interest direct from them. Jesse says the agreed amount was £320 a year. He seems to have got the information from Leveux himself, but the sum is enormous in view of the fact that Brummell's salary, clearly stated in his letter of appointment, was only £400 a year.

By the time that he, with Leveux's help, had satisfied all his creditors, the Paris mob were installing Louis-Philippe on the throne hastily vacated by Charles X. But September brought enough calm for Brummell to be on his way–at any rate as far as Paris, where, as one British diplomatic representative to another, he proposed to pay his respects to his old friend the ambassador, Lord Stuart de Rothesay. He travelled in style and at no cost, Sam Marshall having arranged that he should share the carriage of a King's Messenger. Overcome with relief or exhaustion, he dozed through most of the 180 miles to Paris–sometimes very audibly; though, as the King's Messenger assured Marshall on his return, 'Mr Brummell snored very much like a gentleman.'

His week in Paris was a delirious return to past delights. 'Stuart and several of my friends have spoilt me for at least a year to come.' At the ambassador's table he met the lovely and legendary Princess Bagration, widow of the famous Russian general, now in her fifties but still wearing 'nothing but white Indian muslin, clinging to her form and revealing it in all its perfection'; and Talleyrand, 'who never says what he does and never does what he says, proud as a peacock and venal as a lackey', limping back at the age of seventy-six to complete the astounding record of having served as a minister from the reign of Louis XVI through the Republic, the Directory, the Consulate, the Empire, the Restoration, and now about to leave for London as the ambassador of Louis-Philippe. With Talleyrand was his jackal, 'Handsome' Montrond, once a dandy Muscadin of the Directory; and among the former Bonapartists who had successfully trimmed their sails to ride the Bourbon breakers were Count Molé and the Corsican Minister of War, General Sébastiani, who was shortly to succeed him at the Foreign Office. These last two provided Brummell with letters of introduction which, when he at last managed to drag himself away from the rue du Faubourg St-Honoré, ensured him a very cordial reception from General Corbet, commanding the Military Sub-division of Caen, and the Prefect of the Department of Calvados, Louis Target.

On the morning after his arrival in Caen, Brummell wrote to Lord Aberdeen, to inform him that 'I have this day entered upon my duties as Consul. I will avail myself of this opportunity most humbly to request your Lordship's indulgent consideration upon the subject of my having taken the Liberty to absent myself so long from my post. After a residence of more than fourteen years at Calais I had unavoidably involved myself in difficulties which it was not in my power to surmount at the instant. By making every sacrifice remaining to me I have been at length enabled to leave that place with credit to myself, and in such an honourable manner as, I feel persuaded, Your Lordship would approve.' He stepped outside into the autumn sunshine to survey his parish.

The Hôtel de la Victoire adjoined the south gate of the great castle built by William the Conqueror and faced the church of St-Pierre. Westward, along the rue St-Pierre and rue Notre-Dame lay the great Abbaye-aux-Hommes which the Conqueror donated to his favourite Norman city; and eastward, along the rue des Chanoines, the Abbaye-aux-Dames that was the gift of his wife Matilda. Southward, a bridge connected the place St-Pierre with the rue St-Jean, crossing the canal which looped up from the river Orne, round and down again, converting the centre of the town into an island. Branching off on either side of the rue St-Jean lay the streets where most of the British residents and the leading French families had their homes. Two-thirds of the way down was the rue des Carmes, and almost at the end of the rue des Carmes was the office of the British Consulate–about three-quarters of a mile from the Hôtel de la Victoire.

The distance, as well as the expense of staying at the hotel, made it urgent for Brummell to find lodgings in a more central part of the town. He claimed that he had undergone 'all the horrors and all the more horrible cheating of one of the worst hotels, I am confident, in Europe', and that he had, in his favourite terms, 'gnawed bones upon unwashed dowlas in this charnel house', and spent sleepless nights scratching himself. In fact the hotel was regarded as one of the best in the district, and the truth may be simply that they asked him to pay cash. In any event, he moved quickly and on 28 September signed the lease for a set of rooms at No. 47 rue des Carmes at a rent of 1200 frances a year.

'An admirable lodging,' he wrote to Sam Marshall, 'half a house, the property of a most *cleanly*, devout old lady (the cousin of Guernon de Ranville, one of the condemned ministers), excellently furnished, with a delightful garden, two Angola cats, and a parrot that I have already thrown into apoplectic fits with sugar.' His good fortune had rejuvenated him, for the 'devout old lady' was almost a dozen years his junior, though he probably never conceded this. In the census of the following year he reversed his age, giving it as thirty-five instead of fifty-three.

She was Madame Aimable-Angle Guernon de St-Ursin, doubly related to Guernon de Ranville (the ex-Minister of Education who was currently imprisoned with the Prince de Polignac and other members of Charles X's council in the fortress of Ham) through her father and her late husband, Jean de Guernon de St-Ursin, whom she married in 1813. Her only daughter, also called Aimable, was born in September 1814, and was thus just sixteen–and '*une jolie blonde*'–at the time when Brummell joined them.

No. 47 rue des Carmes was a handsome, double-fronted, three

storied building. The front door opened on to a broad passage which ran right through the house to a small courtyard from which steps led up to the large walled garden. A kitchen and two large rooms on either side of the corridor occupied most of the ground floor; a staircase at the garden end of the corridor led to two large rooms and a small one on the first floor and another three on the second. These last were presumably the bedrooms of Madame de St-Ursin, Aimable, the cook Marie Godard and the maid Marie Vantier, while Brummell occupied half of the rest of the house with Isidore Lebaudy, the valet who took over from Sélègue. A few yards to the west of No. 47, almost at the end of the street, where it opened on to the quayside, was the small office of the British Consulate. Just round the corner was the Customs Office.

The trade which brought British vessels up the Orne was mainly in coal and iron, though they also carried some produce from the West and East Indies–coffee, sugar, spices and fruit. Temporarily dealing with the problems of their skippers and crews, and with those of the British residents, was a naval lieutenant on half-pay, Benjamin Hayter, appointed by Brummell's predecessor, Ogilvy, to perform the consular duties until the Beau belatedly assumed them. Brummell, who intended to devote himself to the social and diplomatic aspects of his appointment rather than mere clerical details, promptly invited Hayter to stay on as his vice-consul, an offer which Hayter, a married man with six children, gladly accepted. 'I am perfectly contented with my *Chancellor* Hayter, who is well versed in his business and, from my investigation, I believe to be an honourable *adjoint*,' Brummell wrote a month later.

Some years afterwards, when it was in his interest to do so, Hayter claimed that Brummell paid him a salary of £40 a year, but this seems too Micawberish even for the Beau who, from an annual salary of £400, was already committed to a reported £320 to Leveux in Calais and an undoubted £50 to Madame de St-Ursin, in addition to whatever wages he paid his valet Lebaudy– and all this without allowing for food, drink, hats, wigs, gloves, unguents, polishes and laundry. There is little reason to doubt Brummell's statement that 'Mr Hayter is remunerated for his official services by the fees that are received. The other Vice-consuls and provisional Vice-consuls at the Out-Ports are also remunerated in the same manner.' These were three French merchants, Le Jolis, Ducoudray and Le Carpentier, at Cherbourg, Granville and Honfleur respectively, and 'an English private gentleman', G. W. Jennings, whom Brummell nominated at St-Malo in January 1831.

Brummell's past fame had flown before him, even to the provincial town, but the letters from Molé and Sébastiani also helped enormously. 'Without a sixpence in my pocket, I am become a great man here,' he blithely informed Marshall a month after his arrival. 'They dine me and fête me most liberally; and I have already been elected a member of their Societé or club, a sort of Brooks's in a much more magnificent house, *without* ballot, an honour not before accorded to any Englishman. All the newspapers and latest periodicals are there taken in profusion, and as much franc whist, écarté and billiards as you please, till eleven o'clock at night. All well-educated, well-mannered and well-conditioned people.' This was the *Salon Littéraire* which occupied the former Hôtel de Londres in the rue de l'Engannerie and had a membership of sixty permanent members and fifteen associate or foreign members.

He was greatly enjoying this quaint new world, with its dissipations of 'franc whist' continuing so devilishly 'till eleven o'clock at night'. 'To morrow I dine at a grand to-do given by the Préfet and Monsieur de la Pommeraye, the député.' (Colonel Adam de la Pommeraye was a neighbour of Brummell's at No. 31 rue des Carmes; he commanded a cavalry regiment at Waterloo and had more recently been appointed by the Chamber of Deputies to escort Charles X to Cherbourg and exile in England.) 'I am preparing a *neat little extempore*, which I shall let off upon success to the commerce of the two countries being toasted.'

He was favourably impressed with the English residents–'they keep large and hospitable mansions'–and in particular with 'Messrs Villiers and Burton, two very good men of independent fortune, with numerous families. Their houses, and without exaggerating they are like Devonshire House or the Embassy at Paris, are generally open at half-past five to a well-provided dinner, and, Heaven knows, I have as yet profited most abundantly by their kindness, and always *portes ouvertes* in the evening. The French of the best class mingle much in this society, and there is always a fiddle for the amusement of the young ladies.' His consular duties were performed with zeal: 'I am doing all that I can do to make all parties satisfied with me. I condole with the outs and agree with the ins: as to my own nation, I have called upon all who are worthy of such a compliment. I shake hands and gossip with the fathers and mothers, and pat all their dirty-nosed children upon the head, and tell them that they are beautiful. What can I do more with my scanty means?...Prostrate my remembrances at the feet of Mrs Marshall, and of all your family. Scribble me what is going on in *your little fishing-town of Calais.*'

There were some sixty-five British families permanently resident in Caen. Colonel Francis Burton lived in the rue Guilbert, whose gardens backed on to those of the rue des Carmes; George Villiers in the rue St-Louis, the first turning on the right going down the rue St-Jean from the rue des Carmes towards the river. Among those certainly worthy of a call from the Beau were the residents in the new expensive houses along the rue des Chanoines, outside the old fortifications: William Cooke, a gentleman of private means; William Cox, a retired colonel about Brummell's age; Dr Kelly and Dr Woodman; O'Connor, a merchant who sponsored Brummell at the Literary Society; John Spencer Smith, a former British envoy to Stuttgart; Colonel Todd; and Mr Denny, the Protestant minister. In the adjoining rue Haute, there were Captain Chambers and a naval officer named Douglas, and Thomas Wells, one of the three English tulle manufacturers in the town. Just outside the ramparts, on the rue des Quais, Miss Eleanor Wheatcroft and her sister Mary kept a school for young ladies, with the help of Miss Davidson; and where the street followed the canal northward and westward until it ran opposite the church of St-Pierre was the boarding establishment for young gentlemen conducted by Mr William Meston.

Neither of these schools lacked pupils. The terrible infantile mortality of preceding centuries was fading; but the fecundity which so much worried the Reverend Thomas Malthus continued unchecked. Astonished husbands, convinced of woman's innate fecklessness by their wives' annual pregnancies ('Bone-weary, many-childed, trouble tried!', as one poet apostrophised his spouse, 'Mother of nine that live and two that died!') sighed and saw no solution to the problem, other than spending more of the daylight hours away from the household increasingly littered with children ('When,' as the comedian Samuel Foote asked one prolific parent, 'do you begin to drown them?'). Among those dirty-nosed children whom the new consul found himself expected to pat upon the head were the Bennetts' seven in the rue de Vaucelles, which continued the rue St-Jean across the river and out on the Paris road; the Darceys with ten in the rue de l'Engannerie; the widow Fitzgerald with her seven in the rue Singer, just below the rue des Carmes; the Mackesons' nine up in the rue des Chanoines, and the Shaws' seven. Brummell's hospitable friends, George Villiers and Francis Burton, had seven apiece; and scattered through the town were six families with six children each and another six with five–to say nothing of the drones with only four or less.

There was one more prominent English figure in Caen, whom Brummell probably first ignored but was later to cultivate as a close friend–Charles Armstrong, the grocer whose double-fronted shop stood at No. 133 rue St-Jean, almost opposite the entrance to the rue des Carmes.

In November 1830, the Whigs returned to power at long last, committed to a programme of retrenchment in public expenditure and of electoral reform. Among the appointments made by the new Prime Minister, Lord Grey, were Lord Palmerston as Foreign Secretary, Henry Brougham (now Lord Brougham and Vaux) as Lord Chancellor, and William Lamb (who had inherited the title of Lord Melbourne in 1828) as Home Secretary. All were old acquaintances of Brummell and amply compensated for the loss of his benefactor Wellington as premier. His old confidence returned. He was soon treating his bureaucratic superiors in Whitehall with nonchalant contempt; well within six months he had established his supremacy. The Foreign Office records contain a report from him, dated 14 February 1831, with a statement from M. le Carpentier (who was Mayor of Honfleur as well as British Consul there) referring to a shipwreck and a payment of £1.18s.2d. which Brummell had authorised to be made to two of the seamen who survived. At the bottom is the pencilled comment, 'This is very irregular'–and beneath this, with the initials of John Bidwell, Superintendent of the Consular Service, the plaintive reply: 'We can't help it–if we row him he will beat us.'

The autumn of 1830 was unusually long; the chilly Norman winter mercifully brief. He was soon able to resume his favourite afternoon perambulation down to the bottom of the rue des Carmes, across the wooden bridge over the canal, and along the Cours Caffarelli, a new tree-lined promenade named for a prefect of the department under Napoleon. On the first Friday in March the Caen Philharmonic Society gave its opening concert of the season and a few days later there was a charity performance in the theatre down by the Champ de Foire. When the weather was too inclement for strolling outdoors there was always the drawing room of Madame St-Ursin, whose heart he quickly won. He helped pretty golden-haired Aimable with her English lessons and lent an attentive ear to her mother's denunciation of the Orleanist usurper. Out of sympathy for his landlady's legitimist views he made it a practice on official holidays never to fly the Union Jack above the Lion and the Unicorn which graced the portal of his consulate at No. 47 but displayed it at the office down the road.

He was blossoming again after a dormancy of almost fifteen years. He got on extremely well with General Corbet, the military commander, who turned out to be a boyhood acquaintance of Tom Moore. Corbet had been forced to flee to France after the Thomas Emmet conspiracy of 1797 and thereafter had fought for Bonaparte in the Peninsula and Germany. The prefect, Louis Target, was a less likable character; his father had gained notoriety by refusing to defend Louis XVI at his trial, and the son owed his appointment to Louis-Philippe. But this was more than compensated, in the Beau's estimation, by having as a close neighbour a genuine *marquise* of the *ancien régime*: Madame de Séran, whom he had first met in London many years ago, when she was a young refugee from the Revolution, and who now entertained him at her soirées at 42 rue des Carmes. True, the company at the *Salon Littéraire* was not quite what it had been at Brooks's and White's; a stroll along the Cours Caffarelli did not really compare with his former progress down St James's Street; and in his less euphoric moments he must have admitted to himself that there *had* been some exaggeration in his comparing the Villiers mansion in the rue St-Louis with Devonshire House. One thing, however, remained the same—the cost of putting on a show. He was rapidly in deep water again. On 14 April he wrote in French to Leveux:

I scarcely expected six months ago to find myself once more reduced to the extremity of having recourse to your kindness. I have relied too much, as you know, on my friends' promises; they have done nothing for me and it may be another wretched age of four or five months before they choose to rescue me from the situation with which I have recently been trying to cope. This situation has finally become most threatening—I am not concerned at being deprived of the luxuries and amenities of life, for I have long been forced to learn to do without them, but at the moment my honour is at stake, my reputation and all my present and future interests, since I have reason to fear that the total lack of means to provide for the official expenditure which is daily demanded of me by my consular office and the ignominy of being continually harried for the small debts that I have necessarily contracted in this town, may shortly be the cause of my losing my appointment.

This was a shrewd argument. Leveux could not recoup himself from Brummell's pay if Brummell was out of a job.

I therefore beg you to consider the difficulties of my situation in your own interests, which I vow to you are more sacred to me than my own; I beg you to reflect on them and to make every endeavour to provide for my pressing need. Be influenced only by those sentiments of liberality and friendship which you have shown towards me for fifteen years, and which I shall never abuse. Pay no heed to the unworthy counsels of those (I know them but shall not name them) who, to satisfy their unjust and miserable claims against me, will seek to injure me in your esteem.

Of course, there never had been any chance that he could make ends meet; and he was certainly not so stupid as to be unaware of this. Writing to Marshall in October 1830 he had said, 'I forsee that little or nothing is to be made of my department', meaning that there was no hope of a rise in salary; but he added confidently, '*N'importe*, I shall try something in the spring to better it.'

And this he did. But first he made one more attempt to raise money from Leveux. 'I have been flattering myself for the past month, my dear Sir, that I should receive news from you.' Instead there had been silence and now he was 'driven to the last extremity, to escape from the importunities of the people of this town, and finally to save the coat on my back, for that is truly almost all that remains to me.' He asked Leveux to accept just one more promissory note, and finally the banker agreed.

The time was approaching for another of his annual summer meetings with his attorney about the mysterious sums of money that he continued to draw from England. On 19 May he wrote to Palmerston, asking permission to put Hayter in charge of the Caen consulate for a period not exceeding ten days. He required leave of absence 'to meet a professional person at Hâvre, upon business of moment to me, and which person cannot be away from London for more than five days at a time' (and could therefore not get to Caen and back). Still cherishing the hope of Sam Marshall's imminent demise, he continued, 'I will take the liberty of availing myself of this occasion in most humbly soliciting your Lordship's consideration of me, should a vacancy occur in the Consular establishment at any of the other Ports of this country, and particularly that of Calais, where I resided during many years of the latter part of my life.'

It was a reasonable precaution to remind Palmerston of his hope and qualifications, but what must have surprised the Foreign Secretary very considerably was the sentence that followed: 'I may represent to Your Lordship that which might be prejudicial to my own individual interests, but, with every zealous anxiety to make myself of use in preserving Your Lordship's protection and the only means which enable me to exist, I will beg unreservedly to state the almost total inutility of the appointment of a Consul at this place, and that the situation might be abolished altogether without any probable detriment to His Majesty's, Service.' This was indeed a bold move to force a transfer to a better-paid post.

The reply came from John Bidwell. 'Your Despatches, not numbered [a sigh, but no rebuke], of the dates noted in the margin, have been received and laid before Viscount Palmerston. I am directed by His Lordship to state to you that he accedes to your request.' The request, that is, for a few days' leave; on the matter of the consulship there was no comment. In the end Brummell did not take the leave because his mysterious visitor was unable to get away from London. He was forced back on whatever resources he could find locally–principally Charles Armstrong, the grocer and wine merchant in the rue St-Jean. Armstrong, though English, was the American Vice-consul. He was the shipping agent for the vessels plying to and from the United Kingdom and America, and he obliged his customers by cashing bills and money-orders drawn on English banks.

Brummell addressed a note to him in August 1831.

I have been reduced to so low an ebb during the last three weeks by delay and not receiving promised remittances from England that it is impossible for me to hold up my head, or to exist in my actual state a day longer. For ten days I have actually not had five francs in my possession, and I have not the means of procuring either wood or peat for my scanty fire, or of getting my things from the washerwoman. A trifling advance would arrange these difficulties, and give me further time, but I know not who to apply to in this place.

I have not anything to offer you by way of security, excepting my signature, if it is not my small stock of plate, for which I paid six hundred francs, and my watch and chain, worth as much more: to these you are welcome, only do not let me be exposed to the most utter distress and want, for my temporary inability to command a few miserable francs. I am not going out, and if you can spare five minutes in the course of the morning you will oblige me by coming down here: these matters are better arranged in person than by writing.

Though neglected–as he claimed–by his acquaintances in England, the news of his appointment stirred their memories. Tom Moore, travelling in the coach from Devizes to London, discovered that one of his companions was 'an old masquerader of other days, Sir Thomas Champneys', who entertained him with an anecdote of Brummell listening to a pompous Cabinet Minister explaining at great length the workings of the Income Tax that was about to be brought in, and remarking at the end, 'Then I see I must retrench in the rosewater for my bath.' Less amiable were the comments of Lady Louisa Stuart, who at this time described Brummell with truly comprehensive denigration as 'the son of the errand boy of my father's secretary's clerks...an idle flattering knave'. (Her description of William Brummell's beginnings was quite accurate–as a boy he had run errands for

Charles Jenkinson, who was an Under-Secretary to Lady Louisa's father, Lord Bute.) The other Brummells were in the public eye that year because of the marriage of the Beau's niece Georgiana, daughter of William Brummell and Anne Daniell, to Sir Thomas Pigott of the Royal Horse Guards.

Mortality continued to thin the ranks of his friends: in April 1831 Lord Walsingham, who had played cricket with him in the Eton eleven of 1793, was burned to death in bed at his house in Upper Harley Street. Another old friend died as an indirect result of the introduction in March of the Reform Bill. The change was more than overdue: Manchester and Birmingham, with populations of around 100,000 each, were not represented in Parliament at all, while some boroughs with less than a dozen electors (Old Sarum had none) returned two members each–entirely at the behest of the great landowners. When Lord Radnor offered Thomas Creevey one of the seats at Downton, Creevey suggested that he should go down and let the electors see him. The startled Earl replied that this was 'quite out of the question, a practice never heard of'.

The Whigs carried the bill through its third reading in September, only to have it thrown out by the Lords. In the Midlands and the West Country there was a wild outbreak of rioting and arson. The Countess Brownlow, recalling this 'time of disorder and dread' spoke of 'incendiary fires all over the country. From Belvoir Castle, standing on its hill, not a night passed without several of these fires being seen.' One of the marauding bands broke into a country house,

plundered it, destroyed everything they were unable to carry away, and finally set it on fire. The master of the house was absent: his lady, in delicate health, was forced from her couch to a precipitate flight. Led by her young daughter to a distant part of the grounds, they both remained for hours on the damp earth, the daughter supporting the mother's head on her bosom, and both concealing themselves under a laurel tree...When servants found them, half dead with cold and terror, there was no apartment, no couch, no bed of that so lately splendid residence fit to receive them, and they were carried in-animate to the only place which had escaped the incendiaries–a groom's bed, over one of the stables.

The description is J. W. Croker's, given in his speech to the Commons when the House met for the new session in December.

The splendid residence was Colwick Hall, where Brummell had so often spent a week hunting. The unfortunate châtelaine was Mary Chaworth, Byron's boyhood sweetheart who had married Jack Musters instead. She never recovered from the shock and died in February 1832.

It had been a miserable autumn and winter for Brummell. His valet, finding that he could get no pay, gave notice and demanded all his back wages amounting to more than 1000 francs. Once more Brummell applied to Armstrong: 'That d——d ungrateful brute, Isidore, persecutes me at every instant: the fellow says he is going to Paris on Thursday, and will not depart without being paid, in money or by Bill, and I believe him capable of employing a *huissier* [bailiff]. I am wretchedly bedevilled, and out of spirits, and hate going out of the house, or I would call and thank you for your note of yesterday.'

Armstrong accepted one of the Beau's gold watches as surety for this loan and another to repay a debt to the bankers, Gilbert and Bellamy. At this inconvenient moment Brummell received instructions from D. R. Morier, the Consul-General at Paris, to go to Granville to investigate a dispute over the detention of some British fishing boats. It meant a round trip of more than 130 miles and one or two nights in a Granville hotel–all to be paid in cash. Since he had none he ignored the instructions; but Morier was not to be put off–the order was repeated. Armstrong received another appeal:

I am positively pressed for two hundred and eighty francs at the moment, that is, before four o'clock to-day, or I shall be exposed to the utmost disgrace. The things, that is the plate, are in the closet in my room, and you may have them by sending any confidential person for them; but I do not like to *trust* my servant with them, as it may be known, or she may be seen with them in the street. It is the urgency of the moment that I am anxious to weather; small difficulties often extend to irreparable destruction of character; such is my situation at this instant.

It would indeed have been a mistake for the world to see him pledging his plate to Armstrong. He was living on credit in every sense of the word; and really living remarkably well, his elegance and wit often earning him more invitations than he could accept. As a bachelor he was not expected to entertain; when he dined at home either alone or with friends he had the meal sent in from Longuet's restaurant.

Except for putting his signature on essential documents he left almost all official business to his vice-consul Hayter. A favourite story in Caen was that there were only two occasions on which he was called upon to officiate personally as consul. The first was when he married a young British couple in his drawing room. The second was when, three months later, the bride's mother called one morning 'to request that he would restrain her son-in-law from beating her daughter and ruining her furniture'. Brummell was outraged at being interrupted at his toilet. He denied that the affair had anything to do with him, dismissed her with 'Call tomorrow, Madam, call tomorrow; I will consult my chancellor,' and gave his servant instructions never to let her in again.

He derived a great deal of pleasure from the supplementary English lessons that he gave his landlady's daughter, in an exchange of notes which became the excuse for a little showing-off and more than a little self-pity.

My Dear Miss Aimable, During the present week I have led a most idle and unprofitable life; never in bed before the moon had retired, and in consequence unable to open my jaded eyes till the morning had almost vanished. I am angry with myself, now that this dissipation is passed, because it has made me inattentive to our correspondence in English. I shall certainly turn over a new leaf, and amend the evil course of these late hours, if it is only in deference to my promise to improve you in the knowledge of my uncouth native dialect. You are anxious to learn, and you merit every commendation for your assiduity...Prosecute your studies with the same amiable attention and emulation that you have already evinced, and you will soon be omniscient. I am half asleep; my ideas are as dense and foggy as the morning; and one might write as well with Ourika's paw, as with the pen with which I am labouring. Very sincerely yours, G.B.

Ourika was one of the St-Ursins' cats. The Beau, meticulous in observing the traditional civility of writing in a clear and careful hand, liked to pepper his prose with scraps of French and seldom missed an opportunity of hinting how popular he was: 'It is in vain I had promised myself a quiet evening at home, I am really *obsédé* to attend a stupid *soirée*, and without being guilty of a palpable untruth, it is impossible for me to send an excuse. I am compelled, then, to defer the pleasure of writing to you, more diffusely, and more *academically*, till to-morrow morning. Good-night, and happy dreams be with you. Always yours, G.B.'

But there were times, such as Christmas Eve 1831, taking his thoughts back to his adored Duchess of York and the festivities at Oatlands, when he made little attempt to conceal his misery.

My Very Dear Miss Aimable, All the plagues of Egypt, in the shape of visitors, have obtruded themselves upon me this morning, on purpose, I believe, to interrupt my transcribing verses, or otherwise communing in manuscript with you: it is not then my fault, though I dare say you will accuse me of idleness, that I am compelled to be brief in writing to you; but you have promised to take a lesson with me to-morrow morning, Christmas Day! What a period of rejoicing and fête, according to the customs of my native country, this used to be to me, some years since: while now 'Of joys that are past how painful the remembrance!' I am out of humour with myself this morning, and more so with those troublesome people that break in upon my domestic tranquility: I have not, indeed, much to enliven me; but, with all my cares and vexations, you are always a consolation to me.

A consolation, and a pretty shoulder on which he now un-ashamedly bewailed his plight, a sympathetic young creature before whom he was not afraid to remove the mask.

The moment I had begun to write to you yesterday morning, one of my usual time-destroying friends came in, and extended his visit and his idle confabulations till it was too late in the day to pursue my letter. I am this instant out of bed, though I am half asleep, knocked up, and tormented with the headache, and I really feel myself incapable of inditing two rational connected sentences to you. My own venial *amour propre* will not then allow me to scribble nonsense, and I must *enfoncer* my shivering knees into the fire, and my crazy head into the back of my *bergère*, while I commune with my inveterate morning companions, the blue devils,–and be assured, my very dear Miss Aimable, that one of the most prominent and vexatious of these evil spirits is the compunction of having neglected my promised duty to write to you: I believe I am falling into second childhood, for I am in-competent to do anything but to ruminate over the broken toys of my past days.

Outside 47 rue des Carmes he was an entirely different man. Captain Jesse, meeting him for the first time in February 1832 at a party in the Burtons' house in the rue Guilbert, found him 'the most light-hearted person in the room', and immediately identi-fiable by

the polished ease of his address and the extreme neatness of his person. It was quite pleasing to see the graceful manner in which he made his way

through the crowded *salon* up to the lady of the house; the profound bow
with which he saluted appeared to be made thus low as a particular tribute
to her. The presence of his other female friends was duly noticed, and I
could almost fancy that his bow to each was graduated according to the
degree of intimacy that existed between them, that to his *friends* being at an
angle of forty-five degrees, while a common acquaintance was acknowledged
by one of five.

He wore a blue coat and a buff waistcoat with a velvet collar
to the coat and his consular badge in the buttonhole; he had
succumbed, no doubt for reasons of economy, to the modern
fashion of boots and black trousers in the evenings instead of
knee-breeches. He wore his perfectly folded neckcloth without a
pin and had no other jewellery than a heavy gold watch-chain and
an antique ring which he bought in Calais from a man who dug
it up on the site of the Field of the Cloth of Gold. 'An attire
which, being remarkably quiet, could never have attracted
attention on any other person.'

His dress by day was just as simple and unvaried:

a snuff-coloured surtout and a velvet collar a shade darker, and a real cashmere waistcoat made from a shawl which, from the beauty of its quality,
must have cost a hundred guineas. The ground was white and, though the
waistcoat had gone through a French washerwoman's hands for many
winters, it was still in as good a state of preservation as himself, partly owing
perhaps to his coat being invariably buttoned up. Dark blue trowsers, very
pointed boots, the unrivalled white neckcloth, a black hat a little larger at the
crown than the circumference of his head, and primrose kid gloves, com-
pleted his attire. In summer the cashmere waistcoat was exchanged for a
light Valentia one.

Jesse cultivated the Beau's acquaintance and was soon allowed
to call on him and marvel at his morning ritual. He had managed
to preserve unpawned the silver toilet articles that Charles
Greville had noted, including the famous spitting-dish (one of his
widely-quoted pronouncements in the old days was that 'one
simply could not spit in clay'). After he had cleaned his teeth and
shaved, Jesse observed, 'two hours were consumed in ablutions
that would have gained him a reputation for sanctity in a Maho-
medan country'. And although Brummell left the door only a
little open so that they could talk from adjoining rooms, Jesse
had a good view of the proceedings through a glass on the dressing
room mantelpiece.

'I think I see him now standing without his wig in his dressing trowsers before the glass, going through the manual exercise of the flesh brush...When the strigil of pig's bristles was laid aside he looked very much like a man in the scarlet fever.' Having put on a flannel camisole, 'the Beau took a dentist's mirror in one hand and a pair of tweezers in the other and, thus nobly armed, closely scanned his forehead and well-shaven chin, and did not lay them down till he had drawn, with a resolution and perseverance truly extraordinary, and totally regardless of the exquisite pain the removal of each elegant extract must have caused him, every stray hair that could be detected on the surface of his venerable mug!'

Brummell was now very bald and, as Jesse remarked, 'Had he known that I had ever caught a glimpse of him without his wig, he would, I think, have had a fit and cut me the next time we met.' However, he remained unaware that Jesse was peeping and eventually, 'every hair [of his wig] being in the right place, and his hat a little on one side, *bien ganté*, with an umbrella under his arm, his body slightly bent, and his tie reflected in his lucent boots, he proceeded, creeping snail-like, on tiptoe down the street, either to make a morning call, or to kill the interval till dinner by lounging with an acquaintance in the rue St-Jean'.

Because of the changeability of the climate in Caen he usually left his cane at home and carried a brown silk umbrella tucked under his arm, its ivory head carved to represent George IV. He never took off his hat to anybody in the street since 'it would have been difficult to replace it in the same position', and there was the added risk of disturbing his wig–'a catastrophe too dreadful to be wantonly encountered.' In fine weather he acknowledged his friends with a bow, or, if they were on the other side of the street, 'by an extension of his arm and a slight movement of his fingers in the air'. When it was wet the whole of his attention was devoted to negotiating the uneven cobble stones, since there was no pavement. 'So cleverly did he pick his way on the points of his toes, that I have seen him travel the whole length of the street without contracting one speck of dirt on his boots, the *soles* of which, by the bye, he always had polished, as well as the upper leathers.' He insisted on this refinement because he had discovered that he could not otherwise be certain that the servants would properly clean the edges of the soles. He refused to wear anything so unfashionable as overshoes or galoshes except under cover of darkness, and when walking through the rain with a companion would always order him to keep his distance for fear of getting his boots or trousers splashed.

In one respect, however, he was surprisingly unmodish. He became a member of the Themis chapter of the Caen lodge of the Grand Orient of France. There is no record of his having been a Freemason in England–nor, with the exception of the Prince of Wales who conformed with the royal custom, were Alvanley or any others of his close friends. In France it was associated with the Bonapartists and Orleanists whom he as a royalist and legitimist abhorred and despised. In England it was irremediably middle class. Yet here he was, on 19 February 1832, being admitted to the degree of Knight of the Eagle (one of the two higher degrees, the seventeenth and eighteenth, conferred in a Chapter of the Rose-Croix) under the sponsorship of a mere grocer, the now ubiquitous Charles Armstrong. It was enough to shatter White's bow-window. The most likely explanation is that he had found membership of the society helped him to borrow money in Calais and he was now strengthening his position at Caen, having given up hope of the transfer that he had asked Palmerston for, ten months earlier.

If so, he quickly discovered how right he had been; for on 21 March he received a letter which put an end to all plans and hopes:

Sir, HM's Government having had under their consideration the present Consular Establishment of the country with a view to effect therein every practicable reduction, they have come to the conclusion that the Post of British Consul at Caen may be abolished without prejudice to the public service.

In acquainting you with the determination of His Majesty's Govt. to abolish the office of Consul at Caen, I have the satisfaction to express to you my approval of your conduct during the period in which you have executed the Duties of that Office.

Your Consular Functions being at an end, your Salary will cease on the 31 May–and you are at liberty to quit Caen as soon after the receipt of this Despatch as may suit your convenience.

It was signed by Palmerston.

CHAPTER SEVEN

Hôtel D'Angleterre

He had, of course, only himself to blame. Palmerston was a member of a government elected on the promise to retrench and economise. Brummell had put into writing his own conviction that the Caen consulate was not worth maintaining, and he had done so in an official letter applying for leave which would therefore be preserved in the Foreign Office files. However much Palmerston–who was widely blamed by Brummell's friends for harshness to a former acquaintance–may have wished to help, Brummell had made it virtually impossible for him to do so.

Still, there was a bitter careless irony in Palmerston's assurance that he was at liberty to leave Caen as soon as he liked. He could not afford to move; and equally he could not afford to stay. With typical kindness he at once thought of Hayter's predicament as well as his own. When he acknowledged receipt of the letter of dismissal he suggested that, since the Vice-consuls at the Out-Ports were unfamiliar with the preparation and submission of reports and returns, Hayter should be retained as Vice-consul at Caen to collect and collate them and forward them to Paris. 'I cannot speak too favourably of the assiduity, skill and accuracy with which he has executed those services entrusted to him by me.'

Unfortunately, Hayter–or his wife–let the news of Brummell's dismissal become public property almost immediately. Instead of having breathing space until the end of May, the Beau found his creditors flocking round the door just as they had at Calais when word got round that he was leaving. One morning Madame de

St-Ursin appeared with the alarming news that there were bailiffs
at the front door with a warrant for Brummell's arrest. She offered
to let him hide in her bedroom, which under French law the
bailiffs were not allowed to enter, but he gallantly refused to
compromise her. Outwardly unruffled he allowed her to take him
to a spare room where she locked him up in a wardrobe. As she
was leaving the room, his composure deserted him. His voice
was muffled by her dresses but she clearly heard him shouting:
'Madame de St-Ursin! For God's sake take the key!'

The bailiffs, possibly set on him by the restaurateur Longuet
to whom he owed 1200 frances for dinners, were called off. It
was an indication of Brummell's popularity in the town that
many of Longuet's customers, especially the younger ones, threatened that they would cease patronising him unless he gave the
Beau more time to pay. But he had reached a point at which not
even time was of much use to him. 'Dear Armstrong,' he wrote
with the brevity of despair, 'Send me seventy-five francs to pay
my washerwoman; I cannot get a shirt from her, and she is really
starving on my account. I have not actually money to pay my
physician, or for my letters to and from England.'

The need to have a physician willing to treat him was pressing.
Not only was there cholera in the town, killing one in every
three affected (it had broken out in London and other large cities
in Europe in January and by April had caused 20,000 deaths in
Paris), but his own general health was showing the effect of the
continuing strain. And almost as important was the ready cash
for postage to England, for this was the only direction from which
he could expect help. Armstrong's name was by now well known
to Brummell's benefactors as the man who cashed the drafts that
they sent over. They had a great deal more faith in his business
acumen and reliability than the Beau's. When Brummell posted
off a new bagful of begging letters, urging them to send him
money individually and to canvass each other on his behalf, one
of them replied:

I really think that a personal interview of Mr Armstrong with the persons
you have named would do more good than letters. All that I can do to insure
his seeing them I will. I don't know how to get at the Duke of Wellington
or Lord Willoughby. I will write to George Anson and his brother Litch-

field, Bagot, Alvanley, and many others that may occur to me, who I may think can be of any use; and among them, by the way, old Allen, who, I assure you, spoke of you the other day in the kindest manner, and I tried hard to get a pony out of Coventry for you when I was in town. Worcester, I fear, is still ill in the country, otherwise, I am sure he would have been more ready to exert himself than anyone.

It is interesting to see that, whatever may have been the shabby trick that Meyler accused Brummell of having played on Lord Worcester, it was quite forgotten and forgiven now. Of the others mentioned, Lord Willoughby was Peter Burrell, who inherited the barony of Gwydir from his father and that of Willoughby d'Eresby from his mother; the Anson brothers had long been contributing to Brummell's upkeep, and George had recently married Forester's daughter Henrietta; Bagot was no doubt Lady Harriet Villiers's husband; 'King' Allen (nicknamed the Half-Sovereign after he went bankrupt and paid only ten shillings in the pound) was the former gallant Guards officer who loved London so much that when they went to Dover together Alvanley hired a coach to drive up and down outside the inn to lull him to sleep; and Coventry was the former Lord Deerhurst, a lover of Harriette Wilson's sister, Sophia, before her marriage to Lord Berwick.

Alvanley was back in London from France and dined with Kangaroo Cooke at Raikes's house on the last day of May 1832, 'both very amusing and full of anecdotes of former times'. For most of them those former times were becoming rosier in retrospect. The continuing agitation for parliamentary reform was accompanied by an equally alarming demand for better living standards for the lower classes. On 18 June 1832, the anniversary of Waterloo, the Duke of Wellington, 'assailed in the streets by a mob of ruffians who hissed and abused him' as he rode from the Tower to Apsley House, had to accept the indignity of a police escort. The next day at Ascot the King was struck on the forehead by a stone flung by a spectator who, to the great relief of the other racegoers, eventually turned out to be a mere 'half-cracked Greenwich pensioner' with no political convictions. In France Louis-Philippe was faced with two days of bloody fighting in Paris by republicans and an outbreak of civil war in the Vendée in favour of the royalist legitimists.

Meanwhile Brummell was trying to collect his expenses, 286 francs, from the Foreign Office for the journey he had made to Granville. 'As it has pleased His Majesty's Government that my functions as Consul resident at this place should cease, I will take the liberty to represent to you that the insignificant sum I have stated is now of the utmost importance to me.' He also took the liberty to ask for a little more: 'It would be intrusive if not absurd in me to talk of past services in the narrow situation I have held here, yet I am sensible that some trifling approbation might be extended to me for having reduced the charges and defrayments of the Out-Ports attached to it nearly one half during the period I have officiated in comparison with previous years.'

He got nothing, and in early summer persuaded Armstrong to go to England on his behalf. The weather turned unseasonably chilly. One Sunday evening he sat down in a mood of black despondency to write his tutorial letter to Aimable.

Oh, this uncomfortable weather! I am freezing *au coin de mon feu*, and my ideas are as much congealed as my limbs. You must not, then, in common compassion, expect either amusement or instruction from a *malheureux* in my torpid state. There are moments too when I am subject to that sort of overwhelming depression of spirits that makes me incapable of anything but to brood over my own grievances, fancied or intrinsic, it does not signify. I cannot shake off its gloomy influence. I should like to retire to my bed, and, if it was possible, to sleep till the spring, or till nature would beneficently animate my dejected thoughts as she regenerates the leaves and the flowers of the earth. I am at the instant subdued by chillness and blue devils, and feel as if I was in my grave, forsaken and forgotten by all those who were once most dear to me. '*Le plus grand des malheurs est celui de ne tenir à rien, et d'être isolé.*' [The greatest of misfortunes is to care for nothing and to be alone.] I am sick of the world and of existence.

He added a quatrain written years before by Fox's uncle, General Fitzpatrick:

> What'er they promised or profess'd
> In disappointment ends;
> In short, there's nothing I detest
> So much as all my friends.

'You must perceive, that is if you have the patience to read these vague saturnine jeremiades, that—'

He got no further. The quill fell on his writing desk. He tried to get up out of his chair and failed. The right side of his face was sagging and he could not speak intelligibly. Dr John Kelly, called in from the rue des Chanoines, carried out the conventional bleeding and blistering. Brummell believed that he was suffering from a more than usually severe attack of rheumatism and for a few days he was so ill that nobody let him know that he had had a stroke. But by Thursday evening he had recovered sufficiently to write to one of his regular hostesses: 'I have risen today with my head perfectly quiet, my chest and all its vicinity composed, and free from that oppression and those excruciating spasms which I thought, and at one time sacrilegiously prayed, would put an end to my sufferings in this world. Once more, thanks to Heaven and a constitution still unshaken, I am returning to my senses and at peace.'

He busied himself with supporting Hayter's application for the vice-consulship. Hayter wrote to Palmerston, offering to work without pay, if he were allowed to retain the fees that he collected. These he assessed at £40 a year, the same as his half-pay from the navy, together enough to support his wife and their 'large family of very young children' who now numbered seven. It was no doubt these fees that he referred to when he claimed on another occasion that Brummell paid him a 'salary' of £40.

Hayter was given the post on these terms and shortly after-wards Armstrong returned from England with the best of good news: he had collected money from all the people Brummell had suggested–Alvanley, Worcester, Anson and the others–and from Charles Greville, Lord Pembroke, Charles Standish and Lord Burlington, Lady Harriet Granville's uncle. There was enough to pay off almost all of Brummell's debts in Caen and the promise of regular contributions in the future, which would assure him at least £120 a year. This would have lasted him about a fortnight in the old days. On the other hand Sir Robert Peel recently laying plans for his police constabulary had calculated that a single man on a guinea a week should be able to cover his lodgings, medical attendance, very comfortable subsistence at his mess, clothing, 'and save out of his pay ten shillings a week'.

It was at any rate a new beginning. To show his determination to turn over a new leaf, the Beau decided to move. He no longer needed the extensive quarters that he had thought fit to rent from

Madame de St-Ursin when he had the dignity of his consulship to uphold. In September he took up residence in the Hôtel d'Angleterre, paying 1500 francs a year for full board and lodging. Madame de St-Ursin later complained to Captain Jesse that Brummell left owing her money: that during the two years he was at 47 rue des Carmes 'with the exception of six hundred francs, she had never received one louis', and that when he left he did not even say goodbye to her. As she said to Jesse:

I confess to you that I was mortified at such egotism; however, I took no notice of it. Six months after, to my great astonishment, he knocked at my door, and entered the *salon* as if he had seen me only the day before: my reception, however, was not very flattering, for I considered that he had not only been ungrateful, but guilty of a great piece of rudeness, *une impolitesse*. On my telling him this, he appeared greatly distressed, and I was wondering how he would get out of the scrape, when he rose from his chair and, taking my hand, said with great emotion, 'Madame de St-Ursin, I would willingly have wished you good-bye, but I was in tears.'

It sounds as if the devout old lady's memory was at fault. Brummell was unforgivably feckless in money matters, but he took great pains not to impose upon people of moderate means and he tried never to be rude unintentionally.

It was not surprising that he should leave in September, for the second year of his lease ended then. That he did not visit Madame St-Ursin for six months is highly unlikely, since he was writing to Aimable on December 10 in terms which suggest that he had never left off: 'You are wrong in supposing that the presence of M. de St-Quentin, or of any other person, interfered with my promise to write to you. "Heu! quantum minus est cum reliquis versari quam tui meminisse." [Alas! how far the conversation of others falls short of the memory of you.] I have been engaged during the last four days with letters upon business, irksome, indeed, to indite, but which admitted of no delay. So, mistaken Miss Aimable, do not unjustly reproach me with negligence or forgetfulness.'

Madame de St-Ursin's claim that he never paid her more than six hundred frances in rent is quite untrue. Charles Armstrong's accounts of his advances to Brummell show an entry of 2000 francs for 'House Rent' in August 1831, which is evidently a year in advance and six or eight months in arrears. (These accounts were prepared for showing to Brummell's friends in England. In some of the entries there is a discrepancy between what Brummell received and what Armstrong set down. For instance, the 280 francs which Brummell borrowed in the autumn of 1831 is shown as 380. A payment to Longuet, the restaurateur, of 800 francs looks as if it had been 'rounded up'. Similarly the 2000 francs paid to Madame de St-Ursin was probably 1800 since Brummell had almost certainly handed over 600 francs, six months' rent in advance, when he signed the first year's lease in September 1830. But these increases are infrequent and were not used to cheat Brummell, who examined and countersigned the accounts, though they may have been intended to persuade the Beau's benefactors that Armstrong was doing out of pure charity what, as a businessman, he was perfectly entitled to charge for.)

The Hôtel d'Angleterre, on the east side of the rue St-Jean between the rue de l'Engannerie and the rue de la Poste, was a large building, the product of amalgamating two former mansions at Nos. 79 and 81. In the front the upper floors extended over the adjoining shops; at the rear there was a pleasant, tree-shaded garden. The proprietor, Hippolyte Fichet, ran it with the help of his second wife, his son and daughter-in-law by his first marriage, his step-son by his second marriage, three cooks, three floor-waiters, two chambermaids, a linenmaid and two ostlers. Among the permanent residents he already had two British families: the forty-year-old Mrs Emma Harris and her five children, Mr and Mrs George Morton and their two.

Brummell took a set of rooms on the third floor of the north wing, facing the street. He had a small *salon* with a tiny box-room attached, a bedroom with the fireplace that was indispensable to him, and a dressing room. These, with breakfast in his room and *table d'hôte* dinner served in the ground-floor dining room, were quite a bargain at a little over £60 a year. He had bought a large supply of shirts in January and he was right up to date with his quarterly subscription of fifteen francs to the *Salon Littéraire* round the corner in the rue de l'Engannerie. With a pound in his pocket (he had been trying, not entirely successfully, to limit himself to twenty-five francs a month for casual expenses) he was at peace with the world, able to devote his whole attention to the local gossip and *soirées*, his correspondence with various young women to whom he made playful avuncular love, and the events in England which he studied in the newspaper room at the *Salon Littéraire*-that 'sort of Brooks's in a much more magnificent house'.

From home there was news in December of the elections for the reformed Parliament, in which the Tories did badly and the proceedings turned out to be almost as corrupt as in the past but a great deal more expensive since there were more electors to be bribed. Lord Feversham's nephew, Tom Duncombe, a Whig and one of the Beau's younger acolytes in the old days, lost his seat at Hertford, because of the lavish bribes distributed by the Tory, Lord Salisbury. Croker noted that: 'He says it has cost Lord Salisbury £14,000, and that for half the money he would have retired. Folks think that he must join Brummell'.

In January 1833 Delmeé Radcliffe died, the quiet little man who had been the best gentleman-jockey in England and latterly in charge of George IV's racing stables. He had been at Eton with Brummell and had never changed his style of dress since–'single-breasted coat, long breeches, and short white-topped boots'. In February it was the turn of Lord John Townshend, a star of the far-off brilliant evenings at Devonshire House. In March Lord Dudley, who had talked so much to his horses and so little to the King on Brummell's behalf, said his final words in the asylum at Norwood to which he had been committed 'under the super-intendence' of a keeper just twelve months before. And in April the generous Lord Foley who had contributed to Brummell's fund for Beckford and so many other worthy causes, died leaving eight children and such impressive debts that the ancestral estates had to be sold to meet them.

Finally, in August, to everybody's surprise, it turned out to be not Tom Duncombe but Tom Raikes, that highly respectable businessman, who found himself in such financial difficulties that he had to retire for several years to Paris, whence he continued to have a solicitous eye on Brummell's welfare. Fortunately Alvanley still kept his head above water in England where he was now playing a more prominent part in the House of Lords, though without neglecting his reputation as a wag. In February that year his friend Jekyll reported that he had 'dined with some grandee whose mansion had recently been fitted up in great splendour, but the dinner was scanty. Alvanley said more carving and less gilding would have been preferable.'

While Alvanley's witticisms remained commendably terse, Brummell's were becoming more and more ponderous–at any rate in the arch notes that he sent to the young women he pretended to have fallen in love with:

During those years that I have vegetated upon the barren moor of my later life, I have sedulously avoided running my crazy head into what may be termed inconsequent distractions; and now, in spite of all my theoretical circumspection and security, I find myself over head and ears, heart and soul, in love with you. I cannot for the life of me help telling you so; but, as all considerate reason has not at times utterly abandoned me, I shall put myself into a strait-waistcoat, and be chained to the bedpost.

Perhaps, after having undergone such compulsatory infliction, and the bereavement of at least half the blood in my veins, I may be restored to my more cool and sedate senses. I shall then turn Anchorite and flee away to the desert. Adieu! I have yet sufficient command over my drooping faculties to restrain any tributary tears from falling over my farewell; you might doubt their reality; and we all know that they may be counterfeited upon paper with a sponge and *rose*-water!

At Christmas he sparkled into a profusion of frenchified English: 'It is the hallowed fête of Christmas, nativity, mince-pies, mistletoe, wind, gentle evergreens, and *étrennes*. Sanction the latter *offrande* with your habitual Christian amenity, and *comblez* the charitable feeling by the recompense of one of those halcyon *billets de reconnaissance* that you know so well to write. I solicit you to prostrate it *aux pieds de Mademoiselle* **** *en boudoir*, as I should not like to hear that she blushed at its insignificance *en société*.' But this was still the season when he most remembered Oatlands and little Princess Fred; he was soon back to

My fire is going to give up the ghost in sighs of smoke from suffocation, and my wayward fancies are congealed by the severity of the breeze that moans upon entrance under my door–I am as cold as the dormouse without a home–my regard for you all may be said to be, just now, as pure but inanimate as the falling snow, and my best friends, in good faith and fair truth, seem to be frozen at the bottom of the well. When addressing you, *c'est toujours un dégel de coeur*, but at this instant my torpid hand and faculties refuse to answer to the grateful summons of more deserved eulogy, and, in timely silence, *sans complimens*, I will bid you good-morrow, peace and welfare, and redeeming thaw to myself...P.S. Madame de Rigny announces a *bal paré* on the 31st. I must elapse from my *sabots* upon the occasion, and *galope* with the rest.

Madame de Rigny, one of Caen's most lavish hostesses, was married to the Chief Collector of Taxes of the department, who was in turn the brother of Count Henri de Rigny, Minister of Marine in Louis-Philippe's Cabinet. Their very large house in the rue St-Jean, the Hôtel du Grand-Manoir, had formerly belonged to Charlotte Corday's aunt, Madame de Bretteville and it was from here that Charlotte had set out to murder Marat forty years before. Because of her husband's official position Madame de Rigny's guests were drawn from all political factions. Brummell, on the other hand, since the loss of his consulship had relieved him of any obligation to be polite to the ruling party, was consorting more and more exclusively with the Legitimists–Carlists, as they called themselves, since they recognised only Charles X as the rightful King of France, even though his last official act had been to abdicate in favour of his grandson, Henri V.

The Carlists of Caen were delighted to receive support from one who had walked so intimately with a King of England, and overjoyed when he refused an invitation to the ball given in honour of Louis-Philippe, who stayed in the city on his way to Cherbourg in September 1833. The Orleanists claimed afterwards that Brummell refused because he had not been invited to the dinner that preceded the ball. The Beau himself, when questioned next day, answered with all his old languid air of astonishment: 'The King? What King?' The French King, he was told–Louis-Philippe. 'Oh–the Duke of Orleans, you mean? No, I did not go, but I sent my servant.'

If he had indeed sent his servant, the man might have received a cordial welcome, for the King was going to extremes in an attempt to court popularity. To the accompaniment of loud but outraged laughter from the notabilities he had tickets for state balls distributed to the ten legions of the Paris National Guard, drawn from tradesmen and the lower middle class. At a ball at the Tuileries in November, 'a lady happened to complain that her shoe pinched her, when her partner immediately presented his card as Bootmaker to the King and offered to wait upon her the

Above Mrs Fitzherbert: miniature by Conway

Below Queen Caroline, wife of George IV, from
a portrait by Sir Thomas Lawrence

Above A banquet
in the Royal
Pavilion

Your Lordships' consideration often, should a vacancy occur in the Consular establishment at any of the other Ports of the country, and particularly at that of Calais, where I resided during so many years of the latter part of my life. I may represent to Your Lordship that which might, perhaps, be prejudicial to my own individual interest; but with every zealous anxiety to make myself of use in preserving Your Lordship's protection and the only Means which enable me to exist, I will beg unreservedly to state the almost total inutility of the appointment of a Consul at this place, and that the situation might be abolished altogether without any probable detriment to His Majesty's Service.

My Lord,
I have the honor to be
Your Lordships' most devoted
and very faithful humble Servant
George Brummell.

Right Extract
from Brummell's
letter to Palmerston

The broken Beau–Bow!

The Broken Beau–Bow: sketch by Brummell

very Sincerely Yours
George Brummell.

Brummell walking in Caen

next morning'. And when Lord Yarmouth called on his coach-maker to have his carriage prepared for a similar function a few weeks later, the man remarked, 'That puts me in mind that I am also invited, and I must get my own carriage ready likewise.'

Brummell naturally felt compelled to support the Carlists, an odd but colourful lot, ranging from the comparatively youthful Henri de Vauquelin, Henri de St-Marie and the comte de Chazot, to the octogenarian countess 'who took quantities of snuff, occasionally dimmed the shining *parquet* with an expectoration' and ceaselessly lamented the passing of the *ancien régime*: 'Oh, how dismal our drawing rooms are these days! I don't understand it at all. When I was young, a woman had her friends and her husband his; each amused themselves in their own way. But now you always see married couples together!–it's true, I assure you. Oh, these dreadful modern customs!'

Brummell would often visit her to play five-sous whist into the early hours, as he did for instance on 2 January 1834. 'Improvident pursuit!' he wrote to one of his corresponding matrons the following morning. 'She made half-closed eyes at me, instead of attending to the game: this afflicted me afterwards with a relative *cauchemar*–I fancied, in the dream, I was struggling with my Aunt Margaret's ghost–I am still *dormant*, and only just able to whisper to you how Sincerely I am yours, G.B.'

A further consequence of the loss of his official position was that the Beau no longer had to pat dirty-nosed children on the head or be pleasant to their plebeian parents, 'How can such people be received?' he would wonder out loud at somebody else's party. 'It is deplorable to be in such society!' Even his Legitimist friends did not escape: after one of them had given a dinner with expensive food brought in from the remote regions of France, somebody asked Brummell how the feast had gone off. 'Don't ask me, my good fellow,' he replied, 'but, poor man, he did his best.'

Those who rashly tried to force their company on him got short shrift. One day when he was walking with a friend he heard a voice call, 'Good evening, Mr Brummell!' On a balcony above them was an Englishwoman, a doctor's wife and zealous social climber whom he knew by sight and heartily disliked. 'Now won't you come up and take tea?' she said. He stared at her in horrified astonishment. 'Madam,' he finally answered 'you take medicine, you take a walk, you take a liberty, but you *drink* tea!' He bowed and paced on.

Early in 1834 Brummell involved himself in a dispute which soon affected almost the whole of the British colony and a great many French residents as well. Mr Hayter, the vice-consul, finding that his fees and naval half-pay were not enough to support a growing family, asked to be paid a regular salary of £100 a year. The Foreign Office turned down his request and he decided to emigrate to Canada where the authorities were offering free grants of land to ex-officers. As soon as Charles Armstrong heard of this, he resolved to apply for the vacant vice-consulship, and asked Brummell to approach Lord Palmerston on his behalf. This the Beau did on 30 January 1834, assuring the Foreign Secretary that 'from having had the honour to hold the employment of British Consul at this place and from my general acquaintance of every thing and person it contains' he could vouch for Armstrong as 'a person universally esteemed by the French residents of the Town and by the English inhabitants, whose interests he is invariably anxious to serve. He has no desire to derive any emolument from the official duties he would undertake. Should other attestations be necessary as to his adequate qualities to fulfil the duties of the charge, I could add the favourable suffrage of almost every respectable inhabitant of this place.'

Armed with this recommendation Armstrong left for London, halting at Paris on his way to canvass the consul-general and the ambassador. There he learned, to his affected surprise, that he should have addressed himself to Archibald Gordon, the British consul at Le Havre, from whom the Caen post depended since Brummell's dismissal. (In his letter to Palmerston, Brummell had disingenuously pretended to be 'ignorant whether the appointment in question is or is not within the nomination of Mr Gordon', but it is reasonably certain that both of them knew that it was—and that Armstrong did not apply to Gordon because he had reason to believe that he would be turned down.) Armstrong sent word to Brummell of his cool reception in Paris, posted an official application to Gordon at Le Havre, and continued on his way to London.

Brummell at once wrote to Alvanley, asking him to support
Armstrong, while one of his fellow guests at the Hôtel d'Angleterre, the noisy, energetic George Morton, organised a testimonial
on Armstrong's behalf, with Brummell's signature leading that of
a score of British residents. Morton at fifty-three was only three
years junior to the Beau, but he was a businessman of extreme
activity and persistence (he had applied, too late, for the vice-
consulship when Brummell was discharged) and within a short
time collected upwards of thirty signatures from French residents,
headed by the prefect, the mayor and four members of the
Tribunal de Commerce, the banker Bellamy and the comte de
Chazot. This he sent off to Gordon. Gordon, meanwhile, on
receiving Armstrong's letter from Paris, wrote to Palmerston
recommending 'Mr Watts, who has been named to me as a
gentleman in every way fit and proper to hold the situation.'

Palmerston now came under a barrage from the rival camps
at home and abroad. Alvanley, writing from Albemarle Street on
11 February, supported Armstrong's application because 'he has
been most extremely kind to poor Brummell in the melancholy
situation to which he is reduced, has treated him like a brother
and indeed saved his life by his attention to him. Brummell is
very anxious about him and if you would give him the appointment if possible or recommend him for it to the Consul at Havre
you would do me a most sensible favour.'

A week later Gordon wrote to Palmerston referring to his
earlier letter and to the application and massive testimonial on
behalf of 'Mr Armstrong, Grocer', which he had hitherto sup-
pressed but now admitted had been delivered to him 'a few days
since by Mr Armstrong's shopman' but which he 'declined for-
warding to your Lordship' because Armstrong was already the
United States vice-consul and (apparently despite, and not in
consequence of, that) 'I have been told that he cannot write a
letter.' He also enclosed a recommendation from Hayter in
favour of Watts. Why Gordon preferred Watts is not clear, but
Morton, who immediately on having the testimonials rejected at
Le Havre readdressed them to Palmerston, made no bones about
Hayter's preference for Watts: not only were they both retired
naval lieutenants but also 'in the event of Mr Watts' success it is

understood he is to become the purchaser of Mr Hayter's house and furniture'.

By 18 February Armstrong was in London and the next morning Alvanley sent him round to the Foreign Office with yet more letters of recommendation and a note to John Bidwell: 'I wish that you would speak to Palmerston and, if he agrees to nominate him, get his commission signed as soon as you can, as he is anxious to get back.' Palmerston agreed to see Armstrong the next day. After that interview Bidwell told him he would receive the appointment. He returned in triumph to Caen, only to receive a day or two later a letter from Bidwell asking him to supply Lord Palmerston with references as to his character.

This ominous and entirely unexpected turn spread gloom along the length of the rue St-Jean from Armstrong's grocery store to the Hôtel d'Angleterre, joy in Le Havre and at No. 4 Venelle Manissier where Hayter and Watts resumed their bargaining over the furniture, and profound indignation at No. 2 Albemarle Street: 'I find by a letter from Mr Armstrong at Caen,' Alvanley wrote to Bidwell, 'that there is a hitch as to his appointment and that, notwithstanding the testimonials sent, Mr Watts is likely to get the place. As Palmerston promised it to me after I had seen you and as I have not been informed of any reasons why he should have changed his intention I must think myself very ill-used if such is the case. Before, however, writing to him on the subject perhaps you will be good enough to let me know how the matter at present really stands.'

Bidwell already knew the answer. When Palmerston told him on 27 February to pursue Armstrong with a request for references, he sent back a memo to his master pointing out that Armstrong had already provided them and, what was more, had been told on Palmerston's authority that he had got the job. Palmerston sent Bidwell's note back three days later with the scribbled comment, 'My object in directing a letter to be written to Mr Armstrong was to see by his answer whether he is as illiterate as the friends of his competitor represent. How does he appear in this respect?' Quite acceptable, as was proved by the letter he sent from Caen on 9 March; though nobody will ever now know whether he wrote it himself or whether, as Gordon and Watts maintained, he had to have all his correspondence done for him by Morton, who privately admitted that Armstrong 'was not an educated man'. At the beginning of April the consul at Le Havre received instructions from Lord Palmerston that, in consequence of the Foreign Secretary having received 'the strongest testimonial to Mr Armstrong's character and respectability', Mr Gordon was to provide him immediately with 'the necessary commission and guidance'.

It was a famous victory and a remarkable demonstration of the faithful support that Brummell could still call upon after nearly eighteen years of exile. Gordon had been vanquished; Hayter was forgiven. He had served Brummell well (and his country, too–commissioned in 1804, four years a prisoner of war, discarded at the peace he had helped to win). When he in turn went off to London to petition for 'the proportionate grant of land so generously awarded to the Officers of the Navy of my rank' and also help in 'transporting myself and family of Nine' to Canada, he carried with him yet another testimonial from the British residents of Caen, with Brummell's signature again at the head.

The two months' campaign had provided the Beau with more excitement than he had experienced for a long time past. One day towards the end of April he entered the dining-room of the Hôtel d'Angleterre, took his usual seat at the table, raised his spoon to his lips and had the extraordinary sensation that the soup was running not down his throat but down the outside of his chin. He dabbed his face with his napkin and, sure enough, found that it was soup-stained. Holding the napkin up as a shield, he rose, strolled into the next room, and examined his face in the glass. One corner of his mouth was dragged up towards his ear. He had had a second stroke. He walked across the courtyard to the staircase of the former No. 79, went up the three floors to his apartment, and then sent for Dr Kelly. It was more than a week before he could be pronounced out of danger.

He spent his convalescence writing to his young lady admirers and drawing.

The sketch is from memory: it is a resemblance of a very amiable person who is now no more–of Georgiana, Lady Worcester. [Georgiana

Fitzroy, whom he had been wooing in 1813. She died in 1821 and it was probably a tress of her hair that was found after Brummell's death in an envelope on which he had written 'Lady W——, *la femme la plus coquette du monde.*' The sketch was almost certainly not from memory but from a portrait that he had kept.] In former days I drew a miniature of her, which Worcester now has, and the traits are still fresh in my remembrance. It is the first thing I have attempted since my resurrection; for you must know that I have been in the other world, and I can assure you I found it no paradise.

It seems that I have recently been in a state of absence, or aberration of mind, and utterly unconscious of it till this morning, when, upon my interrogating him–I mean one of my doctors–he told me that when he came to me eight days ago I was in a high fever, and that during three days and nights I had frequently asked absurd questions, and talked to him in a *distrait* and unconnected manner: in short, that I was wandering in my senses, and 'babbling about green fields and butterflies'. I recollect nothing but their having deprived me almost of daily bread, and my making resistance and wry faces at lancets and lenitives. As I do not like to be regarded as a confirmed lunatic, pray keep this a secret.

It was a hesitant recovery. He was allowed downstairs to dine at the *table d'hôte* but almost immediately ordered back to his room again, and remained there for another four days until permitted to go into the town to dine with Henri de Vauquelin. 'I am unwell,' he confessed. 'I had flattered myself that I was progressing towards my ancient regular health; and now those who look after me professionally will insist upon it that my lungs are seriously affected, and pester me with all the alarming hyperbole of their vocation, upon my malady. They are weaving a shroud about me; still, I trust I shall yet escape.'

And a new ray of hope had come to cheer his sick-room:

It has lately been intimated to me, that I must be prepared to leave Caen; this is from the Government in England; how soon, I know not. I am ignorant also of my destination–that will depend upon, and be dictated by, those in power, who have still the kind consideration to think of me and my broken fortunes. For years, I have cherished the wish to go to Italy; and if what I have solicited in my answer should be accorded to me, I shall take up my wallet and my staff, and seek the suspicious heaven of that country and climate. This is no fairy dream!

But there is a strong possibility that it may have been. There is no such message in the Foreign Office files, nor any trace of the letter from the British ambassador in Paris to which he referred a few days later: 'I have had a letter from Granville...and he tells me there is no vacancy in Italy or elsewhere at present, excepting the one *which he recommends me to refuse*, and which I was ordered to prepare for, ten days since, and I have declined it.' His continuing ill-health may have caused him to imagine the whole episode. 'I am much afraid I wrote some sad nonsense to you on Saturday night. I had been in pain during the day, and had recourse to that deranging drug, at least for the senses, laudanum.'

In July he borrowed the latest novel by J. J. Morier, brother of the Consul-General and famous for his *Adventures of Hajji Baba*: 'Millions of thanks to you for *Ayesha*. I have not quite finished with her; for I cannot now read, nor write, nor do anything in a methodical way.' And again, one Saturday evening in August: 'My existence here has become perfectly dreary, insipid, and unprofitable: I scarcely see anyone, speak to anyone [most of Caen genteel society was spending the summer months by the sea at Luc-sur-Mer]; and I find myself so miserably *abattu* and *distrait* that I am incapable of passing away the lingering hours in those occupations which used to be my resource and my amusement.'

He enclosed a copy of his verses on *The Butterfly's Funeral* and ended, 'I could go on writing all night, but my perverse lamp is getting sleepy and closing its eyes. It will leave me in the dark, as you did, *par parenthèse*, by the abrupt and ungenerous termination of your last amiable note to me. Good night, good night; unfading welfare and happiness be constantly with you, and may you dream of butterflies. Eternally yours, G.B.' A day or two later he was happy again, for Chazot had invited him down to his house just outside Luc and a mile or so north of the ancient pilgrimage centre of La Délivrande.

He accepted with enthusiasm because, he said, 'I detest that vile caravanserai of Colignon's'–the principal hotel at Luc which was crowded during the summer with visitors in search of fresh oysters and sea-bathing. His real reason was that he could not afford to stay there. Although Armstrong had for some time exercised control over his income, there was a good deal of Brummell's expenditure that the grocer could not supervise, and could not be expected to, despite a touching note from Alvanley which accompanied a cheque and said simply: 'I beg that you will protect and assist poor Brummell, and rely on my making it good to you.' The trouble was that, as long as poor Brummell was protected, his credit in the town remained good. He scarcely had to move a score of paces up or down the rue St-Jean to find himself inside the most fashionable little shops in Caen–Mullet the boot-maker, Mancel, 'that ourang-outang of a bookseller' who was always getting him the wrong novels from Paris, Cayoc the pastrycook, a constant temptation to his sweet tooth, Magron the *marchand de nouveautés* from whom he bought occasional little thank-you presents for his hostesses, such as the mother-of-pearl paper knife for the mother of one of his young correspondents named Pearl.

So that when Armstrong was called to London in the summer of 1834 (to testify before the House of Lords to the death of Lord Muskerry in Caen some years earlier) he carried with him yet another desperate appeal from Brummell:

My Dear Alvanley,
   I have examined Armstrong's account of expenditure and receipts for me during the last twelve months, and find it in every respect accurate and just. I have delivered to him the halves of the Bank of England notes; but, alas! my dear fellow, this will provide but in a trifling degree for the liquidation of what I owe for my humble support during the last year. [He owed six months' board and lodging at the Hôtel d'Angleterre and was overdrawn with Armstrong by nearly 2000 francs.] I am suffering from a most severe and apparently fixed rheumatism in my leg [the effect of his two strokes], and I am in dread lest I should be compelled to have recourse to crutches for the rest of my ill-starred days. My old friend, King Allen, promised, at least it was so represented to me, to send me some habiliments for my body, denuded like a new-born infant–and what a Beau I once was! Ever most truly yours, George Brummell.

What a beau indeed he once had been! The greatest, and (despite the recent rise of Count d'Orsay) still the most famous–decaying in a small French provincial town, in late middle age, and in near-penury. Armstrong had given him half-a-dozen shirts a short time before; now he was begging second-hand clothes from his friends; for many months he had bought nothing but twelve pairs of silk socks for sixty francs and four pairs of drawers for half that sum.

It was partly from the need to conserve the remains of his

evening dress, as well as from melancholy, that he accepted fewer invitations to soirées in the town that winter. Yet cheerfulness kept breaking in, as on one occasion when he was playing *écarté* (a game with a family resemblance to euchre and nap, in which two players draw hands of five cards) with a spinster of uncertain age. When she 'proposed', he answered 'yes, dearest', to the amusement of the bystanders. The lady professed to be insulted and next day he sent his hostess a set of unkind verses on the subject.

To Miss Pawlter.

I called you 'dearest,' dire offence!
　　'Twas only said in jest;
For 'dearest,' in its common sense,
　　Means her one loves the best.

But jealous of your virgin fame,
　　And squeamish in a crowd,
With prim reproach, you scoff'd the name,
　　Because–'twas said aloud.

Ah! many a year has run its race,
　　And many a lover too,
Since blush of youth adorn'd that face,
　　And flattering words were true.

Thought you that I, grown old in guile,
　　With faded looks was taken;
And sought to gain a treacherous smile.
　　By others long forsaken?

No, no, 't would reason's self abuse,
　　Immaculate Miss Pawlter,
With you to weave a tender noose–
　　That noose would be a halter!

Good night! but since a thoughtless joke,
　　An idle fib, could fret you,
Believe me, if the truth I spoke,
　　You'd curse the hour I met you!

In Paris the English exiles, voluntary and involuntary, were enjoying themselves in their several ways. Tom Raikes was congratulating himself that 'the climate is better, the living is

cheaper, and you may regulate your expenses on any scale you
please without remark or reference to your neighbours'. Lord
Rokeby, a younger dandy, friend of both Raikes and Alvanley,
and untiring hoaxer, was delighting the aristocratic ladies of the
Faubourg St-Germain, and appalling the British ambassador, with
stories that William IV had gone off his head like his father and
ordered the Guards to take Windsor by storm and with the
rigours of war, looting the castle and raping all its female occupants with the exception of the Queen and her lady-in-waiting.
Rokeby's friends found it a huge joke–and the French newspapers
printed it as a fact.

The news from London was all of sadness and the passing of
friends. Payne Knight, 'the scholar, sensualist and sceptic' who
left the great collection of medals, drawings and bronzes in his
house in Soho Square to the British Museum; Lord Burlington, a
recent contributor to Brummell's funds; the hospitable Michael
Angelo Taylor who was said to have kept the whole of the Whig
Party fed on turbot and lobster sauce at his house in Whitehall;
the witty erudite William Spencer. And some time late in 1834
Brummell seems to have had a third but milder stroke.

As the cold weather settled in, he put out more crumbs for the
birds on his window-ledge and achieved his ambition of training
the mouse that lived behind the wainscot to climb up his trouser-
leg on to the table and eat out of his hand. He still unavailingly
shouted 'Rascals! Scoundrels!' at the brutal Normans maltreating
their horses in the street; and even his cherished Miss Aimable
was sharply reproved if he found her wanting in consideration for
her two cats and the parrot. 'You have recently made such a rapid
progress in the English language, at least in writing it, that I
do not think a partial relaxation from your daily task would be
detrimental to this branch of your instruction,' he wrote to her
when he was still staying at the house in the rue des Carmes.

To improve the head it is not necessary to neglect the natural dictates of the
heart; and I will beg to observe, that for many days and nights there has not
been any fresh straw in the basket-bed of the two cats, Ourika and her *élève*
Angolina. You are comfortably couched, and dreaming probably of butterflies, or of the Château de Ham, while these poor animals are waiting, half
frozen, my return home, to let them into a warmer place of rest. I cannot
resist their mewing supplications, though I have latterly taken care to close

the door, for fear their aide-de-camp Tigre, [a neighbour's tom-cat] might also get in and *houspiller* [overturn] Jacko's cage. I would rather preserve my feelings for humanity and tenderness for these mute domestic creatures, than acquire all the languages in the world! Yours, out of temper, G.B.

He could keep no pets at the Hôtel d'Angleterre, apart from the birds on his window sill and the mouse that breakfasted with him–and even that was slain by a floor-waiter who came in when it was running about the room one day and threw a boot-jack at it. He still worried about the dog he had been forced to leave at Calais, and in January 1835 wrote in French to François Sélègue, his former valet: 'Tell the washerwoman that I will have her sent money through you for Mouton's board and lodging as soon as I get it; and tell her to continue looking after the poor animal. If things go badly for Monsieur Leleux [his former landlord] and he has to get rid of the house, try to get hold of Loro the parrot and keep it for me.'

Then a reference to his continuing dream: 'I hear there is a rumour that Mr Marshall is thinking of leaving Calais, having been offered a better consulate. If you hear anything positive about this, let me know at once.' And his continuing nightmare: 'Monsieur Dalbert, of Paris, writes me that he has a promissory note for 380 francs signed by me and due on the 18th, which will be presented to me here. Tell Valobra that I left with him a little gold box with enamel medallions, whose sale should have covered this claim, and that I will not meet the note in question until I know what has happened to that box and the other in papier mâché that I gave him as a pattern.'

This was evidently the gold snuff-box that he brought with him to Caen from Paris (and, with his usual exaggeration, claimed to have paid £100 for). It was not the fault of Valobra, in Calais, Dalbert had already been paid 450 francs (the transaction appears in Armstrong's books). But everything was becoming jumbled in his mind and he was conscious only of the fact that he was deeply in dept–for, despite the deed of assignment on his salary, when Brummell lost his appointment he owed the Calais banker Leveux more than when he began.

It was a gloomy opening to the year, with a bitter east wind continuing through into April, and made more miserable for

Brummell because his favourite correspondent (her name was Ellen and she was probably one of the Villiers daughters) had left in March for a visit to England. 'The days are short and dense, and they will be more gloomy when you are away,' he told her. '*Farewell*, my *protégée*. May Heaven, in its kindest mercy, make you happy!'

He provided her with letters of introduction to 'two of my oldest friends, high in their office at Court' and to 'some of those exalted female *coryphées* who still control what is termed the fashionable world. ... In this remote place I am apparently sequestered and estranged from those with whom my former life was intimately connected; but I am neither forgotten nor neglected by them. Should you enter into society, let it be confined to the best part; no other is worthy of the most distant *connaissance*; and to the best alone would I venture to recommend you.... My nerves are too shattered, and my rheumatism too inveterate, to enable me to call and take leave.'

He nearly lost the closest, most loyal and most valuable of his friends at the beginning of May. Alvanley in the House of Lords suggested that Lord Melbourne had come to a dishonourable agreement with the 'Liberator' Daniel O'Connell on the Irish Catholic question. Melbourne denied it and O'Connell denounced Alvanley in the Commons as a 'bloated buffoon.' Whereupon Alvanley sent George Dawson-Damer to O'Connell with a challenge to a duel. O'Connell refused and Alvanley threatened to horsewhip him. At this O'Connell's son Morgan picked up the challenge and the two men met on Wimbledon Common on Monday 4 May. After each man had fired three shots without result their seconds called off the engagement.

'What a clumsy fellow O'Connell must be,' Alvanley said to Dawson-Damer in the hackney coach on their way home, 'to miss such a fat fellow as I am!' When they stopped at his door he produced a sovereign from his pocket. 'It's a great deal for only having taken your lordship to Wimbledon,' said the delighted driver. 'No, my good man,' said Alvanley, 'I give it to you not for taking me but for bringing me back.'

Brummell too had taken a ride in a hackney coach that day, but with far less happy results. It was early morning, and he was still asleep, when a noise in his sitting-room roused him. Immediately afterwards his bedroom door was flung open and a bailiff entered with two policemen. The bailiff presented a writ for 15,000 francs (£625) on behalf of Monsieur Leveux and informed Brummell that he must either pay or go to prison.

Brummell stared at him, bewildered and on the verge of tears. The bailiff ordered him to get dressed. Brummell asked that they should leave the room while he did so but the bailiff did not intend to be tricked by this elderly, rheumatic desperado. For the first time since his schooldays, the Beau put on his jacket and trousers in a great hurry and without washing.

He sent the floor-waiter to warn Armstrong and others of his friends of what had happened and, realising there was no hope that they could raise so large a sum at short notice, asked the landlord to summon a cab so that he might go to prison in privacy. After confiding his personal papers to Madame Fichet, the landlord's wife, he allowed the bailiff to lead him down the stairs to the waiting *fiacre*. They set off northwards up the rue St-Jean, over the bridge and left along the rue St-Pierre to the place Fontette and the great gaunt goal.

There he was locked into a stone-floored cell with three criminals. There was no furniture except three plank beds for the existing occupants. After a while somebody brought him a chair.

CHAPTER EIGHT

Straw and Bran Bread, My Good Fellow!

In Prison, 5th May, 1835

I still breathe, though I am not of the living–the state of utter abstraction in which I have been during the last thirty hours yet clouds my every sense. I have just received your note–may Heaven bless you all for your good devotedness in remembering me at such a moment.

His friends, both English and French, had rallied to him immediately they heard the news, the women sending notes of commiseration, the men coming in person. When the first of these entered the cell Brummell threw himself into his arms and sobbed: 'Imagine a position more wretched than mine!–they have put me with all the *common* people! I am surrounded by the greatest villains and have nothing but prison fare.' Though they could do little about the debt for which he was imprisoned (its total now swollen by claims from his creditors in Caen), they were prepared to raise enough money to get him put into a private room. But the prison–which, besides debtors and political offenders, held short-term criminals on their way to the galleys or the gallows or the central prison at Beaulieu–was overcrowded. The best that could be done was to allow him to sleep in a disused corridor on an upper floor and to share a room during the day with a political prisoner, Charles Godefroy. Godefroy, a thirty-eight-year-old bachelor, the son of a goldsmith, made an excellent companion for Brummell. His post was that of managing-editor of *L'Ami de la Vérité* and he was currently serving a sentence of three years for publishing articles attacking Louis-

Philippe and supporting the Legitimist pretender Henri V. It was Godefroy's kindness and tolerance that saved Brummell's reason in the months that followed.

His friends applied for his transfer to the local hospital on the strength of a certificate from Dr Kelly. Buoyed up by this hope he wrote a week after his arrest: 'The kindness of every human being within the sphere of my acquaintance in this town has by degrees restored me to equanimity. How shall I be able to repay you for this benevolence? I am, I believe, this evening to be transferred from my present den of thieves to the towers of Matilda, and to the sainted arms of *les soeurs de Charité*. There I shall again breathe fresh air, and be comparatively in peace. I cannot describe to you what I have suffered *here*.' Next day he wrote again, 'I try to slumber upon the hope of removal to a more salubrious atmosphere and humanized intercourse on Monday, *à l'Hôpital*'.

On the following Sunday, in a letter to Mrs Burton, he was still optimistic:

On the evening of this sacred day it was my authorized custom to sit around your fire, and endeavour to requite your welcome by making you laugh at my nonsense. Most heartily I pray that those happy periods may come again, though I scarcely dare look into future destiny. I try to dissipate the sinister troop of blue devils that haunt me, with the hope that I may be allowed to be transmigrated, the early part of the week, from this den of thieves to the pure atmosphere *de l'Hôpital*, and to the more delightful intercourse of the *soeurs de Charité*, instead of the contamination and blasphemy of the felons that surround me. I am wretched here. I cannot describe the nausea of my sensations when I descend in the morning from my cell, and, from the grate of the window, see miserable outcasts dancing and singing in chains, with every apparent gaiety of spirit.

But during the next week he learned that he must stay in the prison.

It was the food, as well as the '*common* people', that most upset him when he arrived. Armstrong arranged for dinner to be sent in from the Hôtel d'Angleterre, but by the first Saturday Brummell was bitterly complaining of the quality and, since he soon recovered his enormous appetite, of the quantity of the dishes that the Fichet family provided:

In spite of all my friends have said to them in expostulation of the shameful pitifulness of the morsel they send to me by way of dinner, they get daily more meagre and miserable, and it is really not sufficient for the poor cat that keeps me company, neither does it arrive before half-past six, *malgré* your orders to them. I cannot help telling you what was the banquet yesterday despatched to me.

One solitary chop, about the size of an *écu*, enveloped in a quire of greasy paper, and the skeleton of a pigeon, a bird I could never fancy. I must not omit to mention the accompaniment of *half* a dozen potatoes. Such was my meal of yesterday evening, after a fast of twelve hours. It is not, I am certain, the fault of the son, but the *ladrerie* [stinginess] of the *père et mère*, with which I have been so long acquainted.

One of the English familes provided a solution for part of the problem by sending a servant to collect the meal from the Hôtel d'Angleterre and deliver it to the prison gate at not later than five-thirty each day, and Armstrong had a stern word or two with the Fichets. On Monday Brummell wrote to him, 'Many thanks for your unremitting kindness in improving the quality of my humble repast. To your good offices, I had yesterday the satisfaction of being indebted for a sufficient, though homely, dinner.'

He was bouncing back in fine style, determined that loss of his liberty should not entail a lowering of his standards. Almost more important to him than food was cleanliness. 'Henri de Ste-Marie told me yesterday you had sent me a bottle of *Esprit de Savon.—I have never received it*,' he wrote to Armstrong within the first week; and two days later: 'I have sent to you two *serviettes*, which I had neglected, belonging to the Hôtel d'Angleterre; they are the last remaining in my possession from that quarter. You will much oblige me by sending to me *to-day* three towels for my toilette; and the same number every six days, for I cannot procure even a clout to rub myself down in this nauseous place.' Then, after instructions about the furniture he had left at the hotel: '*Let the large basin and water-jug be taken great care of.*' These he eventually managed to have brought to the charitable Godefroy's room, with his razors and tweezers and spitting dish, and dressing case packed with lotions. To Godefroy's astonishment 'he shaved every day, and every day he washed every part of his body'.

When he learned that he was not to be transferred to the hospital the Beau engaged a fellow-prisoner, Paul Lépine, to wait on him for a few sous a day. Lépine, a former soldier who was serving three months for a drunken brawl, collected Brummell's dinner from the servant at the gate and also carried up the materials for the Beau's daily bath–'twelve or fifteen litres of water and'–a source of never-ending wonder and shock to Lépine, Godefroy and the entire prison population–'two litres of milk'. With his familiar toiletry around him he could once more devote three hours to the business of washing and dressing, then perhaps some letters writing at Godefroy's table with Godefroy's quill and ink, before strolling into the Cour de la Pistole, where, in common with the other debtors, he received his visitors. There, too, lay the ultimate and inescapable degradation to which imprisonment condemned him–the row of lavatories along one wall, doorless, screenless, mercilessly exposed to the public view.

The Cour de la Pistole was reserved for those prisoners who could afford to pay a fee (formerly a pistole or ten livres) for better accommodation than those who were forced to sleep on straw (*la paille*). Godefroy's room looked out on to the Cour de la Paille and Brummell would often stand at the window, immersed in 'the forbidding study of the human face, not divine but demoniac, which infests the court beneath my window. Groups of these wretches, condemned of Heaven and of earth, attracted by the sun, have been sauntering in their chains within ten paces of me.' Then one of them would growl a threat and send Brummell back into the obscurity of the room where, right through May and into the unusually hot June and July, he insisted on having a fire burning every evening after dinner. Godefroy, now almost bereft of wonderment, watched him crouch in front of it, rubbing his semi-paralysed leg, saying that this alleviated the twinges of what he still insisted on referring to as rheumatism.

From his corridor-bedroom, served by the same stone staircase as Godefroy's cell, he looked out over the Cour de la Pistole and the women's exercise yard, and beyond them the high prison walls and the roofs of the houses in the Quartier St-Martin. Adjoining the walls was a timber-yard which caught fire one night, sending blazing fragments on to the prison roof and bringing prison guards clattering past Brummell's bed on their way to the attics to deal with the flames. He threw on his cloak and followed them, to stand staring out of a window for two hours.

When the fire died down and the warders withdrew, the Beau found himself in pitch darkness and a strange garret. He tripped over his cloak and entangled himself in a line of washing–all of which, now that he was struggling back to a semblance of good humour, gave him the opportunity to joke to Godefroy in the morning that he had very nearly ended up *'comme un vrai Normand'*–a reference to the Normans' reputed fondness for hanging each other on the least pretext.

He continued to give his friends ample scope for acts of charity. 'You are always good and amiable,' he wrote to one of them,

but you will be the best of beings, if you will have the kindness to renew your benefaction *en forme de gâteau*. I can assure you, it is my principal nourishment, for the *mesquin* repast they usually send me from the hotel would not be adequate to sustain even a *demoiselle* lost in love. I may represent an additional claim upon your bounty at this moment; my companion Minette, *la chatte noire*, who is in the straw at my feet, having produced three hungry kittens–her delicate state disdains the unleavened bread of the prison. I have another favourite belonging to my more private apartment: it is a spider about the size of a bee, which I have so far *apprivoisée* [tamed], that it comes regularly to me from its web every morning at seven o'clock to demand its *déjeûner*. You must forgive then my anxiety for the sustenance of these familiar friends, as well as my own; they are, perhaps, the only ones that will soon remain to me.

The cakes came and, from others of his lady friends, wine, pâtés, jelly, sweetmeats and books. Yet he was still 'sadly out of sorts with the world and with myself; no propitious tidings come to me! Nothing cheers me but the occasional sunbeam that looks in upon me from Heaven; when that retires, all is darkness and despondencey. It seems to me a century since I have been in this intolerable bondage; every week that lingers away is a year in the calendar of my life!' A little later he wrote, 'A *month* tomorrow, I have been *here*, in tribulation, in suspense, and, at length, nearly in broken-heartedness; no news has, as yet, arrived to me from England. I cannot bear up against, nor long survive, the prolonged disappointment. My first *presentiment* upon this infamous farce, this insulting calamity, coming abruptly upon me, was that I should never leave these abhorred walls alive; the despondent *prestige* now gains influence upon me, and I shudder even to think of it.'

His impatience was natural but unjust. From the very first day the devoted, energetic Armstrong had been busy in his cause. He asked Brummell for a complete list of his property and his liabilities. There were two boxes, Brummell replied,

the one mahogany with brass ribs, and G.B. on a plate at the top–the other with a glass on the top, covering worked birds drinking out of a vase; it was the labour and gift of the late Duchess of York, and I have a reverence for it–the latter has a leather case, which is either in the cupboard of the *armoire* out of the sitting-room, or in the other recess where you will find my trunks, etc., etc. Pray send me what remains in the drawers of the bedroom–there are some waistcoats, drawers, pantaloons, etc., and in the upper *tiroir* sundry trifling things which I forgot, but which I may have occasion for. The clock, vases, brown candlesticks and in short everything in the room is my own, not omitting the old green velvet arm-chair. There is one insignificant article which I also wish you would transmit to me; it is under the small *commode* in the sitting-room, with a white marble slab on the top (which also belongs to me), and of which I am every evening in want, a *boot-jack* that shuts up.

Enclosed I deliver to you a list of every debt which I owe in this country of France. You will have the goodness to add your own just and excellent claims upon me, and those due to the hotel. Those in the list to whose names I have attached a cross, I am ignorant of the precise amount of their remaining claims upon me; you can easily ascertain them. Beyond these, so help me Heaven, I have not an existing debt, either in my handwriting or by oral promise, in this country.

Having established the extent of the disaster and protected the Beau's property against sequestration, Armstrong organised a collection among the English residents of Caen and informed Lord Granville. The ambassador sent an immediate gift of 400 francs and opened a fund in Paris. It was clear that these two sources would not provide the £800 which Armstrong calculated was the total of the Beau's various debts. He needed help from England and there was only one sure way of getting it. He must go himself–if he could get permission.

He got in touch with George Boyd in London, who had previously sent money to him for Brummell. Boyd wrote to John Bidwell on 11 June 1835:

You are aware, I believe, that poor Brummell, formerly Consul at Caen, is now a prisoner in the Common Gaol of that town at the suit of a Person of the name of Le Veux, a Merchant at Calais. Mr Armstrong, the Vice-Consul at Caen, has very kindly offered to proceed to Calais for the purpose of effecting some arrangement with this Le Veux for his liberation, and from thence coming to this country to communicate the result of his endeavour to Brummell's friends here. Mr Armstrong however is unable to put his kind intentions into execution without leave of absence from the Foreign Office, which if you can procure for him you will greatly oblige me and do an act of kindness to an unfortunate Individual.

Meanwhile in Paris, Lady Granville was acknowledging a contribution to the fund from her brother, the Duke of Devonshire. 'A thousand thanks for poor Mr Brummell. There never was such an act of charity. I am in good heart about the subscription.' After all these years, and with the autocrat cooped up in a French prison, he was still 'Mr Brummell' to Lady Harriet.

And to Charles Armstrong, for that matter, who must on many occasions have regretted that he had such an imperious and persistent cuckoo under his wing. Brummell's complaints about the food from the Hôtel d'Angleterre became so insistent that Armstrong arranged for his dinner to be sent in by another *restaurateur*. This service had scarcely begun to operate, in the first half of June, when the turnkey, who delivered messages when he came off duty, brought him a letter from Brummell:

My dear Armstrong, You would not, I am sensible, like to be imposed upon yourself, nor that I should be famished with hunger in a prison. I am ignorant both of the name and of the residence of the *traiteur*, or rather *traitor*, whom you have employed to purvey my daily meal; he has indeed but one merit, and that is his punctuality at five o'clock. You shall judge yourself of his liberality, and I will neither exaggerate nor extenuate in my report. Yesterday's *portion* was the following:–*half* of the skeleton of a pigeon, which I firmly believe was the *moitié* of a crow, buried in rancid butter, and the solitary wing of an unfed *poulet*, without even the consolatory addenda of its *cuisse*–half-a-dozen potatoes and, by way of excuse for dessert, half-a-score of unripe cherries, accompanied with *one* pitiful biscuit, that looked like a bad halfpenny–this is the positive total of my dinner's calendar.

Nor was it only the food that Armstrong had neglected:

Twice I have beseeched you to send me *three* towels, and to repeat that number every six days. I have been reduced, for the last eight-and-forty hours, to rub myself down with my dirty shirts, and that resource is now at an end, for they are gone to the washerwoman. Will you have the kindness to speak in a peremptory manner to those about you, if it is owing to their negligence I am to suffer these privations. I only ask for wholesome sustenance for my body, and salutary cleanliness for its outside. It is impossible to find these necessaries within this hell upon earth; and with all my dejection, I should be loath to give up the ghost from famine or filthiness. Amend these indispensable wants before you leave the town *this* evening.

Gaol-bird or not, this is the unmistakable accent of Captain Brummell at the end of his patience with Trooper Armstrong. Throughout his life he had insisted on the maintenance of certain standards by other people as well as by himself; he did not intend to permit any slackening of discipline just because he was in prison.

I am also in want of some old waistcoats and pantaloons, which were in the drawers of the bureau in my bed-room, at the Hôtel d'Angleterre. There was also a pair of patched boots in the closet of the sitting-room; and in the armoire a small glass bottle of Macouba snuff–will you have the goodness to transmit them to me?

Pray tell my friends that I am very fond of strawberries, when they are in full season, and that they always do me good. In the schedule of my debts in Caen, which I wrote to you, I omitted to make the observation that I was utterly in rags, and without the means of procuring better raiment.–Good-bye; I would give half the remainder of my days to go down to the seaside with you this evening.

Armstrong left on 7 July for Calais and London, where, uncouth grocer that he was, 'being unembarrassed by any feeling of delicacy, he undertook the collection of the several donations entirely as a business', and sadly found several aristocratic doors slammed in his face, for, as Raikes said on being told by Lord Granville of the £800 debt, 'after the endless applications that have been made from him to his old friends since he left England, how can such a sum now be raised?' But Armstrong kept doggedly at it. He pushed on as far as the Foreign Office door– and beyond.

On 27 July a clerk set before Lord Palmerston the draft of a letter to the Treasury:

My Lords, on a Revision of the Consular Establishment in the early part of the year 1832, I found that the British Consulate at Caen in Normandy might be abolished without prejudice to the Service; and that the salary of £400 a year, assigned to that Post, might be saved to the Publick.

This reduction was accordingly carried into effect and Consul Brummell's salary ceased on the 31st of May, [sic] 1832.

Subsequently to that Period I have received various representations from

Mr Brummell stating the pecuniary difficulties into which he was plunged by the suddenness of the abolition of his consulship–the stopping of his Salary; and requesting that some pecuniary assistance might be granted to enable him to effect his Release from Prison.

Palmerston picked up his pen, deleted the last nine words and substituted 'him'–no point in raising that unhappy subject. 'Mr Brummell's case appearing to be one of great hardship, I venture to recommend to your Lordship's favourable consideration the grant of a Gratuity, equal to Half a year's Salary, as Compensation to Mr Brummell on the Abolition of his office as H.M.'s Consul at Caen, which he had held upwards of two years.' The Foreign Secretary deleted 'upwards of two' and substituted 'nearly three', then initialled the draft.

Brummell was oscillating between fury–'I have this instant received a visit from Monsieur Target [the Prefect]. He said he *did not know* I was *here*, and hoped I was *à mon aise*!!! Oh, the Saracen!'–and long-forgotten heights of bliss brought on by a free banquet. One of his Legitimist friends, the rich baron de Bresmenil, had been sentenced to five days in prison for shouting *Vive Henri Cinq*! in a public place. The baron celebrated this minor martyrdom by inviting Brummell, the comte de Roncherolles, a Carlist ex-deputy, and two others to dinner and allowing the Beau to choose the meal. The repast was sent in by Longuet and served by three convicts from the Paille. The food was excellent, the wines magnificent and Brummell in his fine old form, regaling his host and fellow guests with story after story, name after name. Only at the end did gloom descend once more– the bottle of rare brandy that should have accompanied the coffee could not be found.

The three waiters, all professional thieves, were the obvious suspects. Bresmenil, a very large man, threatened to throw them out of the window one by one if they did not bring back the bottle–and was prevented from doing so only by the fact that the window was barred. Brummell, brought to high emotional pitch by the unaccustomed beauty of the meal, staggered up from his chair and screamed at them: '*Scélérats! Rendez-moi mon pousse-café.*' [Scoundrels, give me my chaser!] They finally discovered the bottle outside, empty, clutched to the bosom of the dead-drunk turnkey, Brillant, who had been engaged to keep an eye on the waiters.

By mid-July his hopes had risen. 'Not a word yet from England, but I hear, not however, *officially*, that things are *at length going on favourably*...I am almost enjoying this partial sunshine that is glancing in at my *grille*, though it may revive other thoughts of other days.' Other views from his window were less pleasing, for instance the

outré brigand who I saw the day before yesterday attempt to escape, even with his load of chains, over the wall of *our garden*: he is a remarkably good-looking animal, mild, too, in his manners, and has frequently moved my humanity, even to assisting him in my humble way. I shall remember, to my last hour, his cries and struggles to avoid the additional irons that were forced upon his arms and throat, even to the arrival of six *des militaires*, when he was *quieted* to insensibility, and conducted to his eternal subterranean cell. And yet I exist in close adjacency to these outcasts!

His penance was now over. Armstrong had collected enough money to settle with Leveux in Calais and all the creditors in Caen. Alvanley and Worcester were as usual the most prominent in subscribing and persuading others to contribute. Lord Sefton, George Dawson-Damer, Charles Greville and half a dozen others paid £25 each. General Upton–the gay Arthur Upton of thirty years before, when he was keeping Amy Wilson and Brummell was fencing with her sister Harriette–not only sent £25 but also, through Sir Herbert Taylor, the King's Private Secretary, got £100 from William IV. Palmerston's plea to the Treasury eventually produced a further £200. And Alvanley, Greville, Sefton and Worcester promised to make a yearly contribution, on condition that Armstrong would henceforward control the Beau's expenditure as well as his income.

At five o'clock on 21 July Brummell was released from prison and returned to his old rooms at the Hôtel d'Angleterre, which Armstrong had persuaded Monsieur Fichet to keep for him on promise of paying his bills and by pointing out the advantages of having the Beau as a resident tourist attraction–which he long had been and was to continue to be. He dressed for the evening and made his way to General Corbet's soirée, where the whole company rose and congratulated him on his release. Outwardly he was as brilliant and self-assured as ever, but he had aged visibly. He had gone into prison almost broken in health; he came out almost broken in spirit.

Apart from the periodicals and novels that he still read avidly, he was increasingly living in the past. He had given his album to one of his young friends and he rummaged from time to time among his keepsakes for little gifts to repay their mothers' hospitality. A pair of note-keepers: 'the green one was worked by Lady Sarah Saville, subsequently Lady Monson, *en suite* Lady Warwick, the other, of the dove tint, like her eyes, was the travail of Lady Foley'. Or a miniature: 'it is the late poor Duchess of Rutland; we were great friends in those days, you must know, and so, indeed, we remained till her death, ten years since. Pray have a respect for her, and protect her, now she is no more.'

He managed to bring the name-dropping even into his evasions about his age. He never admitted to more than fifty, although now, just short of sixty, he was looking at least seventy. If pressed he would name some prominent member of the aristocracy, at least ten years his junior, and claim that they had been contemporaries at Eton. But he did not conceal from his sympathetic correspondents that he was feeling old and tired, exhausted even by sitting up after dinner to drink tea or play twopenny whist. 'Today I am too much subdued by the shadows of Vallombrosa, at Madame de Séran's last night, to hold up my head if I saw you. I shall take to rouge if this goes on.' And again 'Mine was the "Rake's Progress" last night, and I have but this instant escaped from the sepulture, while the sexton was asleep; I am still in my shroud, and incapacitated for writing to the living in the twilight.'

About this time he enclosed in one of his letters a copy of a sketch he had found in a magazine. The original was captioned 'The Broken Bow' and showed a tearful Cupid with an arrow and a broken bow beside him. Under his copy of this, Brummell wrote 'The Broken Beau', with 'Beau' crossed through and 'Bow!' substituted. It was a moment of self-revelation which he promptly regretted. 'These ridiculous words were written in a moment of haste and with no other idea than being laughed at by *you* as a *mauvaise plaisanterie*, not to be seen by others. I entreat you *instantly* to erase the words in question, or throw the sketch into the fire.'

There was more embarrassment to come. His favourite young correspondent Ellen was back from her visit to England. The exchange of his archly flirtatious letters and her polite pretty replies resumed; but this time he deluded himself into believing the flirtation was serious. He went too far and the poor girl had to tell him so. The maudlin remorse in his letters after that makes sad reading:

'I am no longer the victim of delusion and, with every deep-felt contrition, I am prostrate at your feet; tell me, with all the angel consideration that is innate in your being, that you forgive and will forget *forever* all my past faults and follies towards you...'

'Tell me at once that you forgive me; that, forgetting every past dereliction, spontaneously from your benevolent heart, you forgive me...'

'In regard to my two notes to you which you mention, I have already told you they were the frantic effusions of jealous feelings maddened by laudanum, which rendered me wretched and insensible of what I said to you...'

'I can do nothing but sit and cry over your letter to me last night.'

In the long vacation of 1836 a Cambridge undergraduate stayed for three days at the Hôtel d'Angleterre and noticed at the *table d'hôte* 'a very quiet, very refined, and on the whole interesting-looking elderly gentleman, to whom some of the guests and all of the servants of the house seemed to pay unusual attention. He took him for a French gentleman of the old school, or for some retired diplomatist whose life had been spent in the highest society; but on making inquiry he was told that this was poor Beau Brummell, and that he was then "poor indeed".' Unfortunately the quiet elderly gentleman refused to accept his poverty. The dreadful lesson of prison was growing dim in his memory: 'He had, it is true, brought himself down to one complete change of linen daily; but he could not find it in his heart to renounce his primrose gloves, *eau de Cologne*, oil for his wigs, and patent blacking.'

It was this blacking, the *vernis de Guiton* at five francs a bottle, that precipitated a crisis and jolted him back to reality. 'My dear Armstrong,' he wrote in panic and reproach in November 1836,

Mulet, the boot-maker, has this instant been with me, in an insolent manner, and says that as you have refused positively to pay his account, or the principal part of it, for *vernis*, he shall proceed against me for the amount of this debt, without it is settled the present day. Send me the money on *my own account* and let me instantly settle it. I have, so help me Heaven, not four francs in my possession, and it will utterly destroy me to see a bailiff enter my room, or assault me in the street. I will enter into any promise with you upon the subject of this d——d polish, that you may demand, if you will instantly enable me to pay this scoundrel.

Armstrong paid–but made it very clear to the Beau that he was not happy to do so, and did not intend to come to his rescue in the future–indeed, he would refuse to handle his affairs at all. Brummell was all contrition.

Do not be any more out of temper with me. I do not deserve it from you; I have never trespassed upon the rules of economy which you dictated to me, excepting in one instance, and that has been that d——d execrable blacking. I have now relinquished it forever! You are of too good a natural disposition to be displeased with any part of my conduct in this place, during our more intimate acquaintance in this last year. So help me Heaven, I have never trespassed from the economy you dictated to me...Let our good friendship remain between us as it has ever yet done, and you will never have reason to repent it.

Never is a long time. Only a few weeks later he was writing: 'You have hurt me more than I can express by your note to me this morning. [Armstrong had discovered he had been staking–and losing–much more than he could afford on the lottery.] I am, believe me, sensibly ashamed of myself for this act of past folly–and if you overlook it, and still promise me your services, both here and in England, I give you my sacred word of honour, I will never again commit such an extravagant and senseless error.'

Still he could not make ends meet: 'It is, I can assure you, with the greatest reluctance I am compelled to solicit occasional assistance from you; but I told you the truth yesterday, when I represented the abject condition of my linen to you. I have not a single shirt that will hang to my back, nor are my socks and drawers in a better state.'

It is difficult to believe his statement later in the same letter that 'I am in ignorance as to those who, through your mediation, have befriended me on the other side of the water, nor do I know precisely the amount of their contributions; therefore I am unable to write them my thanks for what they have done, or to make them acquainted with my continued destitute situation; the belly, indeed, is filled, but the hand is empty, and the back and limbs unprovided for.' If this were true, then Armstrong must have ordered him not to write to his former friends any more.

'I have not heard from any one of them, excepting, as you know, from my sister; and I could almost suppose she was laughing at me, when she says she hopes that I "have everything comfortable about me". Surely, my dear Armstrong, I had better immediately write to her, to Alvanley and to others; they may imagine I am living comparatively in comfort, if not at ease, and the positive reverse is the case; and I see it cannot last long with me.' Yet when Armstrong sent him a cotton dressing-gown instead of the silk one he had asked for, he threw it out of the window.

Armstrong let it be known in the town that he would no longer settle bills run up by the Beau unless he had previously sanctioned the purchase. To pay for small luxuries–such as the glass of curaçao and the two *biscuits de Rheims* that he ate every day at two o'clock at the nearby pâtisserie–Brummell began to pawn or sell the small ornaments and pieces of jewellery that remained to him. Two watches, some vases, his last silver snuff-box all went in this way. He took to wearing a black silk cravat–a sartorial abomination that he had denounced all his life–because it was cheaper to launder than the starched white cambric that had made him famous.

In any event, his clothes were now so worn (he had to stay in bed on the days that his tailor mended his only pair of trousers) that he seldom went out into society, preferring to take his second cup of coffee–the terms of his *pension* allowed him only one after dinner–at an obscure café down by the Town Hall where he was still allowed to run an account. Whenever one of the old

ladies who kept the café suggested he might settle the mounting
bill, he would reply, 'Yes, madame, at the full of the moon, at the
full of the moon' and give her the profound bow that used to
entrance the Duchesses of Devonshire and Rutland and York.

It was painful for him to encounter his former friends. Coming
out of the hotel dining-room one day he met an old acquaintance
whom he had not seen for twenty years. 'They immediately
recognised each other. "*On est bien changé*," said Brummell,
"*voilà tout!*" He uttered no complaint, but could not conceal his
poverty and painful embarrassments.'

In June 1837 King William died and the bewitching young
Victoria took his place on the throne. In July Tom Moore came,
bringing his spoilt son for coaching in French. General Corbet
invited him to dinner with a fellow-Irishman, the octogenarian
Judge Rothe who lived in the rue Calembourg, and Brummell
and one or two others. 'The poor Beau's head gone,' Moore
noted in his diary, 'and his whole looks so changed that I never
should have recognised him. Got wandering in his conversation
more than once during dinner.'

His absent-mindedness became more and more of a social
hazard on the rare occasions when he went visiting. At one house
he sat at the fireside apparently lost in thought, while his hostess
discussed with a friend the wisdom of leaving her daughter alone
at Luc-sur-mer. Suddenly they were startled by Brummell's
voice speaking his thoughts aloud while he still stared at the
fire: 'There is no necessity for being alarmed; she is too plain for
anybody to dream of running off with her.' At a dinner given by
the Coxes, he gallantly escorted the hostess in and sat at her right
hand but no sooner had the dishes been brought in than he began
criticising them. He loudly declared them to be too cold or too
tough and finally, glaring at the main course, exclaimed 'What
a half-starved turkey!' He had quite forgotten Mrs Cox, who sat
in tears beside him, and imagined he was back at the Hôtel
d'Angleterre where he now complained of every meal from
beginning to end.

Despite this dreadful deterioration he still had many loyal
friends in the town. When somebody asked Mrs Burton why she
continued to welcome 'such a driveller', she answered: 'He is

never in our way, sir, and though it is true he is no longer the amusing character he used to be, I like to see him take his seat before my fire.'

Soon he was unable to make even the short journey to the Burtons. One evening he fell down in the street and cut himself; when he was carried into the hotel it was discovered that he had pulled his left boot only half on. On another occasion he fell backwards in his room and broke the window with his head. When Colonel Cox called to see him and said that his wife was always asking after him, Brummell smiled, nodded and whispered, 'Ah, Mrs Cox asks after me, does she? I saw her yesterday, and do you know, between ourselves, she very often pays me a visit; but pray don't tell the Colonel–he is such a jealous fellow.'

Since he could no longer get out to spend any money, there was enough to pay for an old woman (whom he hated) or a waiter to sit with him and see that he came to no harm. 'On certain nights some strange fancy would seize him, that it was necessary he should give a party, and he accordingly invited many of the distinguished persons with whom he had been intimate in former days, though some of them were already numbered with the dead.' (Among those who had died in the three years since his release from prison were Lord Robert Manners, Berkeley Craven–who shot himself after a disastrous bet on the Derby–Lord George Germain, Kangaroo Cooke, Lord Sefton and Mrs Fitzherbert.) The waiter set out a whist table, lit the candles and at 8 p.m. precisely opened the sitting-room door and announced the Duchess of Devonshire. 'The Beau, instantly rising from his chair, would advance towards the door and greet the cold air from the staircase as if it had been the beautiful Georgiana herself.' Then he would sit down and stare vacantly at the fire until the servant introduced Alvanley or Worcester or whatever names he had been given. At ten, the attendant told him the carriages had arrived; Brummell bowed his guests out of the door, and went to bed.

Alvanley and Worcester (Duke of Beaufort since November 1835) and a few other survivors of the golden days foregathered in Venice that autumn of 1838, with the Jerseys and Damers and, as Rokeby put it, 'hundreds of unknown Bulls and Cows'.

Alvanley, who intended to stay near the Mediterranean now that
his health was breaking up, had called on another exile in Milan–
Henry Mildmay, who had cultivated 'a most formidable pair of
campaigning moustaches. He is grown fat and, like poor Brummell, has not got beyond 1817 in English affairs–still talks of
Macao at Watiers'. Lord Stuart de Rothesay had called at the
Hôtel d'Angleterre and found that 'Poor Brummell is become an
imbecile. He is grown slovenly and dirty; is, however, otherwise
well, and lives on what we subscribe for him.'

There was even sadder news from Charles Armstrong in
November:

I have deferred writing for some time, hoping to be able to inform you that
I had succeeded in getting Mr Brummell into one of the public institutions,
but I am sorry to say that I have failed; I have also tried to get him into a
private house; but no one will undertake the charge of him in his present
state; in fact it would be totally impossible for me to describe the dreadful
situation he is in. For the last two months I have been obliged to pay a
person to be with him night and day, and still we cannot keep him *clean*; he
now lies upon a straw mattress, which is changed every day. They will not
keep him at the hotel, and what to do I know not: I should think some of his
old friends in England would be able to get him into some hospital, where
he could be taken care of for the rest of his days. I beg and entreat of you to
get something done for him, for it is quite out of the question that he can
remain where he is. The clergyman and the physician here can bear testimony
to the melancholy state of idiocy he is in.

It was another six months before Armstrong managed to get
him admitted to the asylum of the Bon Sauveur on the Bayeux
road. As a ruse to persuade him to go quietly Fichet had previously
invited him to take a drive around the town, but when Fichet,
Armstrong and Armstrong's servant Auguste entered his room
they found the Beau still in his dressing-gown, sitting in his
armchair ('a gift from the Duchess of York, who was a very kind
friend of mine'), with his wig on his knee. He had developed an
obsessive interest in this wig. Sometimes he would mislay it and
create a scene, accusing the old woman attendant of having
stolen it; at others he would dowse it with so much oil that when
he put it on, often back to front, the oil dripped down his cheeks
and on to his dressing-gown. On this occasion he had got out his
shaving brush and was covering the wig with lather.

He ignored his visitors. When Fichet reminded him of the

drive they were to take together, he said that he did not want to go. In the end, they picked him up and carried him down the stairs, kicking and shrieking: 'You are taking me to prison! Loose me, scoundrels! I owe nothing!'

As the carriage clattered across the place Royale, past the café where he still owed the old ladies sixty francs, he suddenly drew back from the window, wrapping himself more closely in his dressing-gown, 'That is Monsieur de Ste-Marie,' he explained, 'I did not bow to him, for I am not fit to be seen in such a *déshabille* as this.' The moment of clarity passed. When the carriage stopped at the gates of the Bon Sauveur and he heard the bolts being drawn he burst into tears again, saying: 'A prison! A prison!'

It was instead a gentle, kindly place, a school for girls, a home for the deaf and dumb, a hospital, an asylum for more than 350 men and women. Brummell, since he was a paying patient, was given rooms in a detached house, where Bonaparte's brilliant and corrupt secretary Bourrienne had died insane four years earlier. There was always a fire in the grate and as much food as even he could cope with. In fine weather the servant allotted to him wheeled him in a chair round the gravelled walks of the garden; when he had to stay indoors there was somebody to sit with him—the servant or one of the Sisters of Charity who had founded the home a hundred years before. Occasionally visitors would come out from the town to see him and, less frequently, he would recognise them. 'Good morning, Fichet! *Table d'hôte* at five as usual?' 'Yes, sir.' 'Very good, very good—I shall be down.'

Cradled at last in warmth and security, his old impeccable manners returned, enchanting the nuns who attended him. With infinite courtesy he did his best to repay them at the end. In the afternoon of 30 March 1840, he was visited by the Protestant clergyman who had long been trying to direct his thoughts to religion. The pastor entreated Brummell to pray. The Beau politely replied, 'I do try'. He was by now very sick and frail. At 8 p.m. the nun who had looked after him ever since his admission noticed that he had 'fixed his eyes upon me, with an expression of entreaty, raising his hands towards me, as he lay in the bed, and as though asking for assistance but saying nothing'.

She asked him to repeat after her the Act of Contrition. 'He immediately consented, and repeated after me in an earnest manner that form of prayer. He then became more composed and laid his head down on one side; but this tranquility was interrupted, about an hour after, by his turning himself over and uttering a cry, at the same time appearing to be in pain; he soon, however, turned himself back, with his face laid on the pillow towards the wall, so as to be hidden from us who were on the other side; after this he never moved, dying imperceptibly.'

He was buried, nevertheless, in the Protestant Cemetery where his brother and sister put up a headstone for him: 'In Memory of George Brummell, Esq., Who departed this life, On the 29th March, 1840, Aged 62 years.' It had only two errors: the date was March 30; his age was sixty-one.

The grave was soon lost in weeds and ivy. Those who had known him died. Even in Mayfair, the scene of his triumphs, all trace of his habitation disappeared. A century later, the Greater London Council, desirous of conferring on him the Cockney accolade of a blue plaque on his house front, could find no proof that he ever lived at 4 Chesterfield Street, the address with which he is most often associated, and those houses which he is certainly known to have occupied–18 Bruton Street, 22 South Street, 13 Chapel Street–have all been pulled down and rebuilt. 'Like the orator, the great actor, the conversationalist,' wrote a later dandy, Barbey d'Aurevilly, 'Brummell left nothing but a name mysteriously sparkling in all the memoirs of his time.'

Though his name would be associated with the Regency as long as that of the Regent himself, there was not, after all, a great deal to remember him for; he had invented a method of keeping a cravat neat and a pair of trousers unwrinkled; he had set high society an example of cleanliness and courtesy; he had encouraged with without rancour; he had directed his impertinence agains those more powerful than himself; he had been loyal to his friends and bilked only those who could afford it; he had been the most brilliant of butterflies, the gayest of grasshoppers. And he had spent the last years of his life miserable, filthy and mad.

As Tom Raikes said when he read the news in his morning paper: 'It is a happy release for him; but when I call to mind his gay career and success in London, a wretched end like this suggests an awful lesson.' The Victorian Age had begun.

Sources

Captain William Jesse spent some time with Brummell in Caen in 1832. After the Beau's death Jesse returned to France, collected more material, and brought out his *Life of Beau Brummell* in 1844. This two-volume work, with some additions in the rare revised edition of 1886, contains the bulk of Brummell's known correspondence. A handful more documents were later published by Lewis Melville, Kathleen Campbell and Willard Connely. To these I have added not only a great deal of scattered published material but also a considerable number of hitherto unknown letters and other documents from the British Museum, the Public Record Office and other collections.

I am grateful for the continuing courtesy and help of the staffs of both those institutions, and of Mrs K. F. Campbell, Foreign and Commonwealth Office Library; Mr S. W. Cole, Paymaster General's Office; Mr R. H. Bridgman-Evans (for permission to consult the Fribourg and Treyer ledgers); Sir William Gladstone, Bart, (for permission to quote from the Glynne-Gladstone MSS); Mr J. M. Hamill, Assistant Librarian, Grand Lodge, and my friend Mr W. S. Rearden (for information on masonic matters); Mr K. C. Harrison, Westminster City Librarian; Mr W. J. Smith, Head Archivist, Greater London Council; Mr A. G. Vesey, Clwyd County Archivist; and Miss Anne Wall, Assistant Press Secretary to H.M. the Queen.

I am particularly indebted to Mrs Peter Martineau and Mrs Barbara Hopton for permission to consult the papers and genealogical tables collected and compiled by their father, the late Major John C. Daniell OBE, whose scholarly and wide-ranging studies of the Daniell family tree led him along the Brummell branch and enabled me, among other things, to trace the wills of the Beau's father and grandfather. I am also grateful to them for permission to publish the portrait of Brummell in 1815.

All the quotations used have been taken, and in some cases abridged, from the following sources:

MANUSCRIPTS

British Museum: Add. MSS 30,115; 36,593; 36,595; 38,223; 38,307; 41,335

Daniell Papers: Letter, Duke of Sussex to William Brummell

Glynne-Gladstone MSS: Letters, G. Brummell to Sir Stephen Glynne

Paymaster General's Office: Assignment of Brummell's Salary to Lewis and James Hertslet

Public Record Office: FO 27/419, 435, 453, 455, 491, 493 and 510; PRO 30/29/417; Prob. 11/958 and 1242

Westminster City Archives: Rate Books, Fribourg and Treyer Ledgers

PRINTED MATTER

The Annual Register, Examiner, The Gentleman's Magazine, Notes and Queries, Public Advertiser, St James's Chronicle, The Times.

The poetical works of Lord Byron, Ebenezer Elliott, Charles Lamb, Thomas Moore, P. B. Shelley, William Wordsworth.

The correspondence, diaries, memoirs, and recollections of H. F. Amiel, Lord Auckland, Grantley Berkeley, Mary Berry, Countess Brownlow, Frances Calvert, Harriet Cavendish (Lady Granville), Alan Chambre, Princess Charlotte, Lord Colchester, Thomas Creevey, J. W. Croker, Joseph Farington, George III, George IV, Lord Glenbervie, Charles Greville, R. H. Gronow, George Jackson, Joseph Jekyll, Julia Johnstone (Storer), Lord W. P. Lennox, Charles Macfarlane, Lord Malmesbury, Lord Minto, Thomas Moore, Amelia Murray, Benjamin Newton, Thomas Raikes, John Richardson, Lady Shelley, Lady Hester

Stanhope, Lady Louisa Stuart, Horace Walpole, Harriette Wilson, Nathaniel Wraxall.

The Bathurst Papers, *Whitefoord Papers*, *Wynne Diaries*; Jane Austen, *Pride and Prejudice*; J. Barbey d'Aurevilly, *Du Dandysme et de G. Brummell*; Charles Baudelaire, *Le Peintre de la vie moderne*; Paul Bailleu, *Preussen und Frankreich von 1795 bis 1807*; E. Bulwer-Lytton, *Pelham*; G. B. Brummell, *Male and Female Costume*; Kathleen Campbell, *Beau Brummell*; Thomas Carlyle, *Sartor Resartus*; Willard Connely, *Adventures in Biography*; F. O. Darvall, *Popular Disturbances...in Regency England*; J. Eardley-Wilmot, *Reminiscences of Thomas Assheton-Smith*; Percy Fitzgerald, *George IV*; A. H. Higginson, *Peter Beckford*; J. H. Jesse, *George Selwyn and his Friends*; William Jesse, *Beau Brummell*; Ernest Law, *History of Hampton Court Palace*; Shane Leslie, *Life and Letters of Mrs Fitzherbert*; R. S. Liddell, *Memoirs of the Tenth Royal Hussars*; T. H. Lister, *Granby*; Thomas Malthus, *Essay on the Principles of Population*; H. C. Maxwell-Lyte, *History of Eton*; Thomas Medwin, *Conversations of Lord Byron*; Lewis Melville, *Beau Brummell*; Clifford Musgrave, *Life in Brighton*; 'One of the Cloth', *Neck-clothitania*; C. S. Parker, *Sir Robert Peel*; Prince H. L. Pückler-Muskau, *Tour in England, Ireland and France*; M-C Renard, *Brummell et son ombre*; J. Roach, *The London Pocket Pilot*; W. M. Thackeray, *The Four Georges*.

FURTHER READING

The two Oxford volumes, J. S. Watson, *Reign of George III*, and E. L. Woodward, *Age of Reform*, with Arthur Bryant's *Age of Elegance* and Christopher Hibbert's *George IV*, will give pleasure, and also guidance to the vast number of other books on the period.

Index